National Pastime

National Pastime

Sports, Politics, and the Return of Baseball to Washington, D.C.

Barry Svrluga

DOUBLEDAY

NEW YORK LONDON TORONTO SYDNEY AUCKLAND

PUBLISHED BY DOUBLEDAY

Copyright © 2006 by Barry Svrluga

Published in the United States by Doubleday, an imprint of
The Doubleday Broadway Publishing Group, a division of
Random House, Inc., New York.
www.doubleday.com

DOUBLEDAY and the portrayal of an anchor with a dolphin
are registered trademarks of Random House, Inc.

Book design by Fearn Cutler de Vicq

Library of Congress Cataloging-in-Publication Data

Svrluga, Barry.
National pastime : sports, politics, and the return of baseball to
Washington, D.C. / by Barry Svrluga.—1st ed.
p. cm.
1. Baseball—Washington (D.C.) 2. Washington Nationals (Baseball team)
3. Sports—Political aspects—Washington (D.C.) I. Title.
GV863.W18S87 2006
796.357'6409753—dc22
2005046629

ISBN-13: 978-0-385-51785-0
ISBN-10: 0-385-51785-8

PRINTED IN THE UNITED STATES OF AMERICA

1 3 5 7 9 10 8 6 4 2

FIRST EDITION

For William J. Svrluga Sr.

Contents

★ ★ ★ ★ ★ ★ ★ ★ ★ ★ ★ ★ ★ ★ ★ ★ ★ ★

Acknowledgments

Before the 2005 baseball season, I had been in exactly one major league press box for precisely one major league game. So, naturally, in order for a rookie baseball writer to be granted the opportunity not only to cover a rookie team, but then write a book about it, there are almost too many people to thank.

First and foremost are the Nationals themselves, without whom there would be no story to tell. Major league baseball players, as a subset of society, have reputations as being ... well, difficult. Washington, and by extension this book, benefited because the Nationals, even in down times, were generous with their time and their stories. Tony Tavares, the team's president; Jim Bowden, its general manager; and Frank Robinson, the manager and resident Hall of Famer, all gave of their time and their insight when they had no particular obligation to do so. Tony Siegle, the assistant general manager, never withheld a story. Several players sat down for lengthy interviews, some of which, unfortunately, don't appear in the text. And others provided key understanding of how the team worked and what playing in Washington meant to them. Thanks, in no particular order, to Jose Guillen,

Brad Wilkerson, Brian Schneider, Livan Hernandez, John Patterson, Jamey Carroll, Jose Vidro, Nick Johnson, Gary Bennett, Endy Chavez, Chad Cordero, Ryan Church, Gary Majewski, Zach Day, and Joey Eischen. Staff members Tom McCraw, Eddie Rodriguez, and Randy St. Claire deserve special mention, as does Jose Rijo.

Alan Alper, super fan, gave of his time, his passion, and his reference materials, all of which were both appreciated and essential, and Katie Hynes was always ready with a tale about the days in Montreal.

The players and fans showed their faith in talking to the rookie writer, but the rookie writer would never have been in that position without the people at the *Washington Post*. Emilio Garcia-Ruiz, the *Post*'s sports editor, somehow saw fit to hire me in the first place, then granted me the right to cover this remarkable story. Why, I'm still not sure (nor, perhaps, is he). Matt Rennie and Tracee Hamilton, the two assignment editors I have worked with at the *Post*, helped me adjust first to the paper and then to my new job, pushing when appropriate, providing reassurance on the, oh, one million occasions when I needed it. All of my editors not only allowed me to pursue the book, they encouraged it, providing a much-needed endorsement. And no rookie ball writer could have better veterans to break him in than Dave Sheinin, the *Post*'s ridiculously talented national baseball scribe, and Thomas Boswell, its eloquent and insightful— not to mention legendary—baseball columnist. Sheinin's contributions are present in this book in his generous advice to the new guy, Boz's in his sheer enthusiasm for the game more than 30 years after he started covering it.

Thanks, too, to the *Post*'s Sally Jenkins, who led me to Esther Newberg at ICM, without whom this project wouldn't exist. My editor at Doubleday, Jason Kaufman, and his assistant, Jenny Choi, showed patience with a first-time author. Chris Wilson provided a huge boost with his exhaustive fact-checking.

Finally, thanks to my family, who managed to cover up their

doubts about sports journalism as a career with pats on the back. My mother, Kay Litten, the old English teacher who considers Strunk and White's *Elements of Style* to be something of a Bible, deserves special thanks for reading the manuscript and offering suggestions. And, mostly, to my wife, Susan, who barely batted an eye during long road trips or days and nights spent hunkered down in my "office," the Starbucks at 3rd and Pennsylvania Southeast. She listened, critiqued, and cajoled. Only I know her true contribution, which is immeasurable.

December 2005, Washington, D.C.

National Pastime

★ ★ ★ ★ ★ ★ ★ ★ ★ ★ ★ ★ ★ ★ ★ ★ ★ ★

Chapter 1

A Team, and the Trailers, Arrive

*T*he nights were the best, really, when the ice on the ramp leading up to the Washington Nationals' offices was slick and
black, undetectable in the darkness. That's when the wind picked up
across the parking lot at Robert F. Kennedy Memorial Stadium,
when the unmarked black van might race over the asphalt, charging
toward an innocent employee. "Jesus, this is it," the employee would
think. "Someone's coming after me." But invariably it would turn
out to be a security guard, a friendly woman protecting the employees, smiling and asking, "Is everything okay?" Going outside on
those nights was at one's peril, but considering the facilities—Oh,
who's kidding whom? They weren't really facilities. They were good
old-fashioned Porta Potties. So, considering the Porta Potties were a
good fifty yards across the parking lot, there was no alternative but to
trudge out into the cold, wave to the security guard, find the plastic
door, hold your breath, and step in.

David Cope headed out one night in December 2004, stared into
the blackness, and turned back around. Cope had been hired a month
earlier as the Nationals' vice president of sales and marketing. He was

a lifelong Washingtonian, a sports business professional who had worked for nearly every franchise in Baltimore and Washington, from the king of them all, football's Redskins, to baseball's Baltimore Orioles, basketball's Washington Wizards, and football's Baltimore Ravens. He drove his bosses crazy from time to time when he would think back on that experience. "When we started the Ravens, we . . ." and he would launch into a tale about relocating the NFL team from Cleveland. But he had never been through something like this. Staring out into the night, Cope couldn't see a thing. He went back into his office, throwing open the door that, in a stiff breeze, might blow open on its own anyway. A flashlight. He needed a flashlight. The absurdity of it all didn't hit Cope then, just as it didn't hit the Nationals' other employees during those sixteen-hour days, when their jobs were simply to build the front office of a baseball team out of . . . well, out of nothing. The venue for such a project: a pair of double-wide trailers that sat inconspicuously in the low-lying parking lot outside RFK. The offices inside the stadium wouldn't be completed for four more months, and if the employees thought too much about the circumstances, all the work that had to be done between those frigid nights and Washington's first baseball game in thirty-four years, they might have cried. So when Cope returned to the metal trailer that held his office, it was a practical matter. The staff tried not to drink too much coffee, too much soda, too much water, too much anything, because lots of liquid meant more trips to the savagely frigid bathroom. Cope had no choice. Grab the flashlight, then head back out. When he arrived at the Porta Potti, the next challenge: where to put the flashlight? He looked around. Finding nothing, he stuck it in his mouth, unzipped his pants, and went about his business. An illuminating experience. "What the hell am I doing?" he muttered, the impediment muffling any actual words.

"The whole thing," he said, "was crazy."

The fact that Washington had a baseball team, the fact that Major League Baseball had decided, *finally*, to move the Montreal

Expos to the nation's capital, was a thought that warmed the souls of lifelong Washingtonians during the fall and winter of 2004, in large part because they were oblivious to those icy treks to the outhouse, to the wind hurling open the trailer doors, to the pizza that arrived night after night from that place down East Capitol Street . . . that is, until the orders stopped, because no one could remember ordering a roach as an extra topping. For outsiders, for Washington's baseball fans, a drive past RFK Stadium, just twenty-two blocks east of the U.S. Capitol, might bring back memories of when the Washington Senators played there, back in the 1960s and '70s. But inform anyone who drove past Parking Lot 4 that basically the entire franchise was being run out of those two double-wides at the bottom of the hill, and that was another story.

"You have to wonder," Cope said, "how it all happened."

Before the trailers, before the Porta Potties and the pizzas, it started at the Hilton Washington, which is rarely referred to as such. It is, rather, the Hinckley Hilton, because it is here that, on March 30, 1981, John Hinckley, Jr., the son of a wealthy Colorado oil executive, emerged from a crowd of journalists outside the hotel, brandishing a .22 caliber pistol. There, too, was President Ronald Reagan, just his seventieth day in office. Hinckley fired six shots. The fifth pierced Reagan's lung. Police tackled Hinckley, Secret Service agents whisked the President away in his limousine, press secretary James Brady was shot in the head and ended up in a wheelchair. Reagan recovered, and the Hilton Washington, perched on the east side of Connecticut Avenue Northwest as the street rises from Dupont Circle, became a landmark.

Yet on a clear October day, nearly a quarter of a century later, the Hinckley Hilton served as a workaday Washington hotel. In the function rooms below the lobby bar, they staged a USO gala. Around the corner, smiling women with dark hair handed out name tags for the meeting of the National Italian American Foundation. And on the eighth floor, in a suite that didn't look or feel like home,

Tony Tavares's cell phone rang . . . just as it had been doing for days. It rang again, beeping out an electronic version of "O Canada." He was, indeed, a stranger in a new land. Tavares picked up his phone, growled a few words, and hung up. As soon as he put down the cell, the phone in his suite let loose its more traditional ring.

"Tony Tavares," he said in his clipped, East Coast, this-better-be-important-or-else tone. And he listened. Just for a minute. "Okay," Tavares said, but it was rushed, abrupt. "Uhkay. If you want a job with me, e-mail me at . . ." and he provided his e-mail address. "I can't guarantee anything, uhkay? Just e-mail me. . . . Yeah. Right. Bye."

Tavares put the phone down and looked through some papers. He had been in Washington less than forty-eight hours. All he had was a suitcase. He was, in theory, the president of a major league baseball team, but what evidence of a baseball team was there here? Kevin Uhlich, dressed like Tavares in a dark suit, was also employed by the Washington Expos, or whatever the soon-to-be-renamed Washington baseball club would be called. He and Tavares had worked together with the Anaheim Angels, Tavares as president, Uhlich rising from bat boy as a kid to CFO as an adult. When Major League Baseball moved the Expos to Washington, the Expos' executive vice president for business affairs, Claude Delorme, had to remain back at Montreal's Olympic Stadium to tend to a twenty-six-page black binder, Delorme's ad hoc document that provided him with a guide that might have been entitled "How to Shut Down a Major League Baseball Team." The baseball operation, the people who dealt with real-life pitchers and catchers, remained at Olympic Stadium, too. There was no point in moving those people to Washington. Tavares needed help on the business side. He called Uhlich.

"Do you want to do this?" Tavares said.

Uhlich had lived his whole life in California, had a family in California, was attached to California, *was* California.

"Yes," he said anyway.

So they hit the ground in Washington, a city about which neither knew anything. Tavares had been there, oh, must have been twenty years ago now. He'd returned once in August, when it looked more and more likely that the Expos would move to the District of Columbia and not to northern Virginia, Norfolk, Las Vegas, or Portland, Oregon. He and Delorme took a cab out to RFK Stadium to get an idea of what they might be getting themselves into should the Expos take up residence there.

"Claude," Tavares said at the time, "I just want to warn you: The neighborhood around there, it's, uh, not the best."

That, Tavares thought to himself, was being gentle. He remembered something worse. He remembered a war zone. So when the cab drove east down Independence Avenue, past the Starbucks on the corner of Pennsylvania Avenue and Third Street S.E., past historic Eastern Market, where residents shopped and ate, and past the row houses that were selling for $500,000, $800,000, even upward of $1 million, Tavares knew the town he would bring the Expos to was different from the town he'd visited all those years ago.

This, he thought, *will work.*

But how? When a new administration takes over a team, the game plan is relatively clear. But here, there was no infrastructure, no one with prior knowledge of how things work, of whom to call in the community. Where in the world do you start? Tickets. Tickets would be a good place to start. So on their first day in town, Tavares and Uhlich met at the Hinckley Hilton with reps from Ticketmaster and Tickets.com. And they needed a place for their employees to work, so they searched for office space in downtown Washington. They ended up with two nondescript rooms at Foley & Lardner, a law firm used by Major League Baseball with offices in Georgetown, on K Street, in the heart of Washington's power center. And, in a move that sounded like a joke, they arranged for those trailers to be installed in the parking lot at RFK Stadium, the kind that contractors use on large projects, because the stadium itself, which hadn't hosted baseball in thirty-four years and had been abandoned by the

Redskins in 1996, was undergoing $18 million in renovations. Had the front office of a baseball franchise ever been run out of trailers? This one would be.

Technically, baseball was back in Washington. But baseball, at this point, consisted of two men jumping into cabs, jetting off to their next unknown destination, confused by everything, even the cab fare system. "How come," Tavares once bellowed, "it's $12 when I took a cab to RFK one day, and the next day, the guy tries to charge me $25?" At night, they returned to the Hinckley Hilton and headed up to the eighth floor, where for the time being, they lived in adjoining rooms.

"It's not much of an operation," Tavares said. "It's a couple of people running around like chickens with their heads cut off."

The chickens went about hiring some sort of a staff. David Cope was at his home in the tony Washington suburb of Bethesda, Maryland, on a Saturday morning in the fall when his cell phone rang. Up popped a 714 area code. Cope's forty-year-old mind, which tends to race, went to work immediately. He is, as he said, "sick with numbers." He knew 714 is a southern California exchange. But it was just after 6 A.M. out there. This call wasn't coming from the West Coast. It was coming from Kevin Uhlich, and he wasn't in California at all. He was in Washington, D.C.

Cope had read about Tavares and Uhlich in the newspapers, and he knew they were starting things up, knew they faced an enormous task ahead in converting the Expos from Montreal's team to Washington's team. Tavares and Uhlich needed bodies. Cope knew the market. He knew the process. And, perhaps his most attractive characteristic, he was available.

Of the entire Expos' front office staff, the only person who came south across the border to continue to work for the franchise in Washington was John Dever, the director of baseball information, the man responsible for assembling stats and notes for the media, for setting up interviews with manager Frank Robinson and the players, for handling the day-to-day information on injuries and hitting streaks and the like. Other than the baseball staff—the scouts and the assistant general manager and the farm director and the people who dealt with actual bats and balls and players—Dever was it. No one from ticket sales. No one from promotions. No one from community relations. No one from marketing. Not even a single secretary who might have known some of the personalities involved, who might have understood the way a baseball team worked, who might have been able to step in and seamlessly run the office. Tavares had consulted an experienced Washington immigration attorney and asked for help. The rules, he had been told, were clear: A person had to have a highly specified skill to be able to earn a visa and be able to come from Canada and work in the United States. Frankly, the attorney said, he wouldn't take on these cases. Tavares would have to hire people from the Washington area, an area without a baseball team since 1971.

So when Tavares and Uhlich hired Cope, Cope, in turn, had to hire his own staff of a couple dozen people. Quickly it became clear that the task of bringing baseball back to Washington wasn't for everybody. Here's the pitch: Come to work for baseball's new team in the District. I can guarantee you . . . well, I can guarantee you that we'll sign you up for six months. Beyond that? Well, nothing. And you'll be working for . . . well, that's not real clear right now. Major League Baseball owns the team, and it'll be sold in the next few months. No, no, I don't even know if I'll be around after that. Oh, and by the way, you'll need to work maybe ninety hours a week. You'll have no life. I'll give you Sunday afternoons off to see your family, and a couple hours for a break at dinner, but then it's back to the office.

Oh, and did I mention that we don't have offices?

"Here's the deal," Cope would tell people. "We're going to do this well. And if you perform, we're going to give you credit for doing a good job. If the new owners come on, and if they want to keep us, great. But if not, you're going to have this on your resume. You're going to get another job."

In the ensuing thirty seconds, Cope would get an idea of whether or not a specific applicant was ready for this.

"Um, what about the health insurance?" some would ask nervously, and Cope would know instantly that he should hire someone else.

"People would ask where we were going to be in four months," Cope said. "I didn't want to hear it. The only answer I could give was, 'I don't know.' That helped narrow down the talent pool pretty quickly."

The chaos of the hiring process was constant. People would hunt down Tavares at dinner, in his office in Georgetown, looking for jobs. There were students. There were lawyers. They were twenty. They were fifty. They sent faxes, e-mails, handwritten letters. They made personal appearances, taped video presentations. They came in all shapes and sizes. They just wanted to work for the new baseball team because it was, to those who didn't know about the trailers and Porta Potties, such a romantic notion. The team outsourced its hiring, enlisting a local sports consulting firm to sort through resumes and set up a Web site. There were forty-five positions available. Fifteen thousand responses poured in. The pace was frenetic. Carleen Martin, a twenty-eight-year-old from Pennsylvania who was working at a cable television station in Washington, heard about the opportunity through contacts at the sports consulting firm. She inquired. Within two days, Uhlich was on the phone.

"When can you interview?" Uhlich asked.

"Um," Martin said, considering her calendar, "I could do it sometime this week."

"Yeah. How about we do it *tonight?*" Uhlich said.

She wasn't wearing a suit. She didn't feel prepared. She was, in fact, nervous. Yet she went down to the Foley & Lardner offices, the Expos' makeshift headquarters. The next day, she had an offer to be the director of marketing and promotions. No owner? No idea about the future? She took it anyway. "It seemed exciting, like an adventure," Martin said. "But I guess everybody had to have some trepidation."

There was, too, the matter of where to work. Tavares and Uhlich were granted their spartan offices at Foley & Lardner that they cluttered with stray baseball memorabilia, but no one else had a permanent home. The team hired two other local men, Joe Deoudes to handle ticketing, Joe Hickey to take on corporate sponsorships. They also headed to Foley's K Street offices, tucked along the Potomac just down the hill from the pulsating bars and restaurants and boutiques along M Street, the heart of Georgetown. But Hickey and Deoudes weren't lawyers. They were salesmen. They didn't have offices. Never mind that they were trying to hire their staffs, to make inroads so they could make sales. They were, as Deoudes said, "just a pair of gypsies." They would find a spare conference room, settle in with a potential employee, begin an interview, and hear a knock on the door. "Sorry," a Foley lawyer would say. "We need this room." And they would pick up their stuff and get the hell out. Hickey worked entirely through his cell phone, often letting calls go unanswered, retrieving the message, then finding a free landline in the office—somewhere, anywhere—from which to return the call, because he didn't have a landline of his own. He made friends with the Foley receptionist, the only person who might at any given moment be able to direct him to an open office or conference room for the next hour or so. "We didn't work there, really," Hickey said. "No one knew who we were."

The Expos had a new home in Washington. But in so many ways they remained a homeless franchise. When the team finally hired a general manager in early November, Jim Bowden, who'd run the Cincinnati Reds for more than a decade, took the baseball staff south and set up shop in Viera, Florida, where the team held spring training and worked out of offices at Space Coast Stadium, a minor league facility that rose out of the brush fields along Interstate 95. "I couldn't ask my guys to work out of trailers," Bowden said. The staff in Washington was flung around the District, scrambling for whatever spare tables it could find, hoping, of all things, that those double-wides could be set up soon. The accounting operation, with Delorme still at the helm, remained in Montreal. "We are," Tavares said at the time, "geographically challenged."

The absurd arrangements made the staff yearn for life in the trailers. Finally, sick of being shooed out of one conference room to the next, Deoudes went to Cope. "Give me the keys to the trailer," he said. And in early December, the staff moved in. There were fifty-eight desks. The Nationals, by that point, had sixty employees. So, naturally, Tavares and Uhlich looked at the situation and said something to the effect of, "You know what, guys? You take the desks. We'll stay down at Foley. Give us a call if you need anything."

The ensuing weeks were some combination of summer camp and boot camp. The staff learned about each other, sometimes more than they wanted to know. Almost none of them had worked in such an operation before, and so they learned about baseball. And they learned about the men they were working for—about Cope, ideas flying a mile a minute; about Uhlich, the even-keeled Californian; and about Tavares, who, everyone soon learned, had just a *little* bit of a temper. "It's vicious," Tavares admitted. "And really, I don't say that boastfully. If there's something I could change in my personality, it would be my temper." Tavares, though, was fifty-five. Even if he had wanted to change his personality, it was highly unlikely he'd be able to. So he, and his staff, lived with his temper. He had two kinds of outbursts. There was the explosion, the one that looks horrific to outsiders but is over rather quickly, the kind, staff members said, where you could be blown out one day but completely back in his good graces the next. "And then," Tavares said, "there's the deep burn." Watch out for this one. When the deep burn arrived, it drove Tavares to tremendous headaches that split through his brain, to trips to his office with instructions, to whoever was around, not to let anyone through that fucking door lest they feel his wrath.

Uhlich, in many cases, was the filter for Tavares's deep burns. He had worked with Tavares in Anaheim. He knew what to take seriously, what not to. When the pair moved out of the Hinckley Hilton, they didn't know when new owners would buy the team, and therefore didn't know how long they would be in town. Neither of their families would join them in Washington other than to visit. "Let's get a two-bedroom place," said Tavares, aware of the bottom-line budget MLB would provide. So they shacked up in an apartment at Pennsylvania Avenue and 24th Street N.W., walking distance to Foley & Lardner. They set up computers at adjacent desks and after coming home from the office, would sit there side by side, going over a budget or an invoice or a proposal. Uhlich stayed up late. Tavares got up early. They tried to leave work at work. They couldn't always do it. But they learned even more about each other. And somehow the partnership worked. One of Tavares's favorite sayings, one he would relate often, is that "intuition is nothing more than accumulation of knowledge over a period of time." Yet if those around him didn't know Tavares well, they'd think he'd be jumping to conclusions, making rash judgments based on nothing but his gut, his intuition. Uhlich offset him. He was more studied, more methodical.

Plus Uhlich balanced out Tavares's temper. Uhlich's idea of being upset was to say, slowly and quietly, "Come on, guys," the pleading, polar opposite of Tavares. There were times, by Tavares's own admission, when Tavares would turn to Uhlich and say, "You go tell that guy I'm going to choke him if he doesn't fucking do it the way I said." And Uhlich would go take care of the situation. "I think Tony's getting upset," he'd say gently, and then impart the instructions.

Given the twenty-four-hour pace of the situation, there were moments, and plenty of them. One day, Tavares stood in one of the trailers, staff buzzing all around. The phones were ringing incessantly, and there simply weren't enough people to pick them up. The answering system that was supposed to routinely put callers on hold wasn't functioning properly. The phones rang, and rang, and rang, each chime representing a customer who was being ignored. Tavares was furious. He picked up a baseball bat. He walked into Deoudes's office.

"If I hear the phones ring one more time," Tavares growled, "I'm going to come into your office with this baseball bat. I'm going to smash the telephone. I'm going to put the phone on your desk. And I'm going to send you a bill."

The staff trudged on. They climbed over boxes in their trailers just to get from one desk to the next. They scrambled to slam the door shut when the wind flung it open. There was one Coke machine, tucked in the area that was supposed to be the bathroom, but there was no running water, so the bathroom did no good anyway, so why not put the vending machine there? Deoudes, worried about security, took copies of the *Washington Post* and taped them to his window, providing a makeshift shade. Hickey tried to sell sponsorships in this environment (though he didn't close any deals until well after the new year, earning him the nickname "Goose Egg" from Tavares). One day, an executive from PNC Bank was coming to town. "I'll meet you anywhere," Hickey said. But the exec wanted to do it at Hickey's offices.

"I'll never forget the look in his eyes," Hickey said. "He couldn't believe we were running a franchise out of these things."

Bathroom breaks, as Cope discovered on his flashlight-enabled foray, became a cruel office joke. Chartese Berry, a refined Georgetown graduate who served as the team's public relations director, grew so fed up with the treks through mud and cold that she took to climbing into her car and driving the fifty yards to the toilets, leaving her Mercedes running the whole time. "It was not," Martin said, "a good place to be a woman." When better facilities finally arrived, the fancy portable toilets with heat and sinks, the staff was so appreciative that they outfitted them with lovely soaps and air fresheners. "You'd have thought it was the Hilton," Martin said.

In a crazy way, though, the whole thing bonded the staff together. The trick, it seemed, was to avoid thinking about the enormousness of the task, although at times that was inescapable. Martin, for instance, would sneak into the stadium from time to time to find a more accomodating rest room. Once inside, she would look down from the stands onto the muddy surface that would one day be the playing field. Sometimes it was covered with snow. Eventually, home plate appeared. She began taking pictures every week, charting the project. "It helped you get a hold of exactly what we were doing," she said.

No one could tell from the outside of those trailers, but what the staff was doing inside was bringing baseball back to Washington.

•   •   •

ALAN ALPER MILLED AROUND the bright, high-ceilinged hall at Union Station, beaming at anything that passed by. He was fifty-one, but at that moment, he was a kid with a lollipop and a soda, staring at a summer of possibilities as if it were the last day of school. Washington was just starting to feel the cold of late autumn. Just three days before Thanksgiving, Union Station bustled with preholiday travelers, men and women scurrying to catch the Acela to New York, looking oddly at a curtain and a stage and the crowd standing in anticipation. The uninformed asked strangers, "What's going on?"

Forget the ignorant. Alan didn't care about those folks. He knew exactly what was going on. The kid was balding, a bit overweight, a professional physical therapist. Who he was hardly mattered, standing in the atrium at Union Station, because he knew there were others like him. Thirty-three years earlier, he'd had his lollipop and soda, his baseball team, stolen from him, snatched away and taken to Texas, someplace called Arlington, stuck between Dallas and Fort Worth, not much of a place for a big-league baseball club, really. But there they'd gone, the Washington Senators, Alper's stability, off to Texas because a man named Bob Short, the owner of the team, was offered a sweetheart deal, and Short didn't really have any attachment to Washington anyway, so he just packed up his team and took off, leaving Alan inconsolable, cold and alone. At the time he was eighteen, insecure, impressionable, scared of girls and his first year in college and whatever else lay ahead. Scared, most of all, of life without baseball.

"I have, at times, been clinically depressed," he said. "And the first time that happened was when they took my baseball team away."

So didn't those passersby, the businessmen and holiday travelers, didn't they know? Today, Alan was getting his soda, his lollipop—his ballclub—back. "I have waited for this ever since," he said, and his eyes were wide at the prospect.

Alan Alper was there for the final homestand at RFK Stadium in 1971, when the men who played for the Washington Senators were his heroes the way baseball players in the '50s and '60s and '70s were once heroes to boys and young men searching for anchors. Take away a boy's heroes, and he becomes a man with a hole in his life, someone who, in middle age, is given to standing in a train station at noon on a fall Monday, wearing a cheesy foam baseball hat and a cheesier white T-shirt, each with a crude rendition of "Washington Nationals" scrawled across the front, the logo someone ginned up during one of D.C.'s previous, failed attempts to bring baseball back. When your heroes are taken away, you become more wistful every day. You become the kind of man who tells complete strangers about the last time you had a baseball team to root for, about the searing pain of its departure, repeating phrases time and again: "It just killed me. It just killed me. I mean, *it just killed me.*"

That he didn't much like the team's new name, the Nationals, mattered little. Yes, the old name, "Senators," reminded him of his youth, "and it just flows so much better," but let's not be picky, not on such a glorious occasion. Nationals and Senators had been used interchangeably for the first half of the twentieth century, so the "Nats" had historical significance. Forget, too, that when he saw the logo, a baseball with a ribbon above it, he was underwhelmed. It seemed to befit a staid Washington institution, perhaps the Department of the Treasury or the IRS. Those details didn't matter. Over the next several hours, there was time only for cheers and smiles, smiles and cheers. He was older than the ballplayers and then some, but who cares? Now his home in Washington's Foggy Bottom neighborhood, already filled with posters and programs and books and baubles from Senators' teams gone by, would welcome fresh trinkets, symbols of Washington's new baseball team, where they would join Hondo, one of his two dogs, named, of course, after former Senators' slugger Frank "Hondo" Howard. The new memorabilia would blend right in. Heroes would return, and they would be his.

Adam Eidinger arrived at Union Station that morning not sure he would go in, pretty certain he wouldn't stay for the naming ceremony, because he had no interest in it. He was supposed to be in France with his wife and eight-month-old daughter on vacation, but a series of snafus and oversights at Washington Dulles International Airport delayed his trip by a day, then another, and now into this Monday morning. Since he was around, he figured he'd help out his friends, friends who were, like him, political activists in the District of Columbia, people who fought for the District's statehood or for the legalization of medicinal marijuana or whatever seemed worth fighting for at the time. In this case, they would hang up posters protesting the use of public funds to build a new baseball stadium in Washington. The way Eidinger saw it, the city, with crumbling public schools, with lead in its drinking water, with more than occasional shootings involving teenagers, had a plan to spend $440 million—or $530 million, or $614 million, depending on the source you asked—on a baseball stadium so that rich men could run a private business, a baseball team, in their town, making even more money for themselves.

"Is this what Washington needs?" Eidinger asked.

Eidinger grew up playing Little League baseball and attending Pittsburgh Pirates games. He remembered, as a very small child, the

Pirates' victory in the 1979 World Series, remembered even better the heartbreak of 1992, when the Atlanta Braves beat the Pirates in the seventh game of the National League Championship Series. So Eidinger didn't come to Union Station teeming with hatred for baseball per se, but rather furious that such a deal was being force-fed to the people of the District. Eidinger sensed resistance to the plan to use a tax on businesses to generate funding for a new ballpark, and a month later, a poll in the *Washington Post* revealed that most District residents believed at least half the funding should come from private sources, even if it meant losing the team. Yet as Eidinger saw it, the men staging this ceremony—the mayor of Washington, D.C., Anthony A. Williams, and the president of the ballclub that was scheduled to take up residence in the District, Tony Tavares—were simply pushing forward, oblivious. The Montreal Expos were coming to Washington, and though the players wouldn't arrive for more than five months, and very few people in the District knew their names anyway, they would be christened the Washington Nationals amid pomp and circumstance and the kind of good feeling Alan Alper wore on his face.

"They weren't listening to the people," Eidinger said.

So while Alper and the others prepared to watch Williams and Tavares tug on a rope, lowering an enormous curtain to reveal the brand-new logo of Washington's brand-new baseball team, Eidinger got to thinking. He had been through all the official avenues of protest, speaking at a hearing in front of the District Council, handing out fliers. He wasn't sure the message was getting across. He had said to friends in the preceding weeks that it was time for some civil disobedience. And who better? Eidinger had made something of a career of it. Arrests? No big deal. Once, Eidinger said, when a government official spoke at the National Press Club against the legalization of medicinal marijuana, Eidinger interrupted the speech by holding up a sign, forcing a Secret Service agent to pick him up and remove him.

Now, standing at Union Station, watching the baseball fans

gather, noting the bank of television cameras ready to record the event for posterity and the six o'clock news, Eidinger formed a few ideas. There was no security by the stage, no one guarding the microphone.

This, he thought, *is too good an opportunity to pass up.* He had a sign tucked under his arm. If he could get to the stage, if he could speak into the microphone, he could make sure the day wasn't just a faux celebration of the new team's new name. He weighed his options. *If I do this right,* he thought, *they'll have nothing to charge me with. This is a private event taking place in a public space. I have every right to be here, and they have every right to kick me out. But I can't be arrested, can I?* So he worked his way through the crowd, past Alper, whom he didn't know, and the others like him.

Eidinger arrived at the side of the stage. And before the people in the hall knew what he was doing, he was at the podium.

"This is a bad deal, people!" Eidinger screamed into the microphone, which was on, and his words, somewhat to his surprise, blared through the hall. "It's a bad deal!"

He held up his sign, a simple white posterboard with caricatures of men in tuxedos sitting inside a stadium counting their money. In one corner, in red letters, were the words "Stop the $540 million stadium giveaway!" but the $540 was crossed out, replaced with a crudely drawn $614, a reflection of the latest estimate, given by the District's own chief financial officer. In the poster's other corner were the words "Call your council member today."

It's unlikely anyone in the hall, given the awkwardness of the moment, took time to read the sign. As Eidinger screamed, someone clicked the microphone off, a deadening thump. The crowd booed a bit, then a bit more. But where was the security? And then Eidinger saw a man approaching from his left. The man put his left hand on Eidinger's chest, his right hand on his side, and pushed. It didn't matter that the hands belonged to Charlie Brotman, the bespectacled, seventy-six-year-old former public address announcer for the

Senators. Brotman came to the event in much the same way Alan Alper arrived, tingling. And some punk kid wasn't going to interrupt it. Eidinger didn't care. His goal: "Make myself as big as I could. I wanted to act like I weighed a thousand pounds." A thousand pounds, with a 150-pound man more than forty years his senior hanging off his back. It was a comedic, pathetic, symbolic, ridiculous scene, the kind that lasts for seconds but seems eternal.

Harold Brazil, a D.C. Council member, ran in to help out, hands-on government at its finest, and the tussle continued. Finally, a Union Station security guard wearing a round, flat-brimmed hat stepped in, too, and the three men—Brotman, Brazil, and the guard—wrestled Eidinger, still screaming, off the stage. John Fogerty's "Centerfield" began playing through the speakers again, and police escorted Eidinger down a back hallway, behind the Au Bon Pain and the Body Shop, away from the travelers and the baseball fans. As police began to question him, Eidinger leaned against a wall, sweating, the adrenaline still pumping. He spewed questions of his own. "Ask them why there's so much corporate greed!" he said to no one in particular. Then, to the cops: "What law did I break?"

Twenty minutes later, Williams, the mayor, and Tavares, the ballclub president, tugged at that ornamental rope. The curtain fell. The logo was revealed. Alan Alper cheered. Adam Eidinger stewed.

Baseball, gone for so long, was, indeed, back in Washington. It might have been run out of a couple of trailers set at the bottom of a parking lot. It might have faced significant opposition from a town that wasn't entirely ready to welcome its return. But even in the cold of winter, amidst the hustle and bustle of a train station, with actual games more a hope than a reality, it was back.

Chapter 2

★ ★ ★ ★ ★ ★ ★ ★ ★ ★ ★ ★ ★ ★ ★ ★ ★

The Big Train, the Old Fox, and Baseball Departs

When Washingtonians think of the day the city lost baseball, they typically reflect back to September 21, 1971, the night the owners of the twelve American League teams gathered in a hotel suite in Boston, the night they voted to allow the Washington Senators to bolt for Texas. It is an accurate, painful recollection. Yet representing it as *the* day Washington lost baseball is woefully misleading, because it is just one instance. The reality: By 1971, baseball in Washington had started up, sputtered, and evaporated over and over and over again.

Start back before the Civil War, back when government clerks played on the lawn near what was then known as the President's Mansion, a space in the backyard that was called the White Lot. Today, that same swath of grass behind the White House is referred to as the Ellipse, and it's just across the street from the makeshift diamonds where present-day government workers and lobbyists and interns and all manner of Washingtonians engage in softball games that pack the area during summer evenings. It is there that the first organized teams in Washington, the Potomacs and the National

Club, hosted games, initially against each other, then against teams from other towns. The first intercity game in the District of Columbia came in 1860, when the Potomacs suffered a 40-24 loss to the Excelsiors of Baltimore, then went drinking at the Ebbitt Hotel, just across 15th Street.

And thus it was established early on that there would be one overriding constant in Washington's professional baseball existence: failure. In 1872, Washington had two entries, the Nationals and the Olympics, in something called the National Association. Neither returned for 1873. The Washington Nationals were reborn in 1886 and had a run in the National League under the names Statesmen and Senators, but poor attendance and mismanagement led the league to strip Washington of that franchise. The town, though, tried again. This time, it was at the whim of two brothers from Philadelphia, George and J. Earl Wagner, and the Senators entered an expanded, twelve-team National League in 1892. But in eight years of owning the club, the Wagners only twice fielded a team that finished better than tenth in the league, and never did the Senators have a winning record.

So in a way, baseball in Washington turned into a sideshow act. The most notable events of the Wagners' ownership occurred away from the park, such as that summer day in 1894 when Cap Anson, the manager of the visiting Chicago Colts, boasted that his catcher, Bill "Pop" Schriver, would be able to snare a ball dropped from the top of the Washington Monument, 555 feet up. A Colts right-hander named Clark Griffith scaled the monument, which had been dedicated only a decade before, to toss out the balls to Schriver. The spectacle was performed without the approval of the authorities, who quickly caught a whiff of what was going on. They shot up the elevator to chase after Griffith, and though the local papers credited Schriver with a catch on the second toss, no such catch actually occurred, Griffith later told noted *Washington Post* columnist Shirley Povich. It would take fourteen more years before someone, a Washington catcher named Gabby Street, caught a baseball from the monument, thus giving the District perhaps its finest moment in the sport to date. By 1899, the Wagners' tenure had run its course. They were no longer trusted, neither by Washingtonians nor by the men who ran the National League, and in early 1900, Washington was dropped from the NL, having failed at baseball again.

It was at this time, though, that the most important man in the history of baseball in Washington, D.C., conspired to help form a league that would bring the sport back to the nation's capital. Clark Calvin Griffith, the same Chicago pitcher who had thrown those balls from the top of the monument, was a baseball man before there were baseball men, an accomplished pitcher who had grand ideas about his place in the game. He was born in Clear Creek, Missouri, in 1869, and took an itinerant path through baseball outposts from coast to coast before arriving in Washington.

Before he was thirty, Griffith became such a crafty pitcher that he earned the nickname "Old Fox," sly as he was, well beyond his years. Late in 1900, Griffith joined two longtime minor-league baseball men, Byron Bancroft "Ban" Johnson and Charles Comiskey, in starting a circuit that would rival the established National League. On December 7, 1900, Ban Johnson awarded franchises in the new American League to eight cities, including Washington. The team would be called, interchangeably, the Nationals or the Senators. And the chaos that characterized the ownership in years gone by—and, come to think of it, more than a century later—marked the beginning of the Senators' tenure in town. The American League named Jimmy Manning, who ran a minor league club in Kansas City, as owner of the Senators. The reality, though: Ban Johnson owned 51 percent of each and every franchise in the AL.

Yet Washington, even with this odd arrangement, had baseball. And Griffith, after stints managing the New York Highlanders and then the Cincinnati club in the old National League, came to the District to manage the Senators in 1912. He took over a team that had never posted a winning record, had never finished higher than sixth in the American League. But he had to thank one of his old minor-league teammates, Joe Cantillon, for Washington baseball's most important asset. Cantillon managed the Senators for three years, a dismal tenure in which he twice lost more than 100 games. But what if another man had been in the manager's chair when the letters trickled in, beginning early in 1907, from a baseball outpost in Idaho? What if a Senators catcher, Cliff Blankenship, hadn't broken his finger, making himself available for a scouting mission? What if Joe Cantillon hadn't been so desperate for help on the field that he failed to send Blankenship west?

What if Walter Johnson had never come to Washington?

As with any legendary figure, sporting or otherwise, myths swirl around Walter Perry Johnson, the polite, plain-spoken Kansan with the chiseled face and broad shoulders. Johnson grew up on a farm near the town of Humboldt, east of Wichita. Like Clark Griffith, another plainsman, he spent his early years as a hunter and gained a reputation as a marksman with a slingshot. But he made his career in baseball, moving to Olinda, California, with his family as a teenager, then branching out on his own, winding up in someplace called Weiser, Idaho, a hard-drinking, rough-and-tumble mining town of three thousand residents, laced with bars and saloons, not the kind of place where young Johnson, straitlaced and square, would figure to flourish. He did anyway. At one point, he threw seventy-five straight scoreless innings for Weiser, and people sent Cantillon letters, raving about "the strikeout king of the Snake River Valley League." One letter, perhaps apocryphal, reported, "This boy throws so fast you can't see 'em . . . and he knows where he is throwing the ball because if he didn't there would be dead bodies strewn all over Idaho." So when Blankenship, the catcher, suffered a broken finger and couldn't play anymore, Cantillon sent him on a mission: Go west to Wichita and sign a young outfielder named Clyde Milan. And while you're at it, head up to Weiser, Idaho, and bring back this kid Johnson.

When Johnson made his first major league appearance in August 1907, nearly everyone at the Senators' stadium, American League Park, was struck by his presence. He stood 6 feet 1 inch and had the sturdy build and leathery skin that comes from a life spent outdoors. His arms, though, defined him. They looked longer than they should have been, out of proportion to the rest of his body. When he threw, he did so easily, a fluid motion in which he turned his body clockwise until he nearly faced second base, then slung the ball in a modified sidearm fashion all his own, resulting in pitches shot not from the mound but from a place with which hitters were unfamiliar. No one else had such a windup, but Johnson made it look comfortable, as if that were the way a man was meant to throw a ball.

Johnson lost that first game and won only five times in fourteen games during his rookie season. But the Senators had their first true burgeoning star. Johnson would go on to pitch for twenty-one seasons and win 417 games, all in a Washington uniform. In the history of the game, only Cy Young himself won more times. Yet until Griffith arrived as manager and part owner, the Senators continued to stink, even with Johnson. The Old Fox, though, began to assemble talent in his own image, scrappy, small, fearless ballplayers. He snared a young second baseman named Stanley Raymond "Bucky" Harris, a slick-fielding first baseman named Joe Judge, and a consistent .300-hitting outfielder named Sam Rice. And prior to the 1920 season, he solidified his place in Washington baseball history, taking out a loan to buy a controlling interest in the Senators. He would step down as manager after 1920, but he would have his hands on the club until his death in 1955.

By the 1924 season, Griffith had his most talented team yet. Surprisingly, he turned it over to his twenty-seven-year-old second baseman, Bucky Harris, who was named the manager. He swiped an exceptional hitter, Leon Allen "Goose" Goslin, from the Baltimore Orioles, then a minor league club. He had tough and durable Muddy Ruel behind the plate; veteran Roger Peckinpaugh, late of the Yankees, at shortstop; twenty-three-year-old Ossie Bluege, a bit error-prone, at third base; Harris himself at second; Sam Rice in the outfield; and on the mound, none other than Johnson, who late in the season won thirteen straight decisions. And that group brought Washington its first pennant. On September 29, 1924, with the Senators in Boston beating the Red Sox, the news of the accomplishment was reported on a scoreboard downtown. Thousands of fans greeted the team's train at Union Station, and thousands more lined the streets for a parade unlike any the town had seen before. The *Washington Post* reported that "Pennsylvania Avenue has been the scene of many a spectacle. Presidents, kings and potentates have trod its path. But the return of the Senators was different. The joy of the cheering crowds was boundless."

Even so, the Senators were heavy underdogs in the World Series to the National League champion New York Giants, who won the Series in 1921 and '22 and lost to the Yankees in 1923. It seemed, then, that if the Senators were going to bring a World Series title to Washington, D.C., they were going to have to do it behind their one true star, Walter Johnson. But Johnson was by now thirty-six, and at times during the Series, he appeared old and tired. He lost the first game in twelve valiant innings, then dropped the crucial fifth game, looking rather unlike the pitcher from his younger years, and the Senators had to win in game six to force a seventh and deciding contest at what by this point was known as Griffith Stadium, the park on 7th Street N.W., where Howard University Hospital sits now.

Johnson wasn't supposed to pitch that day, but the Senators scrapped for two runs in the eighth to tie the game. By then, Harris had made so many moves he was running out of players. He had no choice. Johnson entered the game in the ninth. Each inning, he found trouble. Yet somehow, his arm seemed restored. In the ninth, then again in the tenth, the eleventh, and finally the twelfth, he wiggled his way out of problems. And in the bottom of the twelfth, a twenty-six-year-old rookie named Earl McNeely came to the plate for the Senators, runners on first and second, the score still tied, 3-3. He lunged at an 0-1 pitch, sending it toward third base. The crowd, not to mention the players, was sure it would be an out, and possibly a double play. Muddy Ruel, running from second, looked to see the Giants' third baseman, Freddie Lindstrom, make the play. But wait. Where was the ball? Lindstrom was leaping in the air, lunging at something above his head. The ball had hit something—a pebble, perhaps. It skipped high over Lindstrom. And there it was, in left field.

When it came time for Washington to win a World Series, it figured the city had its slowest runner on second base. But here came Ruel, chugging to third, now hitting the bag and moving home. To most in the stands, and certainly to people like Clark Griffith and Walter Johnson, the play must have taken an hour, maybe two. But when it was over, Ruel had crossed the plate, the Senators had their fourth run, the Giants stood stunned on the field, and a great roar broke out over the nation's capital. The Washington Senators were World Series champions.

The events of October 10, 1924, were, and still are, the high point of baseball in Washington. There is, unfortunately, little competition. The Senators would never again reach such heights. They won the American League pennant again in 1925, but with Walter Johnson on the mound and the Senators leading the Pittsburgh Pirates in the seventh game, Roger Peckinpaugh made a key error, and Washington lost, 9-7. They won the pennant again in 1933, but again lost the World Series, this time to the Giants in five games. And after that, nothing. The Senators had only three winning seasons in the next twenty-eight, after which Clark Griffith's nephew, Calvin, long since entrusted with Washington's baseball fortunes, moved the franchise to Minnesota.

An expansion team replaced it immediately. They were still called the Senators, and they played like them, too. They managed one winning record in the next eleven years. That lone winning season came in 1969, the same year baseball put an expansion franchise north of the border, in Canada, in the province of Quebec, in the city of Montreal.

•   •   •

THE MOST OBVIOUS KEY DATES in the history of the Montreal Expos, the ones anyone assembling a timeline would have to include, are May 27, 1968, when the city of Montreal was granted a franchise by the National League's expansion committee, and September 29, 2004, when Tony Tavares gathered the Expos' staff in the team's offices at Olympic Stadium and broke the news, amidst teary eyes, sniffles, and outright sobs, that the franchise was moving to Washington, D.C. The Expos played their last game in Montreal that night, and when a rookie outfielder named Terrmel Sledge popped up for the final out, baseball in Montreal, a tradition more than a century old, died.

In between, though, there might have been a more important date: August 12, 1994, the day baseball's players went on strike. The previous night, the Expos lost to Pittsburgh, a 4-0 shutout that was just Montreal's third loss in its last twenty-three games. The Expos were 74-40. There was no better team in baseball. The strike pulled the rug out from under the team, from under the city. The players wouldn't return until the following spring, 232 days later. In Montreal, the sport never recovered.

Katie Hynes didn't recover, either. "Every August twelfth," she said, "I still become ill." The pain, more than a decade later, is still acute for Hynes, a Quebecer all her life, a woman who turned forty-eight during the last month the Expos played in Montreal. She is as emotional about "my 'Spos," as she calls them, as Alan Alper ever was about the Senators or his brand-new Nationals. And in the summer of 1994, it was all there for her, what she had waited for since she first became a baseball fan as a young girl. Baseball, Hynes came to understand, just like Alper did nearly 600 miles south in Washington, D.C., is the most personal of sports. It grew into her heart, became part of her soul, helped her breathe, overtook her brain. At its worst, it became a distracting obsession. At its best, it gave her direction. She worked as a property manager, she said, only so she could afford to go to baseball games.

When the National League's newest expansion team came to Montreal, Katie Hynes, just a girl, awaited its arrival breathlessly. She watched as the team was christened the Expos, an ode to Expo '67, the World's Fair that had taken place the summer before. There was no new stadium, so Jarry Park, which held just 3,000 fans, had to be expanded swiftly to hold more than 28,000. It is where Katie Hynes fell in love with the Expos. Mack Jones, the left fielder on that first Expos team who drove in five runs in the team's first home game, used to scoop her up in his arms and toss her about. There was Rusty Staub, the red-haired Louisianan adopted by Montrealers as "Le Grand Orange." Bill Stoneman was the workhorse pitcher, and that he lost nineteen games that first season hardly mattered. Staub and Stoneman, Coco Laboy, Gary Sutherland, and Gene Mauch, the manager, all brought baseball to Montreal, and more than 1.2 million people filed into Jarry Park to watch them, even as they lost 110 games. The Expos became, in short order, *Nos Amours*, "Our Beloved Ones."

It was all just a natural extension, Montrealers figured, of the city's baseball heritage, which extended back at least to 1897, when the Montreal Royals took up residence in the Eastern League. In 1939, the Brooklyn Dodgers took over the franchise, and until 1960, they played in the International League, just a level below the majors. The top prospects of the Dodgers made their way through Montreal, from Roy Campanella to Duke Snider. And it is no accident that when Dodgers president Branch Rickey decided to prepare a young second baseman named Jackie Robinson to be the first African American to play in the major leagues, he figured he could ease the process by signing Robinson and sending him, for a year, to

Montreal, even then one of the most progressive and cosmopolitan cities in North America. It was there, with the Royals, at the park on the east side of town called Delorimier Downs, where Jackie Robinson made his home in 1946, leading Montreal to the minor league championship, a victory in the Little World Series.

Yet the major league experience was something different, something bigger and better. In the 1970s, after the Expos moved from Jarry Park to Olympic Stadium, the hulking edifice built for the 1976 Summer Olympics, Katie Hynes went there night after night to see the teams that became contenders in the 1980s, with stars such as Andre Dawson and Gary Carter and Tim Raines and Jeff Reardon. She was there on "Black Monday" in 1981, when the Expos made their only appearance in the playoffs, when they went to the ninth inning of the decisive game against the Dodgers tied 1-1, when Los Angeles outfielder Rick Monday sent a pitch from Montreal's Steve Rogers over the wall in right-center field at the park known as "the Big O." The Expos' best chance to reach the World Series went with it, and Katie Hynes cried before she left the park, cried on her way down into the subway, cried all the way home.

There was nothing, though, quite like the summer of 1994. It was the Expos' year. There were no questions about it then, and there are no questions about it now. That spring and summer, the team averaged better than 24,500 fans at the Big O, fans who were treated to some of the best young players in the game. Two veterans, Ken Hill and Jeff Fassero, anchored an exceptional pitching staff, but the most intriguing arm belonged to a lithe twenty-two-year-old from the Dominican Republic, flamethrowing Pedro Martinez. The outfielders were all accomplished twenty-seven-year-olds: Larry Walker, a Canadian with a rifle arm, in right; Marquis Grissom, a graceful and fleet runner, in center; and Moises Alou, the manager's son and a .339 hitter, in left. John Wetteland and Mel Rojas shared the closer's duties, and either would have dominated the role on another team. Jeff Shaw set them up, and he was talented enough that he would go on to become a closer himself. The manager was Felipe Alou, a former star player who became known during his ten-year stint as manager in Montreal as "the Master." By the end of play on August 11, the Expos held a six-game lead on the Atlanta Braves.

Katie Hynes was there for all of it, squarely in her seat at the Big O, Section 107, Row SS, Seat 1, the seat that eventually had a plaque affixed to the back, one that read simply, "Kate." "All my life, I've waited for this," Katie said of the summer of 1994. There is no overstating what the strike did to her. "All I ever wanted was a season like that." The emotions are still raw, perhaps even more so because the Expos are gone now, and there will never be another situation that might warrant that type of frenzy.

"A lot of people all over baseball, even people I see here in Montreal, they think 1981 was a real killer," Hynes said. "I disagree. When Rick Monday hit that home run, it was a crushing blow. I know. I was there. But I can accept that, because that happened on the field. I lost that game because Steve Rogers threw that pitch over the plate.

"What I can't handle is when my team is up six games on the Braves, and they cancel the balance of the season and the World Series when there wasn't a war, there wasn't a natural disaster. What was there to prevent that from happening? Those friggin' suits. We have suffered such abuse in this town."

The strike didn't end till April. When it did, the Expos were fundamentally different. Walker signed as a free agent with Colorado, where he won the National League's MVP award in 1997. Grissom, Wetteland, and Hill were all traded within a week of the strike's end. The average attendance at the Big O fell to 18,189 the following summer, and by the end of the season, Shaw had been traded, too. Moises Alou was gone by the end of '96, Martinez after '97. The cycle was clear: The Expos could develop some of the best players in the game. But they couldn't hope to keep them.

And in 1999, the team's owner, Claude Brochu, was forced out by Jeffrey Loria, a billionaire from New York who made his money dealing in twentieth-century art. "You could just tell," Katie Hynes remembered, "that they were bad people." The team finished last in the National League in attendance in 2000, last again in 2001, failing to draw even a million fans. Loria, meanwhile, moved aggressively to take on a greater financial stake, a power play that alienated not only his limited partners, but Montrealers themselves. Baseball officials, frustrated with the lack of television revenue and attendance in Montreal, were already working on plans to eliminate the Expos altogether. But Loria dug in, and the implication was plain: If he was forced out, he would sue, and the antitrust exemption that allows baseball to exist as a monopoly, that allows it to skirt regular commerce laws in the United States, could come under more scrutiny.

To appease everyone—everyone, that is, except Montreal baseball fans—the sport began a game of musical franchises. John Henry, the former owner of the Florida Marlins, took over the Boston Red Sox. Loria, the former owner of the Expos, took over the Marlins, piling Expos' computers and scouting reports and files and even cut-out figures of old Expos players into trucks and shipping them south to Miami.

And Major League Baseball, eyeing a future that clearly didn't include Montreal, took over the Expos.

•   •   •

THE NIGHT IN 1971 when Bob Short made his plea in a suite in the Sheraton Plaza in Boston, arguing that he could no longer run the Washington Senators in the District of Columbia, the Senators hosted the Cleveland Indians at Robert F. Kennedy Memorial Stadium. The Senators won, 9-1; just 1,311 lucky souls were on hand to take it all in. Perhaps an hour after the game ended, Short appeared in front of television cameras in Boston. The American League owners had voted to allow him to move his team, the Senators, to someplace called Arlington, Texas.

"I face you all in failure," Short said that night, "because I was not able to do what I wanted to do."

With that, Bob Short's name was cursed among baseball fans in Washington. When he returned to the area, as owner of the new Texas Rangers, a fan at Baltimore's Memorial Stadium promptly poured a beer on him. When he spoke at the National Press Club on 14th Street N.W. prior to the Rangers' first season in Texas—the first year when Washington had no baseball—he was introduced with awkward jokes. "If you think long enough," the emcee said, "you can think of something nice to say about Bob Short."

Robert Earl Short was born in Minneapolis, where he became a powerful trucking and hotel magnate. He grew intensely interested in sports—not as a fan, but as a businessman, so much so that when he heard the hometown basketball team, the Minneapolis Lakers, was in danger of leaving for Kansas City, he led a group to buy the franchise. In 1957, Short took over the Lakers, and in some sense became a hero in his hometown. Three years later, in a precursor to his run as owner of the Senators, he became disenchanted with dropping attendance, and he stripped the Twin Cities of professional basketball, moving the team to Los Angeles.

But Short was a politician too, and perhaps that is why he was attracted to Washington. After a stint in the Navy, he ran for Congress in his home state and lost. Still, he began a lifelong affair with politics. Short ran for lieutenant governor in 1966 and lost. In 1968, when his friend Senator Hubert H. Humphrey ran for president, Short became the treasurer for the Democratic National Committee. Humphrey lost to Richard Nixon, but Bob Short never really left Washington, and it is there that he became the first villain in modern Washington sports history. Prior to the presidential election in '68, a Washington attorney named Stanley Bregman was arguing with Short, always volatile, in Short's office at the DNC. Bregman ran Humphrey's campaign in more than a dozen states, and he needed more money to drum up support in a couple of key areas. Bregman remembers, "If you argued with Bob Short, it got heated."

Bregman saw Short's temperature rising. So, somewhat casually, he made a suggestion.

"Bob, instead of you and I arguing over money," Bregman recalls saying, "why don't you take some money and buy the Washington Senators?"

Short's demeanor changed immediately. He calmed down. His face brightened. He was no longer angry. "Do you think we can get them?" he asked.

Washington had already lost the franchise once, back in 1960, when the owner, Calvin Griffith, grew tired of losing both in the standings and at the gate and moved the team to the Minneapolis suburbs, where the Washington Senators became the Minnesota Twins. But Griffith escaped largely unscathed, because one condition of the move was that the American League would award Washington an expansion franchise. The District would continue to have baseball. By 1968, though, the expansion Senators were up for sale, this time by James H. Lemon and the estate of James M. Johnson, two of the partners who brought the team to the District. Since the new version replaced the originals, the Senators had never finished better than eighth in the ten-team American League in attendance, drawing scant crowds of seven thousand or eight thousand people to D.C. Stadium, the new multipurpose monstrosity that housed both the Senators and football's Redskins. Short won the team, outbidding entertainer Bob Hope, for $9.4 million.

"Tell the Washington people that, like Winston Churchill said of the British Empire, I did not buy the Senators to preside over their dissolution," Short proclaimed. Yet even with such assurances, some in town were wary of Short. Immediately after he gained control of the Senators, Short declined to make a commitment to the city in writing. And there were other issues, not the least of which was Short's knowledge of baseball. He had none. He called the umpires "referees." He knew he had to hire a manager, but he referred to the position as "coach." And when he wanted a list of candidates for that spot, he flipped through all the baseball names in his mind. "I think he only knew one," Bregman said. So he hired him, the legendary Ted Williams.

Somehow, Williams managed the 1969 team to a winning record and a sixth-place finish, drawing more than 918,000 fans. Short wanted to believe that was just a start, that attendance would continue to grow. But the 1970 team was lousy, losing ninety-two games, finishing in last place in the American League's East division. Attendance fell by more than 90,000, and Short began dropping heavier hints: If this continued, if there weren't changes, he'd pick his team up and move it somewhere, anywhere. He muttered that he didn't make enough revenue from parking, from concessions, from television and radio. On October 8, 1970, he held a press conference in his office at RFK Stadium, attempting to outline his predicament. It lasted three and a half hours. "I'm not threatening to move and I don't want to," Short said, "but I have the votes to move to Dallas."

Because Washington is a political town, and because Short had a reputation for being a stubborn and relentless politician, the fact that his campaign to paint a picture of futility for the public grew more aggressive is hardly surprising. And because Washington doesn't mind a conspiracy theory or two, there remains a belief that Short intentionally undermined his own team to more easily and hastily facilitate a move. After the 1970 season, he traded Eddie Brinkman, a fixture in Washington and the shortstop on the original expansion Senators in 1961; up-and-coming third baseman Aurelio Rodriguez; and pitchers Joe Coleman and Jim Hannan, the former a rising star, to the Detroit Tigers. In return, the Senators received third baseman Don Wert, who would play twenty games and hit .050 in 1971; infielder-outfielder Elliott Maddox, who hit .217 the following year; right-hander Norm McRae, who never appeared in another major league game; and fading star pitcher Denny McLain. The move was at best a curious one, at worst a thinly veiled attempt to submarine the Senators. McLain, whose troubles ranged from associating with gamblers to carrying a gun to dumping water on sportswriters, feuded constantly with Williams. Worse, he lost twenty-two games that year, his only season with the franchise.

Still, on Opening Day in 1971, the seventy-first consecutive year in which Washington hosted an opener, none of the 45,061 fans who filled RFK Stadium could have known it would be the last for a generation. That day, there seemed to be at least a modicum of positive energy at the District's ballyard, for right-hander Dick Bosman pitched a six-hitter to beat the Oakland A's and their young fireballer, Vida Blue, 8-0. The Senators hadn't won an opener since 1962. Spring was in the air. Baseball was still in Washington. There was, again, that most valuable of baseball commodities, hope.

It was short-lived. From behind the scenes came indications that Short was already trying to move the team, and Tom Vandergriff, the mayor of Arlington, Texas, was ready to pounce. Baseball Commissioner Bowie Kuhn noted in his autobiography a phone conversation he had with Short in April of 1971.

"No one can keep me in Washington, not Nixon, not [American League president Joe] Cronin, not Kuhn," Kuhn recalled Short ranting. "I will cannibalize the club if necessary. I will move wherever I want. I'll go to St. Paul, Dallas or Toronto." And in September, Short sat down for a long, rambling interview with Shirley Povich, the legendary *Washington Post* columnist whose time in town dated back all the way to the 1924 World Series, which he covered. "I don't know what the hell to do," Short complained to Povich. "Nobody believes I'm trying everything to keep the team here. . . . I've been through politics, and I'm not thin-skinned, but I can recognize an unfriendly press. Why do they have to keep rehashing all my mistakes and sowing dissension on the team?"

On September 20, President Nixon called the possibility of not having baseball in the nation's capital "heartbreaking." Speaking at the Oval Office, he said, "I hope something can be worked out so that major league baseball does not leave Washington. It has been a great tradition, going back to Walter Johnson."

Yet the following day, the American League owners gathered in Boston. The meeting lasted thirteen hours, running late into the night. The commissioner, Kuhn, made a last-ditch effort to arrange a deal that would allow Washingtonian Joseph Danzansky, the president of a supermarket chain, Giant Foods, to buy the team. The plea was as much personal as it was professional, because Kuhn had grown up in the District and had once earned $1 a day working the scoreboard over at old Griffith Stadium. But the owners were unimpressed with Danzansky's offer for the team, in large part because he would have to borrow more than $6 million of the $9 million he was offering. Plus, Short wanted upward of $12 million if he was going to sell. And Vandergriff, the mayor of Arlington, stood by anxiously. The Texans' offer was a lucrative one. Short would get a $7.5 million loan at low interest, an expanded stadium for which he would have to pay $1 annually for rent, and a $1 million television pact, not to mention favorable deals on food and parking revenue.

At 11:20 P.M., after a second vote left only Baltimore and the Chicago White Sox as dissenters, the owners ushered Vandergriff into the room to tell him the news: The Washington Senators would be moving to the town over which he presided, Arlington, Texas.

Baseball was shaken. Washington was shaken. The following day, the dispatch from Boston in the *Post*, written by George Minot, began: "The Washington Senators died at age 71 tonight."

And in his dorm room at the University of Maryland, a piece of eighteen-year-old Alan Alper died, too.

"I was an immature, lonely kid," Alper said. "This was my sense of belonging. This was my sense of identity, being a Senators fan, having a baseball team. They took my identity away from me that night."

•   •   •

IT WAS THE BOTTOM of the eighth inning when Ted Williams, the greatest hitter who ever lived, turned to Tom McCraw, a journeyman, and told McCraw to pinch-hit. McCraw went up to the plate, and he sensed something in the crowd at Robert F. Kennedy Memorial Stadium. For one thing, it was larger than normal, 14,660 paying fans and, by most estimates, some 4,000 gate-crashers. Thirty-four years later, had RFK held that crowd, it would have gone down as the smallest of the 2005 season for the Washington Nationals, a club for which none other than Tom McCraw served as hitting coach. But in those days the Senators didn't draw, and thus they were headed out of town. It was September 30, 1971, the last of the Washington Senators' 10,861 games.

When McCraw stepped to the plate in the eighth, the Senators were tied with the New York Yankees, 5-5. The fans, though, were less interested in the game—one out, runners on first and second—than they were in the larger picture. There was history to be witnessed, albeit of the dubious, depressing sort. "It's like they were angry," McCraw said.

The day was an odd one for the fans, for the players, for the city of Washington. This was an era when ballplayers frequently lived year-round in the towns in which they played, one in which many of them held off-season jobs in the area, where they raised their families. Frank Howard, the Senators' mammoth slugger who launched home runs into RFK's upper deck that are still marked by stark white seats more than thirty years later, was particularly distraught before the game.

"This isn't exactly a pleasure," he told the press. "I've been playing for the Senators for seven years and I think of this city as my home, no matter how bad we were." He called himself a "D.C. kid" but lamented the Senators' history of losing. "Nobody's going to buy a horseshit product, and that's what we've been the last two years."

The Yankees, too, were well out of the pennant race by that point, some twenty games behind division-leading Baltimore. So in a sense, the game didn't mean much to them, either. In the sixth, Howard led off against New York's starting pitcher, a lefty named

Mike Kekich. And Kekich provided Washington with perhaps its final fine moment for the next thirty-four years. "Let's just say I tried to throw him a straight pitch," Kekich told reporters afterward. "I felt sorry for the fans." In those days, Howard didn't miss many straight pitches, and he launched it into the upper deck in left, the last of his 237 homers as a Senator. It was a tiny bit of salvation. He tossed his helmet into the crowd. He blew a kiss as a curtain call.

"What can a guy do to top this?" he asked afterward. "A guy like me has maybe five big thrills in his lifetime. Well, this was my biggest tonight. I'll take it to the grave with me. This was Utopia. I can't do anything else like it. It's all downhill the rest of the way."

And it was all downhill the rest of the night. Bob Short wasn't at RFK Stadium that night. Rather, he holed up in his home in the Minneapolis suburb of Edina, listening to the radio broadcast via a special telephone hookup. He had ordered his workers back in Washington to give no indication that it was the Senators' final game. The national anthem was a tinny recording of Robert Merrill, and Povich, in the next day's *Post,* lambasted the whole affair. "The Star-Spangled Banner never before sounded so much like a dirge," he wrote. "Francis Scott Key, if he had taken another peek by the dawn's early light, would have seen that the flag ain't still there, and lyricized accordingly." Moreover, Povich characterized Arlington, Texas, as "some jerk town with the single boast it is equidistant from Dallas and Fort Worth."

So it was likely a good idea for Short to stay at home, because most of the fans, and many of the media, came merely to spew their venom at him. The signs were everywhere throughout the stadium, from "Goodbye Boob Short" to two gigantic ribbons draped from the upper deck in left field, one with "Short" and the other with "Stinks" scrawled upon them. A huge sheet draped below a section of the upper deck blared, "Bob Short Fan Club." The seats above it sat completely empty.

Alan Alper had his signs that night, too. One, on red posterboard, reflected his inner feelings, so sad: "Washington Senators: First in the hearts of their fans, 1901–1971." The second was more aggressive, a black posterboard with a wooden stick and a rope noose taped behind it: "Let's give Short a Texas send-off." Alan drove to the park alone that night, just as he had the previous two games against the Yankees, just as he had the previous week, the night after the vote to move the Senators, when Alan joined 1,457 others at RFK to watch his team beat the Indians. He could sense, just as the players could, the unrest growing in the crowd. He thought they might rush the field. "I was too chicken," Alan said.

When Tom McCraw got to the batter's box, he remembers the home plate umpire, Jim Odom, telling him, "I'm getting ready to get the hell out of here." But it was only the eighth inning. The score was still tied. Still, McCraw's response was swift. "If you go," he said, "I'm going to be in your back pocket."

They remained, though, even as the crowd grew more restless. The fans had one more cheer in them, because McCraw delivered a single against the Yankees' Jack Aker, scoring Dave Nelson with what looked like the winning run. The Senators managed a sacrifice fly to extend the lead to 7-5, but McCraw's hit would go down as the last in Senators' history.

Reliever Joe Grzenda took the mound in the top of the ninth for the Senators, his job just to record three outs, to leave Washington without a baseball team, but at least with a win. He got Felipe Alou to ground out. One down. He took a comebacker off the bat of Bobby Murcer and tossed it to McCraw, who was now playing first. Two outs.

And then it happened. The fans started pouring over the fences, onto the field. They pried loose the bases. They ripped out shreds of turf. Celebrating? Not quite. But if Washington was going to lose baseball, it was not going to do so quietly. "We couldn't control them," said Jim Honochick, the head umpire. "There was nothing we could do."

Look up the result of the Washington Senators' last game in the record book, and the score doesn't read Senators 7, Yankees 5. Instead, it is Yankees 9, Senators 0, the official score of a forfeit. The Senators needed one more out to move officially to Texas, and their fans, what few remained, wouldn't allow them to get it. That night, Merrell Whittlesey of the *Evening Star* typed out the beginning of his story. "Those die-hard fans who never leave the game until the last man is out," Whittlesey wrote, "can always say in their hearts that the Senators never left town."

The following morning, the *Post* was full of news on the final game, on Howard's homer and McCraw's single and the crowd rushing the field and the forfeit. And tucked in a corner of the front page of the sports section was the following news: Earl Foreman, lawyer and owner of the American Basketball Association's Virginia Squires, was in the process of trying to bring the San Diego Padres to Washington. There was hope anew, the kind of false hope that would tease and taunt baseball fans in the District of Columbia for the next three decades. There would be headlines over the next two years, big, bold letters proclaiming, "Washington Wins a Fresh Start in Baseball" and "DC Triumvirate Returns Baseball to RFK."

But each deal, somehow, fell through. The Padres never came. The San Francisco Giants never came. The Houston Astros never came. Baseball expanded to Miami and Denver, to Phoenix and Tampa. All the while, the nation's capital remained without the national pastime.

★ ★ ★ ★ ★ ★ ★ ★ ★ ★ ★ ★ ★ ★ ★ ★ ★ ★

Chapter 3

Washington's Gain, Montreal's Loss

*J*im Bowden had never been out of baseball in his entire adult life. But when he finally was, he moved to Hollywood, California. He always had more than a little Hollywood in him anyway, so the kid from Massachusetts who made his name in baseball in Cincinnati decided to follow his girlfriend to Tinseltown so she could chase her dream. She, like thousands of other pretty faces, figured she'd become an actress. Bowden had been the general manager of the Cincinnati Reds for more than a decade. Remaining in Cincinnati, though, wasn't getting any easier. It was where his five boys lived with his ex-wife. It was where he would always be the ex-GM. It was where he was known around every corner, in every restaurant, at every function. It was where he built his identity, and where, ultimately, he was let go, fired in the summer of 2003. To anyone who knew baseball from the inside out, Bowden was a polarizing figure. Some thought he had one of the sharpest, most creative minds in the entire sport. Others thought he was one of the most devious, conniving men in the game. Some considered the two opinions and said, "They're both right."

Whatever the take, this much was clear: Bowden was out of base-ball, and there were no assurances he would ever get back in. The sport was all he'd ever known. He'd graduated from Rollins College in Orlando, taken an internship with the Pittsburgh Pirates, and that was it. He was in, never to get back out. He was so consumed by the sport that, in his entire adult life, he had never really had a true vaca-tion. So being out of baseball was hardly an option. Within days of his dismissal by the Reds, Bowden was on ESPN, spewing opinions before that summer's trade deadline, sharing his thoughts with the public on deals he might have made when he ran the team in Cincinnati, an instant analyst. That turned into a regular gig on *Cold Pizza,* a morning show on ESPN2, and it fit Bowden well. He had always been a complex combination of image and substance, show-ing up at Reds games in a dapper suit or, from time to time, leather pants. But his mind was constantly working, usually three times as fast as the next quickest in the room, and as the postseason wore on, as he went to games on assignment for ESPN, he wrestled with his future. He loved the television work. Late at night, he would sit in a hotel room on the road, practicing his lines, analyzing his camera presence, holding forth about fictitious deals so that he could get just the right tone, just the right inflection, just the right delivery. It was fun and all, but it wasn't being *in* the game. That's where it was at, where it would always be at, for Jim Bowden: running a team, mak-ing the moves, selling the product. He was a general manager when he was thirty-one, at that point the youngest in the history of the game. He had been a general manager ever since. You don't get the nickname "Trader Jim" if you stay on TV.

During the 2004 World Series, Bowden was in St. Louis, watching the team he'd rooted for as a kid, the Boston Red Sox, sweep the Car-dinals for their first championship since 1918. When the final game ended, Bowden stood up and hugged the man at his side, longtime *Boston Globe* baseball writer Peter Gammons, who was now Bowden's colleague at ESPN. "What a moment," Bowden said. If he were going to be an analyst, he would have to get used to the moments like these from the press box, from the studio. He would have to make do.

Earlier in the week, baseball officials were hoping to put someone else in the job Bowden *really* wanted. Bob Watson, the old major league first baseman, had served as general manager for the Houston Astros and the New York Yankees. He worked in the commissioner's office, and with baseball officials cognizant of the importance of racial diversity in assembling a front office for Washington's new team, the fact that he was experienced and a well-known African American worked in his favor. Robert DuPuy, baseball's president and Commissioner Bud Selig's chief lieutenant, met with Watson, and it was widely presumed that Watson would accept the job, with the understanding that after the yet-to-be-renamed Expos were sold, he would return to the commissioner's office, where he worked as the man who meted out suspensions and fines when there were on-field altercations.

But Watson said no.

"I just don't think it's right for me," Watson said at the time. "I think it's better that I stay in the commissioner's office."

So Bowden had his opening. The job, of course, was not for everyone, because there was no security in it. A new owner could, and presumably would, come in and replace whoever was keeping the seat warm with his own, hand-picked choice. Yet to someone like Bowden, in need of an avenue back to baseball, it was a perfect fit. Dan Duquette, the former Red Sox GM, also spoke with DuPuy because he, too, wanted back in. Pat Gillick, who built a World Series champion in Toronto and successfully helped build both the Baltimore Orioles and Seattle Mariners into playoff franchises, campaigned for the job as well. But over the final week of October, Bowden placed a call to DuPuy. He wanted to do this. In some ways, he *needed* to do this. DuPuy called Tavares, asking what he thought. Tavares said, "Fine." He had never met Jim Bowden, never spoken to him. Yet at forty-three, a dozen years after he landed his first GM job, Bowden was hired to be Washington's first general manager since 1971, when Bob Short, the miserly owner, had served as his own GM. It was a Sunday, Halloween night, when Bowden got the official word. The announcement wouldn't come until Tuesday. But Bowden was working already. On Tuesday morning, before most of baseball was aware Bowden was back in the game, he called Bill Stoneman, the general manager of the newly renamed Los Angeles Angels of Anaheim. There was one player Bowden wanted.

"Bill?" Bowden recalls saying. "Jim Bowden. How are you?"

Stoneman, a bit mystified, said he was fine.

"I just want you to know," Bowden said, "if you're going to move Jose Guillen, I have interest in him."

In the old days, this call would have been routine. Bowden was always interested in players who might be available, and even some who weren't. He was always checking in to see what was going on, always annoying his fellow general managers because he would call, call again, call a third time, even if the answer was always the same. The idea was simple: If you keep calling, then, when that other GM is finally ready to move a player, whose name will pop into his head? Why, yours, of course.

"We have a limited budget," Bowden continued in his conversation with Stoneman. "Our payroll is probably going to be somewhere in the $45–50 million range. And I know Jose has worn out his welcome there."

Bowden hadn't even been officially named Washington's general manager. He was just trying to have a little fun, trying to catch Stoneman off guard. It was all part of the show, all part of being Jim Bowden. He took baseball seriously, but he also took it as entertainment, and he had a significant amount of ham in him. His critics said he made deals for the sake of making deals. His pals believed he thought everything out carefully but then juiced up the entertainment value while analyzing a deal for the press. On the day after Bowden was hired by the Washington club, Paul Daugherty, a columnist for the *Cincinnati Enquirer*, summed it up this way:

Jim Bowden was always about showing off, often in the best sense.

Look at me: I traded my Opening Day pitcher the day before Opening Day. I got Sean Casey for Dave Burba. Casey is a living legend in Cincinnati. Where's Dave Burba now? I got Ron Gant for peanuts, because you wouldn't take a chance on him recovering from a broken leg. I got Pete Schourek from the recycling bin and he won 18 games. I got Pete Harnisch and Denny Neagle. I brought in Kevin Mitchell and Deion Sanders. . . .

Admit it: Wasn't life just a little better around here with Ol' Leatherpants behind the big desk?

So as the show went on, Stoneman, the same man who'd lost nineteen games for the first version of the Montreal Expos back in 1969, could only sit there and wonder. He asked Bowden who the heck he was with.

And Bowden told him he was taking over the Expos as they moved to Washington, that it would be announced later that day, that he wanted—no, he *needed*—Guillen for his new club. The funny thing was that this was the second time the Expos had contacted Stoneman about Guillen. At the end of the season, Tony Tavares, who hired Stoneman as the Angels' general manager when Tavares ran that club, told assistant general manager Tony Siegle to call Stoneman about Guillen. Siegle talked with Stoneman at the World Series. Neither man could know that within days, Jim Bowden would be making the same request—for the same club.

Bowden knew Guillen, knew his history. Guillen had caused problems nearly everywhere he went, from Pittsburgh as a teenager to Tampa Bay to Cincinnati and, finally, to the Angels, where it came to a head: where he was removed for a pinch runner in the heat of a pennant race, where he tossed his helmet in the direction of manager Mike Scioscia, and where he was finally suspended even though he was a valuable member of a team bound for the playoffs. To Bowden, all that wasn't a problem. Rather, it was an opportunity. When Bowden got the Washington job, he called the Expos' manager, Frank Robinson, asking what he needed. Robinson ticked off the list: A shortstop. A third baseman. A left-handed starting pitcher. Some veteran help on the bench. And a right fielder with some power.

With Guillen, Bowden had anticipated the request for a right fielder. Yet there were several complicating issues. The job as Expos' GM, the chair in which Bowden now sat, was open in the first place because Omar Minaya, whom Major League Baseball had hired when it took over the Expos in 2002, left near the end of the 2004 season to take the same job with his hometown New York Mets. Now, needing some power for his new club, Minaya was ready to trade with Stoneman, too. At the general managers' meetings in Key Biscayne, Florida, where the executives met at the posh Ritz-Carlton, hosting each other in their suites, mingling with agents, Minaya talked with Stoneman. Bowden talked with Stoneman. Each tried to lay the groundwork to get Guillen. The Angels wanted one of two young Expos' relievers, either Chad Cordero or Luis Ayala, and the Expos' young shortstop, Maicer Izturis. Bowden said no, because the two pitchers figured to be part of the foundation of his club, and he didn't have another shortstop in the system who was ready for the major leagues. He preferred to give up supplementary parts, perhaps outfielder Juan Rivera. Minaya, with a new job and new money to spend, continued his pursuit as well.

Bowden, though, had one advantage: He, too, lived in southern California. So when he and Stoneman flew back from the general managers' meetings, they happened to be on the same plane. They happened to be picking up their luggage from the same carousel. When Stoneman retrieved his stuff, Bowden was waiting. He couldn't part with Cordero or Ayala, not with the lack of depth in the Expos' farm system. But Bowden said he wanted to find a match. Stoneman looked at him and explained, in simple terms, his parameters for any deal. He told Bowden that if any leak appeared in the press regarding Guillen and the Washington franchise, then the potential for a trade was off. Bowden, who had a reputation of being fairly open with the press, was taken aback, yet took it seriously. And he sat on it. "I didn't even discuss it internally," Bowden said. One thought guided his silence: *I've got to have this guy. I can't afford to lose him.*

And he went about pursuing other priorities. There was no shortage of issues to address with the Expos, who were the National League's second-worst team in 2004. The previous year's third baseman, Tony Batista, earned $1.5 million, but hit thirty-two homers, was a free agent, and wanted a hefty raise. But Bowden identified two other free agent targets for third base, Minnesota's Corey Koskie and Colorado's Vinny Castilla. They needed a shortstop because Bowden believed Izturis would struggle if he had to play every day. But the market for shortstops was the hottest of any position, with St. Louis's Edgar Renteria and Boston's Orlando Cabrera—who, three months earlier, had been an Expo, having been shipped to the Red Sox because Montreal had little chance of signing him when he became a free agent—commanding as much as $10 million annually. The Expos would have to look elsewhere. They needed, too, a leadoff hitter, because Brad Wilkerson, who filled the role the year before, was better suited to hitting down in the order, and the other choice, Endy Chavez, didn't appeal much to Bowden.

So Bowden went to work. Tavares had not given him a final payroll number, because Tavares hadn't yet received one from DuPuy, who, with no owner, played the largest role in determining such matters for the franchise. Tavares and Bowden figured they could spend around $45 million, maybe a bit more. No Renteria, no Cabrera, no Nomar Garciaparra, the top shortstops on the market, all too expensive. So Bowden went for what he thought was the next best thing. Minnesota's Cristian Guzman could make a flashy play in the field.

He could hit a triple. His batting average, over a six-year career, was .266. He had played on winners with the Twins. There was, Bowden thought, enough there to overlook an abysmal on-base percentage of .303.

There, too, was another element. The franchise's farm system was bereft of talent, and there was almost nothing to trade. Bowden thought ahead. Sign Guzman, and Izturis could be trade bait. Anaheim liked him. Would that be enough to spring Guillen?

Bowden made the decision to try to land Guzman quickly. The goal: Get him for $3.5 to $4 million annually. Guzman's representative, Stanley King, balked at such a proposal. Why sign for that in November, before the shortstop market had even begun to heat up? But Bowden pressed, in effect bidding against himself, and he pushed the price up.

And there were other items to pursue, too, right at the same time, in rapid-fire succession. Washington hadn't experienced a hot-stove league in a generation, had never experienced one during the free-agent era. The town hadn't yet met the players it would be rooting for, hadn't grown attached to the ones who might depart. "It's so exciting to think that these players, the ones they're pursuing, will be playing for Washington, D.C.," Alan Alper said. "I think, if the pitching holds up, I think we could surprise some people." It was official: For a few in Washington, baseball's annual off-season extravaganza was back. Listen to Alan Alper describe his new team as "we," and there was little doubt.

Koskie quickly rose out of the Expos' price range, and eventually signed for three years and $17 million with the Toronto Blue Jays. So Bowden turned his attention to Castilla. Most in baseball were scared off because Castilla's success seemed to be limited to Denver's Coors Field, where he launched the ball through the thin air. Though he led the National League in runs batted in in 2004, he struggled away from home. Some teams were willing to give Castilla, who would turn thirty-eight during the season, a one-year deal.

Bowden, mindful that Castilla still played superb defense, was willing to offer two.

Simultaneously, he pursued his shortstop. It was clear by now that the Twins would let Guzman walk. "We can't pay that kind of money for him," general manager Terry Ryan said. "Other teams might be able to, but the Minnesota Twins can't." The Twins would do what they always did—fill in with a prospect.

Bowden didn't feel like the Expos could wait. He upped the offer for Guzman to four years, $16.8 million. In the meantime, he called Robinson: Whom would he rather have at third base, Castilla or Batista? Bowden figured the two players would, in the end, cost about the same. Robinson didn't hesitate. He chose Castilla. Washington offered Castilla what no one else would, two years for $6.2 million.

"We're not a big-market club," Bowden said at the time. "We had to move fast. We can't wait—and then end up competing for these guys anyway."

So in a single day, November 16, 2004, Jim Bowden, the general manager who didn't know whether he would be a general manager or a talking head in two months, committed $24 million of a new owner's money, a new owner who had yet to be identified, to Vinny Castilla and Cristian Guzman. Others around baseball rolled their eyes. The Expos, they said, had paid too much. Castilla was too old, his numbers inflated. Guzman was too lazy, too unfocused, and didn't get on base enough to be worth that kind of money.

Bowden, though, shrugged it off. "Time will tell if they're overpaid," he said. The franchise's situation, he said, played a role. Not everyone was willing to come play for a team that had no owner. Not everyone was willing to come play in a city that hadn't yet approved legislation for a new stadium, thus making its mere presence in Washington unstable. The ex-Expos, still a week from being renamed the Washington Nationals, were inherently fragile, and that fact led to some questionable deals.

"This franchise wasn't a destination," Bowden said later in the season. "We felt we *had to* overpay to get players to come here. This is a 67-win club. This is not the first choice of free agents. You don't have a definite home. We *think* it's going to be Washington, but nothing is definitive. And we need to get better. We thought revenues would be better than they were in Montreal, and that would help provide some of that money. And we thought we could make Guzman a better player."

Washington's new team was still dealing with an old stigma, the stigma that came with being the Montreal Expos.

•   •   •

BEING THE EXPOS over the previous three years had meant being a part of something unprecedented in the highest levels of pro sports in North America. Consider that in February 2002, Tony Siegle sat in his office, new to his job, though he had been in baseball thirty-seven years, starting as a scoreboard operator at the old Astrodome in Houston before learning the rules of the game backward and forward. Not three strikes and you're out or the infield fly, but the minutiae of contracts and free agency and waivers and options, the items fans read in the tiny print in the newspaper under "Transactions," the stuff a scant few really understand. Tony Siegle, baseball administrator, understands them all. At the time, he was the assistant general manager in Montreal under Omar Minaya, the twenty-second general manager for whom Siegle had worked. Sometimes that gnawed at him. Why was he never the choice? Other times, though, he reveled in it, because more than anything, Tony Siegle respected the game, revered the game, loved the game.

With a new job came new faces, new personalities, so on the greaseboard in his office Siegle wrote the names of players in the Expos organization, their positions, and their contract status. And that day, Tony Tavares walked into Siegle's office at the Expos' spring training facility in Jupiter, Florida. Tavares, by this point, had resigned as president of the Anaheim Angels and hockey's Mighty

Ducks in January, worn out after nine years in which he gained a reputation for being outspoken and a tad controversial. Little more than a month later, the bizarre baseball transaction that ended up with Major League Baseball purchasing the Expos led Tavares to Jupiter.

Only once before, when the Philadelphia Phillies were late on their rent payments at Shibe Park in February 1943, had the commissioner's office ever taken such a step, seizing control of a franchise that still intended to field a team that season. Such an arrangement could exist only in baseball, which even in the twenty-first century is protected by an antitrust exemption that dates to 1922, one that doesn't apply to the National Football League, the National Basketball Association, or the National Hockey League. In baseball, one man, Bud Selig, could simultaneously be owner of the Milwaukee Brewers and commissioner of the sport. In baseball, Selig and the other owners could all have stakes in one of their competitors.

So with the Expos under baseball's control, Selig appointed, in one fell swoop, Tavares as the team's president; Minaya, who had worked for the New York Mets and had a reputation as a sterling evaluator of talent, as the GM; and Frank Robinson, a Hall of Fame outfielder who at sixty-six had thought he was through with jobs on the field, as the manager.

"This is a one-year shot for me," Robinson said, and that it was supposed to be for everyone. Selig hired Tavares, Minaya, and Robinson just to mind the store for the 2002 season. The Montreal Expos wouldn't exist beyond that. They would be eliminated. Gone. Poof! Into thin air, a process known at the time as "contraction," and it had been approved by baseball's owners, 28-2, the previous November. The only two franchises to object were the two targets, the Expos and the Minnesota Twins, two franchises baseball believed couldn't generate enough local revenue, largely through television contracts and the sale of luxury suites in their ballparks, to compete with the other twenty-eight. There was no pretense about it. "We are going to contract," Selig said on February 12, 2002, the day Tavares and his underlings were installed, when the Expos headed into what would surely be their last season. "The road map is out there very clearly so everyone knows what the intentions of the 30 clubs are."

So part of Tavares's appearance at spring training—indeed, in Siegle's office that day—was to make sure the Expos' employees understood the direction of the franchise. He grabbed a green grease pencil and in large letters wrote "CONTRACT" across the names and positions and people neatly laid out on Siegle's board. With a sweeping motion, he underlined it.

"There's no way this team is not going to contract," Tavares said. As Siegle remembered it, he was getting animated now. "You can take that to the bank." This is how the two men met, an awkward introduction that fit the circumstances perfectly, because never in baseball history had there been a situation this awkward.

But when baseball didn't contract, when the players' union objected and the Twins won their division and the entire "road map" to which Selig had referred fell apart, the Expos were left with a reputation as the least desirable franchise for which to play. The situation was at best dysfunctional, and it had nothing to do with the city of Montreal, with the few fans who showed up or the droves that stayed away. Rather, it had everything to do with the structure Selig put in place. In a normal situation, the owner would hire the president, the president would have significant input on the general manager, and the GM would have his say on the manager. In Montreal over those last few years, all three men believed they had been singled out by Selig, that they were untouchable unless the commissioner himself wanted them out. Tavares thought he had been given the right to run the franchise as he would any other, and he bristled when Robinson didn't follow his orders. Robinson, who had spent nearly half a century in the sport and was proud of it, bristled under Tavares's leadership. Minaya, an affable man in a position of leadership for the first time, couldn't decide with whom to side and was left in the middle.

That Robinson was even involved in the situation at all was a surprise not only to Montrealers, not only to Tavares and Minaya, but to Robinson himself. Selig had originally approached him backstage at a dinner in New York honoring the memory of Jackie Robinson. He was much closer to retirement age than to his playing days. He hadn't managed since 1991 and had never overseen a truly successful club. His legacy in baseball, though, was secure. He'd hit 586 home runs, the fourth-highest total in history until Barry Bonds blew past. He'd won the National League Most Valuable Player award as an outfielder with the Cincinnati Reds in 1961 and the American League Most Valuable Player award as an outfielder with the Baltimore Orioles in 1966, and was still the only player to have earned the honor in both leagues. He'd won two World Series titles, become the first African-American manager in the history of the game, and been enshrined in the Hall of Fame in 1982. Baseball, in turn, had taken care of him, and in the winter of 2002, he remained the sport's director of on-field operations, doling out fines and suspensions, a cop who prosecuted crimes such as throwing at batters' heads or brawling. He didn't much like the job, but it kept him in the game. His on-field duties, he figured, were long since done.

"I had my shot," he said. "But if that's what he wanted me to do, I'd do it. That's the way I've always been, basically. I've been what they call a good soldier."

It is a self-characterization that makes those who know Robinson, who have worked with him, laugh. Robinson, even in his playing days, had a reputation as a hardheaded, independent thinker. The idea of Robinson falling into line, even to appease the commissioner, seemed absurd. Plus, there was the matter of mulling over the decision with his own closest advisors, his wife, Barbara, and his daughter, Nichelle.

"You're nuts," Barbara said. "Stay where you are."

This is the kind of conversation Frank Robinson had frequently with his wife and daughter. He would ask for their advice, and they would gladly give it. Then he would go the other way. "Why don't you listen to us?" they would ask, and Frank would respond that he *did* listen, that he took what they said into consideration. But he had always done what he thought was right, regardless of what others said, so he would continue to do just that. They might think he was nuts. It didn't matter.

"I think they've come to the point, sometime in the years that have gone by, that this is my life," Robinson said. "Baseball. It's in my blood. And they've come to accept that."

Robinson, though, was never really accepted in Montreal, and his stint with the Expos was tumultuous. He had legendary fights with a third baseman, Fernando Tatis, who bristled every time Robinson removed him from the lineup, be it for a pinch runner or a new defender. It grated on Robinson. "Here's a guy who can't cover his shadow out there, range-wise, and he made the statement that he's the best defensive third baseman that we had on the ballclub," Robinson said. "I just looked at him and said, 'You got to be shitting me,'" and the conflict filtered through the locker room. Robinson had a brusque relationship with the Montreal press, which had doted on former manager Felipe Alou. He was questioned for all sorts of strategic missteps, such as inserting pinch runners too late or removing pitchers too early. In 2004, cameras caught him dozing in the dugout; he blamed his heavy eyelids on taking too much Sudafed to relieve a sinus problem.

Even with all that, there was no more dramatic, controversial night during Robinson's stint in Montreal than July 16, 2002, the night Frank Robinson quit as the Expos' manager. A right-hander named Tony Armas Jr., son of a former major league slugger, couldn't find the plate, walking five men and throwing three wild pitches. When Robinson emerged from the dugout to remove Armas, the pitcher walked off the mound before Robinson arrived.

This, any good baseball man knows, is unacceptable, and Robinson laid into Armas in the dugout. The situation reached a full boil by the end of the game, a miserable loss for the Expos, and the clubhouse remained closed for half an hour. Inside, Robinson took off his jersey, ranting to the team. He didn't need this shit, he said. And he tossed his jersey to Minaya. He quit.

"People say, 'You were a superstar, so you don't understand,'" Robinson said three years later. "I don't give a shit about that. I don't have to be a superstar to understand that you should do things the proper way. I don't have to be a superstar to know that when a guy doesn't have it, he doesn't have it. You throw the ball over the plate, or you come out. It's that simple.

"But then they say, 'Well, you have no confidence in me.' No confidence? I have confidence in you because I give you the ball. That's all the confidence you should need. But some of these guys, that's not enough."

He sighed. "Yep, those are the things that drive me crazy."

The conversation in Robinson's office lasted deep into the night, and it involved the hitting coach, Tom McCraw, one of Robinson's oldest friends, as well as Minaya and Siegle and, intermittently, a player or two, veterans Wil Cordero and Andres Galarraga. When Robinson left that night, he told Minaya and Siegle he'd let them know the next day whether he wanted to remain.

He stayed. The Expos went on to finish 83-79, second in the division. The following year, they matched that mark. In 2004, they dropped to 67-95, last place. But through it all, Frank Robinson rediscovered that, even though his frustration frequently was piqued and his disdain for certain players was plain, he liked this job. He wanted this job.

"What I found," he said, "was that the players' effort, their energy, gave me energy. I drew off that. And it made me want to come back. So I did."

Robinson, though, didn't offer the Expos any true stability, because it was widely perceived that he could retire at any moment. The franchise, too, annually finished last in baseball in attendance, drawing just 812,000 fans in 2002. By the time 2003 rolled around, Major League Baseball needed to raise the Expos' revenues any way it could. There was seemingly no way to stem the losses. But then a Puerto Rican promoter, Antonio Munoz, approached the league. They could stage some of the games in San Juan. They could bring in an extra $350,000 a year. They could fix up forty-year-old Hiram Bithorn Stadium and make it the Expos' second home.

And so the final chapter in the Expos' existence began. On April 11, 2003, the franchise held its home opener more than 1,900 miles from Montreal. They beat the New York Mets, 10-0. That the event even took place was something of a minor miracle. The Expos had a tiny suite of offices at the stadium, in which the air-conditioning worked infrequently, the computer lines even less often. The team ordered washers and dryers to clean its uniforms on site, but they didn't work, so each night the clubhouse attendants hauled the filthy laundry back to the hotel. The day before the first game, there were no towels in the clubhouses, and Tavares pulled out his own credit card, handed it to a clubhouse attendant in front of one of the local workers, and said, "Listen, go across to the mall and buy towels, and we'll bill them back to Señor Munoz." The worker looked on, shocked, as Tavares continued instructing his clubhouse attendant: "Get the most expensive, plush towels you can find. The best, and we'll just bill Señor Munoz." New towels arrived in the clubhouse by 4 P.M.

The artificial surface would bake in the sun over the course of an afternoon, leaving the players to cook on it. After one game, catcher Brian Schneider, badly dehydrated, had to be taken to the clubhouse and quite literally packed in ice, his body almost in shock. On its daily trips from the hotel, the El San Juan, the team bus was accompanied by a police escort, because there was no telling what might happen en route. The hotel was perfectly acceptable, save for the occasional cockroach the size of a small rodent, a staple of island life. And the hosts took care of the Expos as best they could. The players from Latin American countries loved the postgame meals of goat meat; those from the United States, not so much.

Tavares, who oversaw the project, occasionally grew furious with the stadium's staff. In the days leading up to the opener, he walked through the stadium and happened upon a group of men fixing some broken seats. From a distance, it appeared that only one worker was tending to the project, while seven others stood and watched.

Tavares shot up the stairs. "Guys," he said, and he started pointing and counting in Spanish, *Uno, dos, tres, quatro,* ticking off the number of men. "What's going on?" The workers shrugged, pointed to the man doing the work, and held out their hands, palms up. There was just one wrench. What else could they do?

The Expos players became the butt of baseball jokes, though the situation was totally out of their control. Many of them didn't even rent apartments in Montreal those final two seasons because they weren't in town enough to make it worthwhile. Instead, they stayed in hotel rooms. Never has a major league franchise been so itinerant. On May 25, 2003, the Expos left Montreal following a win over the Phillies. They played three games in Miami against the Marlins, three in Philadelphia against the Phillies. They headed to San Juan for a six-game "homestand" against the Angels and the Texas Rangers. Their flight left Puerto Rico on June 8, bound, naturally, for Seattle. "And we had to stop for fuel in Atlanta," pitcher Joey Eischen said. "By the time we got off the plane, we were delirious. We were talking about hunting moose and whether we'd see a bear. We could hardly stand." They played three against the Mariners, flew south for three more at Oakland, then jetted cross-country for three more in Pittsburgh. In all, they played twenty-two straight games away from home, and it didn't even count in the books as a road trip. At the end of the season, the players voted not to allow a repeat of the experience the following year, but they were forced to do so anyway.

"At the end of the day," Tavares said, "the biggest problem with the players was no matter how you cut this, it's another twenty days on the road."

The Expos didn't know it, but their fate was being decided during road trips like that. The two stints in Puerto Rico in 2003 and 2004 were the final indication that baseball in Montreal was over. By then, suitors for the franchise had been identified. There was Washington, D.C. There was northern Virginia. There was Portland, Oregon. Later, there came Monterrey, Mexico; Las Vegas; Norfolk, Virginia; and even San Juan itself.

Baseball officials, led by Selig and his chief negotiator, Chicago White Sox owner Jerry Reinsdorf, demanded that any new home for the Expos provide a fully funded stadium. The league would then sell the team to new ownership, earning a return on its investment of $120 million, the sum it paid the Expos' former owner, Jeffrey Loria, back in 2002. The primary complication for Washington, it seemed, was Peter Angelos, the owner of the Baltimore Orioles, a staunch opponent of baseball in the nation's capital because, quite simply, he considered Washington part of his territory, and any new franchise there would have an adverse impact on his own team. Selig, the man making the final call, had a reputation as a consensus builder among the owners, an exclusive club that was fiercely loyal to one another. He needed the approval of only three-quarters of them to make such a move, but he preferred 30-0 votes. The Angelos issue was Washington's major hurdle.

Yet as the Expos crisscrossed North America and crowds in Montreal dwindled to 4,000 or 5,000 a night, there was no viable alternative. Washington Mayor Anthony A. Williams drew up a plan to provide a $440 million stadium in a run-down neighborhood along the Anacostia River. Northern Virginia, it seemed, might be more palatable to Angelos, and the area offered a plan for a stadium near Dulles International Airport, nearly thirty miles from downtown Washington and even farther from Baltimore. Williams felt like he was being set up. "I thought the process was rigged," he said. "I thought we would lose." But when Virginia's governor, Mark Warner, told the organizers of his state's bid that the commonwealth could not provide funding for a stadium, that it would be left to the local municipalities, Virginia's bid collapsed. Immediately, baseball officials began to work on a package that would compensate Angelos for the mere presence of a team in Washington, D.C. The deal guaranteed Angelos $130 million annually in revenue, and it set the minimum value of the Orioles at $365 million should he decide to sell.

Suddenly, one day shy of thirty-three years since the Senators played their last game at Robert F. Kennedy Stadium, Washington stood alone. The sense of anticipation in the District of Columbia on September 29, 2004, was palatable. In Montreal, the mood was miserable. The Expos were to play their last home game of the season that night. This time, it seemed final. It wouldn't just be the last game of the season. It would be the last game. Period.

That day, Katie Hynes woke up late. She called her mother. "I'm about to go to my last game, Ma," she said. It wasn't official, but she could sense it. She put on her Gary Carter jersey, the one she normally wore only on the road. She didn't ride her bike that day. Too shaky. The metro would be better. Once aboard, people looked at her, the jersey on her back, the white Expos cap on her head, and nodded. She knew. They knew. This was it.

The rumors swirled that day inside the Expos offices at Olympic Stadium. Frustrated, Tony Tavares called Bob DuPuy, MLB's president.

"Bob," Tavares said, "what the hell's going on?"

"Oh," DuPuy said. "Nobody called you?"

Um, no, Bob, nobody had. "I was not the happiest camper," Tavares said.

So DuPuy told Tavares what everyone already seemed to know: The Expos would move to Washington, D.C. Selig signed the paper that day. And in Washington, Mayor Williams was joined by District

Council members Jack Evans and Linda Cropp, two baseball supporters, in donning red Washington Senators caps from years gone
by and screaming to an adoring crowd at the City Museum downtown. Methodically, through his lisp, Williams slowly shouted the
words, "After thirty years of waiting"—pause—"and waiting"—
another pause—"and waiting"—the crowd cheered—"and lots of
hard work and more than a few prayers"—now the final pause—
"there will be baseball in Washington in 2005!"

The joy in Washington was perfectly offset by the misery in Montreal. It was left, then, to Tavares to assemble the team's employees and
relay the news. Tavares's eyes watered when he told them their team, in
their city, would be no more. "It's as tough a thing as I've ever done in
business," Tavares said, but there it was. It was done. The only way to
get through it, the employees decided, was to stage that night's game,
the final one, because that's what they were supposed to do anyway,
and the crowd had already begun to gather outside. This wouldn't be
one of those nights when a home run could hit the back of a seat in the
outfield and fall to the floor with no one there to retrieve it. For the
Expos' final game, there would be some 31,395 fans at the Big O.

As Katie Hynes completed an interview with a television station
outside the gate, someone came up and whispered in the inter-
viewer's ear. She turned back to Katie. "Madam," she said, "I have
to tell you that Tony Tavares just announced that this is your last
game." Katie lost it. She went inside the stadium, and she sobbed.
She found her seat, and she sobbed. She saw the ushers, the same
people she had seen for years, and she sobbed. They let the fans on
the field to talk to the players, to exchange stories and handshakes
and hugs, and Katie Hynes sobbed through all of it. To each game,
she had always brought a bag including her Walkman and her score-
cards so that she could listen to the broadcast and meticulously keep
score. She would then total up the card on the metro on the way
home, balancing it out, making sure each play was recorded correctly. She knew the details of games her friends and even the play-

ers had long since forgotten. But about this day, the toughest day of her life, she can't remember a thing that happened in the game. The scorecard, which she still has, remains unfinished, with no totals recorded. It is, however, dotted with smears, wet marks from her tears shed throughout the course of the game.

After the last out, after the Expos lost and prepared to head for New York for the final three games of their existence against the Mets, a video montage appeared on the scoreboard, one that was set to Green Day's "Good Riddance (Time of Your Life)" and Sarah McLachlan's "I Will Remember You." Katie Hynes watched it through her tears. To this day, she can't listen to those songs without breaking up. They remained in the stands for maybe two hours, Katie and her friends, and then they headed to Hurley's, their favorite pub, to mull it all over. The winter would be excruciating, but she would continue to do interviews, continue to talk about her 'Spos, because "I want to make sure everyone knows it's our team. I want to make sure everyone knows Montreal *is* a baseball town."

In February, Alan Alper picked up a newspaper in Washington, D.C., and read a reference to Katie Hynes, the woman who'd lost her baseball team. Alan looked her up and called her. "I know what she's been through," he said, thinking back to the day his Senators left for Texas.

As the weeks went by, and Opening Day—such a joyous occasion for Alan, such a miserable affair for Katie—grew closer, Alan bought a ticket for the Nationals' first game at Robert F. Kennedy Stadium, an exhibition the day before the season started. He bought it in Section 107, the number of Katie's section back at the Big O. And Alan called her. "Come to a game," he said.

She couldn't.

• • •

THIS, THEN, WAS THE TEAM to which Jim Bowden was trying to lure players, the ex-Expos. Casting a further pall over the situation, even after Bowden signed third baseman Vinny Castilla and shortstop Cristian Guzman, was the fact that the team hadn't even yet been renamed the Nationals, didn't yet have a new owner with deep pockets. Yet Bowden had no choice. He had to look for more ways to fill more gaps. Next up: a leadoff hitter.

Manager Frank Robinson had enormous respect for Brad Wilkerson, the versatile kid from Kentucky who'd batted first more than any other player for the 2004 Expos. But Robinson knew Wilkerson had done so out of necessity, not because it was a position that suited him well. Wilkerson got on base regularly, a coveted quality in a leadoff man, but he wasn't particularly fast, didn't bunt and steal bases. Rather, he hit thirty-two homers in 2004. If Wilkerson could show that pop from a spot lower in the lineup, he might be able to drive in more runs. So Bowden called the Red Sox about Dave Roberts, the swift center fielder who, as a reserve, helped Boston win the American League Championship Series by swiping a key base against the New York Yankees and scoring from second on a single. The Red Sox, though, wanted the Expos' young shortstop, Maicer Izturis, in return. That was fine. With Guzman in the fold, Izturis was expendable. Bowden would have made the trade. But he had to call Bill Stoneman, general manager of the Anaheim Angels, again. He had to check on Jose Guillen.

"It was the first time," Bowden said later, "I had legitimate leverage in a deal."

The Angels were going to lose their shortstop, David Eckstein, to free agency. They had not yet signed free agent Orlando Cabrera, a move that wouldn't happen until nearly two months later. Izturis would be a decent stopgap, a kid who could catch the ball, if nothing else. Bowden called Stoneman yet again. If he could use Izturis, coupled with outfielder Juan Rivera, to land Guillen, he would. If he couldn't, he'd try to ship the shortstop to Boston for Roberts.

"Bill," Bowden recalled saying in a phone conversation, "I just want to make sure that you won't do this deal with Guillen if Izturis is in it. Otherwise, I'm going to move Izturis, because I have another deal. But I'm not going to make that deal if you'll take Izturis and Rivera for him."

Bowden's obsession with Guillen would have seemed inexplicable to other general managers given Guillen's history of troubles, troubles that long ago had stripped him of his status as one of the top prospects in baseball when the Pittsburgh Pirates signed him as a teenager out of the Dominican Republic. But just when Guillen looked like he would wash out of baseball, having been released by the Arizona Diamondbacks in 2002, Bowden signed him to a minor league deal with the Cincinnati Reds. It was a classic Bowden move, taking a discarded player who had obvious talents and trying to resurrect him. Sometimes it worked. Other times it failed. "I never forget that," Guillen said. "When no one else believed in me, Jim Bowden believed in me. That's very important."

Bowden was in the stands at Angel Stadium the day Guillen blew up, tossing his helmet after being replaced by a pinch runner and going into the clubhouse and spewing venom at Mike Scioscia, his manager. Bowden thought he could handle Guillen. "He's high-maintenance," Bowden said. "But I know him." The two met for dinner, along with former Cincinnati pitcher Jose Rijo, at The Forge, a trendy steakhouse in South Beach, in Miami, where Guillen lived in the off-season. Rijo, who would later be named an assistant to Bowden, grew up in Guillen's hometown in the Dominican Republic, and he knew the kid's temperament. The group met, Bowden said, as friends. "We talked," Guillen said. "Jim said he had faith in me."

On November 19, the trade was made with Bill Stoneman and the Angels. Baseball's winter meetings, where most of the off-season deals truly begin to take shape, were still three weeks away. Yet the Expos had reshaped their team. They had a new third baseman in Castilla, a new shortstop in Guzman, a new right fielder in Guillen, a new look altogether. Their new town awaited.

On the field, there was no telling how Bowden's moves would pan out. But off the field, there was still more confusion surrounding the eternally confused franchise. The front office continued to work out of trailers in Parking Lot 4 at RFK Stadium. Occasionally, though, to alleviate the stress and provide for a change of scenery, David Cope would bring his sales and marketing staff to his home in Bethesda. Their after-dinner work sessions might last till late at night, but Cope had Internet connections, phone lines, and a warm room to work in, not a trailer.

On the night of December 14, Joe Hickey, Joe Deoudes, Carleen Martin, and others had just packed up their computers after a long night at Cope's house. It was after 11 P.M., and Cope went to check the voice mail on his cell phone. He had a message, someone asking a question about how the team would go forward "now that the legislation had changed."

Cope wasn't sure what the message meant. Legislation? He knew the District Council was meeting that night to approve, finally, the bill that would provide public funds, largely through a new tax on the District's businesses, to build the team a new stadium. Had something gone wrong? Cope turned the radio to WTOP, the all-news station. He flipped on the television. He called Tony Tavares, his boss, to find out what was going on.

Tavares had been glued to his computer all night, watching a live Internet broadcast of the council meeting. At 10 P.M., Linda W. Cropp, the council's chair, introduced a wrinkle, an amendment to the existing legislation. No more of this public giveaway, she said. Half the financing, at least $220 million, must come from private sources.

Tavares leaned back in his chair, stunned. *Have I been through all this craziness for nothing?*

The team had hired a general manager. It had signed players. It was taking orders for tickets. It was moving forward. Baseball had been back in Washington for all of seventy-seven days. Yet suddenly, it looked like it might never really return.

★ ★ ★ ★ ★ ★ ★ ★ ★ ★ ★ ★ ★ ★ ★ ★ ★ ★ ★

Chapter 4

The Mayor, Mrs. Cropp, and Chaos

*T*he most discussed piece of land in Washington, D.C., in the fall of 2004 wasn't the area around the Washington Monument, fenced off while undergoing renovations, an unsightly patch that didn't befit what is supposed to be a symbol of national pride. Rather, the most talked-about sliver of real estate was bordered on the south by piles of sand and stone, by sickly trees, and eventually by the Anacostia River, the neglected tributary of the more heralded, more pristine Potomac. On the east, the D.C. Water and Sewer Authority's O Street pumping facility provided another boundary, and when the breeze blew in the right direction, the stench was unmistakable. Walk through the middle of it all, at your own peril, and you'd dodge dump trucks and cement mixers and the like, all kinds of heavy equipment. On one corner, a portable toilet invited any daring soul in for a break. The Quality Carry-Out offered, judging by the crude sign outside its dilapidated door, potatoes, bacon, sausage, and ham and egg. A block away, the New Good and Plenty Carry-Out provided competition. And on O Street, the clubs that seemed a world away from the chic Georgetown bars favored by Washington's elite lined up side by side, Secrets next to Club Washington next to Heat. The Mercedeses and sport utility vehicles that parked outside, even in the middle of the day, all seemed to bear Maryland or Virginia license plates. They were owned by people stealing away into a nook of the city that wasn't on the bus tours that carted visitors from all over the country around the nation's capital, fourteen acres tucked in an obscure corner of the District, less than a mile south of the U.S. Capitol, which was clearly visible to anyone driving over the Anacostia and continuing north on South Capitol Street.

By the time winter was on its way, Linda Cropp had spent countless hours thinking about those fourteen acres, more than she'd ever believed possible. When the District of Columbia made its initial pitch to Major League Baseball officials, telling them that Washington was the place for a team, they had offered four sites for consideration: a plot of land adjacent to Robert F. Kennedy Stadium, due east of the U.S. Capitol on East Capitol Street; the intersection of North Capitol Street and New York Avenue; a slice of land in Southwest Washington near L'Enfant Plaza, where a spectacularly expensive stadium would have overhung Interstate 395; and this patch just to the east of South Capitol Street, where nothing much of anything was going on.

The L'Enfant Plaza site drew early attention but was eventually deemed too expensive. So baseball selected the South Capitol site, much to the delight of the District's mayor, Anthony Williams, who for six years had been spearheading Washington's drive to bring baseball back. Williams believed that the Anacostia waterfront should, somehow, thrive with businesses and parks, and just across First Street from the ballpark site the federal government was already developing forty acres. Baseball, Williams believed, would spur development in the entire area. "It was a critical piece," he said, and he talked frequently of restaurants and retail shops, a completely new destination for visitors, who might walk from the

National Mall on a nice day to take in a game, eat out at any number of places nearby, then head back to the suburbs, leaving their money in the District.

But by the time a crisp, sunny day three weeks before Christmas arrived in Washington, the site and the sport had fallen under a great deal of scrutiny. Cropp, who'd stood with the mayor at the City Museum when he made the announcement that baseball would return to town, who'd belted out, "Take Me Out to the Ball Game," was a different character now. She sat in her office on the fifth floor of the John A. Wilson Building, Washington's city hall, not three blocks from the White House on Pennsylvania Avenue. She waited for a letter from Major League Baseball, one she had been told would offer the District some concessions on the stadium project. Twenty minutes passed. She had no choice. Without the letter, she moved on to the council chamber. She was, after all, the chairman, and the day's legislative session wouldn't start without her.

So much had happened since she'd sung "Take Me Out to the Ball Game" less than three months earlier, back on September 29, back when Washington celebrated the return of baseball. "I had no idea," she said, "it was going to be the level of controversy that it was. I had no idea of the storm that was a-brewin'."

By December, Cropp had become the face of the movement against the sport's return to Washington, because she offered alternatives to the deal to which she had already agreed. Williams's pact with Major League Baseball called for a stadium to be built with funds generated by a gross receipts tax on the city's largest businesses, a tax on concessions, and rent paid to the city by the tenants, the team. But in November, Cropp suggested the District's new baseball team abandon the proposed stadium site along the Anacostia River in favor of rebuilding on the grounds near Robert F. Kennedy Stadium. The public was in an uproar. Cropp had been at the negotiating table with baseball officials, had been part of what she called "the dog-and-pony show" the District put on for baseball.

Yet in the ensuing weeks, she had gone home night after night and been unable to sleep. Her fifty-eight-year-old bones felt weary because of this one sport, because of that one slice of land, because of an issue that, by December, had divided the city like none she could remember.

"It was," she said months later, "a horrible time in my life."

Who knew it would get worse?

•   •   •

In 1958, THE HOUSE OF REPRESENTATIVES considered a bill proposed by Representative Oren Harris, a Democrat from Arkansas, to provide Washington, D.C., with a multipurpose stadium east of the U.S. Capitol, one that would house both baseball's Senators and football's Redskins. Later, such monstrosities would be considered "cookie-cutter stadiums," and they popped up everywhere in the 1960s and early '70s, from San Francisco's Candlestick Park to Philadelphia's Veterans Stadium to Cincinnati's Riverfront Stadium. They all housed both baseball and football teams, and all looked relatively the same. But during the discussions that preceded the construction of what would originally be called D.C. Stadium, a Republican from Iowa, Representative H. R. Gross, warned Harris about the project.

"I am still not convinced that this will not someday become a burden on the taxpayers of the country," Gross said. "The gentleman and his committee I hope are not depending on the American League baseball club to provide revenue for this stadium."

The House had appointed a team to look into the economics of professional sports. Ben Okner, an economist at the Brookings Institution who was part of the team, argued that sports clubs enjoy what amount to public subsidies because of their sweetheart deals to use municipal stadiums. And indeed, in its first decade of existence D.C. Stadium lost money each year. Then, of course, it lost the Senators.

When baseball returned to the nation's capital nearly half a century later, it did so in the midst of the same discussions, the same debates. And no two figures were more publicly tied to the struggle than Anthony Williams, the bow-tied mayor, and Linda Cropp, the round-cheeked Council chairman.

Williams grew up one of nine children in Los Angeles as a troublemaking kid put through Catholic schools, and his earliest memories of baseball are from those times, when he said he rooted for the St. Louis Cardinals rather than the hometown Dodgers because, he believes, his older brother was a Dodgers fan, and he wanted to be different. Plus, the Cardinals had Bob Gibson, the great African-American pitcher. "He dominated that plate," Williams said. He remembers being sent to the principal's office and waiting for the ire of one of the nuns, who was listening to the Dodgers game on the radio. Tony Williams would get his spanking. But it would have to be between innings.

But any effort for Williams, the mayor, to paint himself as a baseball aficionado would have come off as disingenuous, because he was not. He exuded, rather, the demeanor of a distant intellectual, not a personable man at all, but one who mastered the issues. He meandered through an itinerant early portion of his adult life before finally finishing undergraduate work at Yale in his early thirties. He went on to get two graduate degrees from Harvard, and dabbled in public service along the way. He was, in fact, something of an accidental mayor. He'd arrived in Washington with a deep background in finance and didn't seem politically inclined, at least not on such a large stage, because he was reserved in groups. He went to work for the Department of Agriculture as its chief financial officer. And in 1995, with the city in crisis, then-mayor Marion Barry turned to the bookish Ivy Leaguer for help. Barry was already a wicked combination of beloved and notorious in the District, having been caught on videotape smoking crack cocaine with a lady friend in 1990, uttering that most famous of D.C. political sayings: "The bitch set me up." He was, of course, elected again anyway.

But by the mid-'90s, Barry's administration had Washington on the brink of financial ruin. Congress stripped the mayor of most of his power over city money, though Barry was allowed to nominate a CFO. He chose Williams. In an editorial on the choice, the *Washington Post* said Williams "brings an interesting resume to the table," but wondered about his experience. Williams said he envisioned himself as a "gifted navigator" to Barry. "The last thing the city needs," the editorial said, "is another Barry sycophant."

Williams proved he wasn't, and he frequently bucked the charismatic and controversial mayor. Barry's underlings took to calling Williams "Bow Tie," snickering at his image. Though he was shy, though he didn't seem *of* the District, Williams was convinced to run for mayor in 1998, and he won the Democratic nomination, which in that heavily Democratic city virtually ensures election. But the demographics of his electorate showed how different Williams was from Barry, who drew his support from the city's poor, predominantly black neighborhoods, particularly those in Southeast Washington, east of the Anacostia River. Williams ran well in upscale Northwest, where the population was universally wealthy and overwhelmingly white.

In office, he pursued issues ranging from fixing potholes to getting government agencies to run more smoothly. Most of all, he pursued things for the District. He wanted downtown to thrive again, and, with help from a new convention center and an arena for basketball and hockey, it did. He helped organize Washington's bid for the 2012 Olympics, which failed. He had an open disdain for the political nature of his job, and members of the D.C. Council had varying levels of trust in him. And even before it became apparent that the Montreal Expos would be moved to another city and not eliminated, he made a decision: Washington, D.C., should pursue baseball. If the Expos moved, the nation's capital should have them.

"You're paid all these dollars to take calculated risks," Williams said. "I thought it was a calculated risk. I thought it was good for the self-esteem of the city. But even more importantly, I think I understand well the economy and the finances of the city, and I think I've

been vindicated on this. I think it's good for the city from an eco-
nomic point of view, from a jobs point of view, for small businesses."

By the time Williams was elected mayor, Linda Cropp had been
on the council for eight years, another beneficiary of Marion Barry's
missteps. Ten months after his arrest in January 1990, Barry, ever
presumptuous, ran for an at-large seat on the District Council. By
that point, Cropp had accumulated a history in the city, arriving
from her native Philadelphia as a student at Howard University,
where she stayed long enough to receive a master's degree in education. She became a teacher in the District's schools, then a guidance
counselor, then a school board member, then the board's vice president and, eventually, its president. Cropp beat Barry. By 1997, she
was the Council chairman.

Yet prior to the battle over baseball, and unlike Williams, Cropp
had never dominated the spotlight. Quietly, she'd developed a reputation as a consensus builder on the council, but for the most part,
she steered clear of controversy. "The way I usually do things is try
to talk about it under the radar," she said. Her style, though, drew
the ire of some colleagues. She was methodical, plodding. She listened. To everything. And that also gave her a reputation for being
rather pliable, even on issues about which she felt strongly.

Cropp had no deep, emotional connection to baseball. Her
grandmother listened incessantly to Atlanta Braves games on the
radio, and her mother followed suit, picking up the Phillies in
Philadelphia. But save for trips to watch cousins play in Little
League, Linda was untouched by the sport. "I know, and I've been
reminded, that I don't know a lot about baseball," she said. But in
January 2003, during a train ride to New York, where she and
Williams and others would meet with officials from Major League
Baseball, another dog-and-pony show, Cropp pulled out a huge
booklet her staff had prepared on baseball's impact in cities, perhaps
five or six inches thick. She plowed through it. What she discovered,
she said, was that if a city already had a team, there's no use being

strong-armed into building a new stadium. But if a city needed a stadium to land a team, building the stadium could be beneficial. It
provided new jobs in construction, she said, and the team would
bring with it new jobs as well, though most of them would be part-
time, seasonal work. She read and she read, and she thought about
it. She went to Williams and described her situation. If they could
figure out a way to generate money for a stadium without dipping
into the District's general funds, then she would support the pursuit
of the sport.

"I would like to have baseball here," she said. She was on board.

•   •   •

LONG BEFORE THE NATIONALS became a reality, before they won or
lost a single game, their story gripped the city of Washington. In the
weeks after they stood together and swayed while singing "Take Me
Out to the Ball Game," Anthony Williams and Linda Cropp went in
vastly different directions. Williams had, over the summer, accepted
an invitation for an eleven-day trip to visit Beijing and Bangkok, two
of Washington's sister cities. It was, in essence, a cultural exchange, a
diplomatic mission that many back in Washington believed could
have been shelved. Less than two weeks after the announcement that
baseball would return, Williams and five councilors took off on the
trip. The mayor left behind a group of staffers armed with a Power-
Point presentation on baseball, people who were supposed to
address the community's concerns while the mayor was halfway
around the world.

Cropp, meanwhile, began attending community meetings. She
would, as always, listen. But she was, at the time, in favor of bringing
the Expos to town, and the misinformation on baseball was overwhelming. No, she had to explain, this money wouldn't exist unless
the team arrived. No, she said, we can't just take this $500 million
and turn it into schools or hospitals or roads, because the business
community would not agree to be taxed for such development. The

businesses had signed up for a tax for baseball, and if there was no baseball, there was no money. "But what you began to sense," Cropp said, "was that people weren't behind this, or didn't understand it, or both."

When Williams returned from Asia at the end of October, the storm, as Cropp said, was a-brewin'. David Catania, a councilor who was on the trip with Williams, was staunchly opposed to the stadium deal, and he told Cropp so. Adrian Fenty, a councilor who vowed not to vote for a dime of public money to be spent on a stadium, worked on Cropp as well. Each of them railed against the plan in public, from the Council dais, whenever they had an opportunity. Catania at one point called the mayor's plan "madness."

"David Catania is very, very bright," Williams said. "And the combination of David Catania and his intellectual firepower and histrionics, and Adrian's histrionics—I don't know whether the intellectual firepower's there on Adrian's side—coming in stereo and hitting Linda put her in a siege situation. It's almost like she's sitting there, and the two battleships are raining in fire, and it was a very difficult situation for her. . . . I think what happened in the council was a result of fermentation of what was going on because we weren't out there in the chicken coop."

Cropp *was* in the chicken coop, and people were pecking at her. Business owners, the backbone of the stadium deal, came to her office and said the legislation could put them under. There were loopholes all over the place, she said. Oncologists, for instance, would be taxed on their gross receipts, which were astronomical given the high cost of radiation treatments. But their profit margins were tiny. Same for car dealers. Some businesses that were split into three or four or five smaller companies were to be taxed multiple times. By this point, the Council chairman wasn't sleeping well. Her mind, she said, was consumed by, of all things, baseball.

"I started worrying at night, wondering, 'Are you doing the right thing here?'" she said. "The more it came to me, it was clear I was not. I had to live with myself on this, and this was a biggie. . . . But I truly had no idea what I was walking into with that thing."

On October 28, the Council chamber on the fifth floor of the Wilson Building was full by 10 A.M. And for the next sixteen hours, citizens of the District of Columbia filed through, in painstaking fashion, allowed to comment publicly on the stadium proposal. "It was ridiculous," said Adam Eidinger, one of those who helped organize a protest outside the building in the morning. "You could talk, but no one was listening." More than 250 witnesses signed up to speak. At one point, Jack Evans, Williams's strongest ally on baseball and the councilor in charge of overseeing the hearing, said, "You know, guys, we're going to have to do something different here. We're only on witness fifty-five." It was 9 P.M., eleven hours into the meeting.

"It was a low point," Williams said, and he thought about the old remark of Otto von Bismarck, the first German chancellor from the nineteenth century, about the legislative process. "If you like laws and sausages," the saying went, "you should never watch either one being made." Everyone, Williams felt, was playing to the camera, and he would know, because for most of the day he sat holed up in his office, watching the proceedings on television. After four in the afternoon, who walked into the chamber but Marion Barry. In typical Barry fashion, the former mayor was running for a seat on the Council—again. He had already taken the Democratic nomination, which basically assured him a seat when the new Council took office in January. Some in the crowd cheered Barry's arrival, because he had already established himself as a stadium opponent. "This is the biggest stickup by Major League Baseball since Jesse James was doing train robberies," he said at the microphone.

Eight days later, on the morning of November 5, Cropp met with Williams and his top aides at the Wilson Building. She unveiled a plan. In a couple of hours, she was going to present a new proposal to the public. She wanted to explore building a stadium at the RFK site. She said it would cost the city $200 million less than the plan for South Capitol Street.

The mayor fumed. How could this be? He, Evans, and Cropp had been at the table with baseball. They had a deal with baseball. *They had a deal.* But over the next month, the deal would change, then change again, thrown off course, then put back on, then be dumped aside. The next Tuesday, when the Council was to vote on the mayor's plan, Cropp blocked the vote. She said she had met with private financiers Richard A. Gross and Michael Sununu, the son of John Sununu, the White House's chief of staff under former President George H. W. Bush. According to Cropp, Gross and Sununu would pay two-thirds of the cost in exchange for rights to build the stadium—back at the old South Capitol site. "I'm going to tell you," Cropp said months later, "all of the ins and outs, I didn't understand. But that's why we have a CFO. I understood the broad picture of it, and it seemed like something. It seemed like it may work."

In their meeting, Williams urged Cropp not to put forward the RFK proposal. He was initially incensed by the private financing plan. "My point was: If we had made a deal with baseball, and we reneged on our deal," Williams said, "that sent a horrible message to the public, because if you think it's a bad deal, then you shouldn't have supported it." And the Council agreed. The private financing package was rejected. Cropp was undeterred.

"I'm pushing a concept," Cropp said, "that we look at alternative ways of financing a stadium."

At that point, no one, including Linda Cropp, knew how far she would go.

•   •   •

On december 2, Linda Cropp sat at a dais at the Hinckley Hilton, the same building on Connecticut Avenue in Northwest Washington where, seven weeks earlier, Tony Tavares had set up shop, trying to bring the Montreal Expos to town. But on this afternoon, the

Greater Washington Board of Trade was holding a luncheon, and the keynote speaker was none other than Bud Selig, the commissioner of baseball. Go down the dais and read the place cards, and wouldn't you know it: Bud Selig and Linda Cropp had adjoining chairs. Here they were, face-to-face, the man who ran baseball and the woman who was making it very difficult to bring baseball to Washington.

"We have made a deal," Selig said at the luncheon, his back pushed to the wall by a group of reporters at the rear of the ballroom. There were myriad other issues on the commissioner's mind that day, for that morning the *San Francisco Chronicle* reported that New York Yankees slugger Jason Giambi had admitted in grand jury testimony that he had used steroids for three years. The next day, the *Chronicle* would report that Barry Bonds, the record-setting home run hitter of the San Francisco Giants, may have—unknowingly, he said—used banned substances as well.

But in the ballroom at the Washington Hilton, in a town that hadn't hosted a major league game since 1971, Selig was plain about where he stood on baseball in Washington. "Certainly," he said, "you have every right to expect that we'll live up to our end of the deal. So, you know, a deal's been made, and I'm satisfied that the deal that both sides agreed to will take place. . . . A deal's a deal." And as he stood before about a thousand people sipping iced tea and eating cake, he delivered an address that tried pointedly to say, *I've been here before, and I've won. I intend to do so again.*

"As each ballpark is built," Selig told the crowd, "and the fans' appreciation of the new edifices is apparent to all, the opposition . . . dies away. Then, the new ballparks become points of pride."

During lunch, however, Cropp laid out her concerns with Selig. "What difference does it make to you," she said, "where the money comes from, as long as you're getting your stadium? Why should you care?" Selig called over John McHale, baseball's executive vice president, and asked McHale to speak with Cropp afterward. She went through her list. She wanted the District to be able to pursue public financing. She wanted the city's liability to be limited if the new stadium didn't open by its target date, the beginning of the 2008 season. McHale listened.

On Monday, December 13, Williams's staffers, and even Cropp herself, hailed the arrival of a letter from baseball officials that, they said, offered concessions, allowing the city to use the new stadium more frequently, providing free tickets for District kids, giving $100,000 to renovate a community center in Southeast. "I am very positive," Cropp said at the time. "We have things in writing from Major League Baseball." But even then, she wanted a little more. She and Williams met that night. And here, they both agree, there was a miscommunication. Cropp wanted the mayor to go back to baseball one more time, to get baseball to be more specific about how it would limit the damages the city would have to pay should the stadium not be delivered on time. Williams thought Cropp would bring the votes on the Council, that she would deliver baseball, and they would talk about the city's responsibilities afterward.

So on that Tuesday morning, the day of the vote, Cropp remained in her office, awaiting a new letter from baseball. She waited, and it didn't come. She waited a bit more, but by then she had to start the meeting. It was a theatrical scene in the Council chamber that day. Baseball supporters sat in the crowd wearing red Nationals caps. Detractors wore blue caps, many of them donning T-shirts that said, "No Stadium Giveaway." Harold Brazil, a councilman in favor of baseball, strode to his seat carrying a sign that read, "D.C. Baseball '05," a Nationals cap on his head.

Cropp spoke early in the hearing, and, per Council protocol, she wouldn't be allowed to speak again until she had worked her way through the entire list in front of her, a list bearing the names of each of her twelve Council colleagues. At noon, she said, she received the new letter from baseball. Chaos ensued.

"At the same time I'm chairing the meeting, I'm trying to decipher this letter," she said. "To the best of my ability, the more I looked at this letter, the more I realized: There was nothing in it." With the mayor in the chamber, she started thinking. She came to a conclusion. She called over one of her staffers. She whispered in his ear. *This is what I'm going to do. Alert the mayor's staff. Talk to the D.C. Sports and Entertainment Commission. Here we go.*

At 10 P.M., after the hearing had dragged on for eleven hours, Linda Cropp dropped the bomb. She proposed an amendment that would require half of the financing for the stadium to come from private sources. She said she would vote against baseball unless her amendment was approved.

"I don't think this is unreasonable at all," Cropp said as reporters besieged her afterward. But the chamber was in an uproar. Evans's head fell into his hands, and he covered his face. The mayor rose from his seat and stormed out of the chamber. Reporters chased after him for his reaction, and he pushed one out of the way. They needed to talk to him, they said. "Too damn bad," he seethed. Police officers surrounded Williams as he headed to his office. "I don't want to talk to anyone," he said, "okay?"

"That was stupid," he said later. "I should've left the building." He called it "a low point."

Back in the chamber, Cropp was adamant: She simply wouldn't support the stadium legislation without this amendment. They had come this far. They were on the brink of baseball returning. Yet she wouldn't budge. The amendment passed, 10-3. Then the bill to approve baseball's return passed, 7-6. One problem: The deal was dramatically restructured. It didn't resemble the version Williams had cut with baseball, the one Cropp had helped to forge. "I knew," Tony Tavares said, "that the whole deal was in trouble."

The next morning, Cropp's office was flooded with phone calls and e-mails. Some expressed support. Others decidedly did not. Some attacks were personal. Some were professional. Others were sexist, racist, offensive, scary. At 8:26 the morning after she fashioned her amendment, the following e-mail arrived in the inbox of three members of Cropp's staff:

> ... thanks for that stupid woman that you call council member to vote against the baseball stadium. Do you really think that that dumb ass jungle monkey and her socialist ways is going to win? Why are you people full of envy for upstarting and growing a community that needs something like this? No wonder so many of you kill each other, none of you dont [sic] have brains and feed off like animals. Nice job socialists!!!!

The next night, Kevin Uhlich and David Cope, two of the Nationals' top executives, were walking out of a restaurant in downtown Washington. Cope's old habit that annoyed Uhlich and Tony Tavares, the Nationals' president, came back to be used against him. "In Baltimore, we . . ." and he would unveil some story about how, when he helped the Baltimore Ravens move from Cleveland, the franchise dealt with a situation. As they walked out of the restaurant, Uhlich's phone rang. It was Tavares. Robert DuPuy, baseball's president, had called. Cropp's amendment, essentially, was a deal breaker. The Nationals were to shut down all of their operations.

"All right," Uhlich said to Cope as they piled into a cab. "How'd you deal with this in Baltimore?"

"Uh," Cope said, "this is new."

The team was to stop selling tickets, stop selling merchandise, shut down the store that sat in one of those double-wide trailers in the parking lot at RFK. Zach Day, one of the team's pitchers, and Terrmel Sledge, an outfielder, had arrived in Washington the day of the vote and were holed up in a hotel, ready to head to the ESPN Zone restaurant downtown to unveil the team's uniforms. They were sent home, never appearing in public. Tavares himself headed west to California, where his first grandson was born, and then to Lake Tahoe, where he made his home. Uhlich, too, headed to his home in

California. Cope got sick, went Christmas shopping, and stayed at home in Bethesda. Baseball officials were working the phones. Could they play in Las Vegas? Northern New Jersey? Puerto Rico? "I'm not sure what would have happened," Tavares said.

Williams, meanwhile, was livid. He would not speak with Cropp for days. "I had never seen him that mad with me," Cropp said. The political undertones rang through the city. Williams hadn't yet decided whether to run for a third term as mayor. Cropp, too, was rumored to be contemplating her own candidacy. Fenty was clearly going to run. Those subplots swirled around the story. But whether he was going to run or not, Williams needed the baseball deal to be completed. Whether it broke down or succeeded, it would be part of his legacy. It had become, through all the politicking and rhetoric, a defining issue.

The staffs for the mayor and the council began to meet soon after the breakdown, and Cropp and Williams eventually came together, too. The gap, they knew, had to be bridged. And they bridged it. They worked with Jerry Reinsdorf, the owner of the Chicago White Sox and Selig's chief bulldog on the relocation project, to come up with a compromise. The city and baseball would purchase insurance that would protect the District against cost overruns, and they'd split the cost. Cropp, in turn, dropped her requirement that half the stadium be funded privately, replacing it with a pledge that the mayor would continue to *seek* private funding. Baseball was appeased because either way the stadium would be built. The pair, standing together, made the announcement at the Wilson Building after 11 P.M. on December 20. The next day, the Council voted, 7-6, to approve the stadium package.

"Was our bid rich?" Williams said. "I'm not an idiot. Of course our bid was rich. We're building a stadium for them. But this is what it took to get baseball here. And if this is what it took to get baseball here, given the fact that even though we're spending a lot of money, I think we're going to get more money from it than we spent, then we should do it."

At RFK Stadium, the refurbishing efforts started again. The team store, stashed in one of those trailers, opened its doors again. And in a steady drizzle that week, just three days before Christmas, a line snaked through the parking lot, people seeking their Nationals hats and Nationals jackets and Nationals clocks. Opening Day, it seemed, was still almost four months away. But it finally seemed like it was going to happen. Say it again to convince yourself: There would be baseball in Washington. Really, there would be.

"This is quite a town," Tavares said. "There's no other place like it."

★ ★ ★ ★ ★ ★ ★ ★ ★ ★ ★ ★ ★ ★ ★ ★ ★ ★

Chapter 5

Viera, and a Team Takes Shape

W hen men wearing baseball jerseys representing Washington gathered for the first time in a generation, they did so in a place that a decade earlier had been little more than sod farms and cattle ranches, where half the population is over fifty years old, where progress is measured by the opening of a Chili's or a Cracker Barrel. The former was under construction in spring 2005, the latter a stop for tourists and truckers along Interstate 95. The area is known as the Space Coast, for Cape Canaveral is close enough that when the space shuttle launches, it's easy to see, even easy to hear, just off to the northeast. And the little baseball park that rises out of the cow pastures, visible from miles around because there's nothing to interrupt the view, is aptly named Space Coast Stadium, with an address in a town called Viera, a planned community that didn't even exist twenty years ago. Mention the spring training complex to any National, and he'd likely roll his eyes. They could, if there were time, head twenty-five minutes up to Cocoa Beach, where cruise ships dock and bars line the beaches. Or they could go to the mall in Melbourne, or the one that grew out of nothingness, the Avenue Viera, just across the sod farms from the stadium.

But really, once you get past the Brevard Zoo and the strip malls, each one seemingly with a Blockbuster and a Publix and a Walgreens, once you cruise through the Super Target and compare the prices to those at the Wal-Mart just across the street, there isn't much to do, not much to see. The Nationals wound up here only because of the bizarre transaction that led to Major League Baseball owning the franchise, one in which the owner of the Florida Marlins became the owner of the Boston Red Sox, the owner of the Montreal Expos became the owner of the Marlins, and all of the rest of the owners became the owners of the Expos. In that deal, there lay a detail. The Expos for years had called Jupiter, Florida, their home for spring training. Yet Jeffrey Loria, the man who owned the Expos but would take over the Marlins, preferred Jupiter for his new team because it was closer both to Miami and to Loria's home in Palm Beach. The Expos would be left with the Marlins' old haunts in Viera.

So it is Viera where Jim Bowden first set up shop in December 2004, gathering his staff together, men he did not know whom he inherited from the Expos organization, the men who would now run the Nationals' baseball operation. Bowden was wary of them, just as they were wary of Bowden. The feeling-out process began in those sod fields in a dreary winter along the Space Coast, where Bowden, more than once, thought about his Hollywood home where his fiancée, Joy, remained, or thought about his five sons in Cincinnati, or looked at his BlackBerry—which could keep him in touch with anyone at any time—and wondered, "Why am I here?"

It is also here where Frank Robinson arrived in mid-February, uncertain of what would come. In the weeks leading up to spring training, people back at Robinson's home in Los Angeles, friends and passersby, would ask him, "Are you getting excited?" Washington awaited, after all. A new city would bring new hope, right? Right? Robinson would purse his lips. Excited? Listen, he was about to enter his fiftieth season in pro baseball. He was sixty-nine years old. He hit 586 home runs, won two MVP awards, won the Triple

Crown, became the first black manager in the majors. Excited? About another spring training? Puh-leeze.

"I got time," he would tell the people. "I got time."

Robinson knew how spring training worked, that there is an ebb and flow to the whole thing, that the veterans arrive at the ballpark at 7 or 7:30 in the morning, more often than not toting a cup of coffee and a breakfast sandwich from McDonald's or Burger King, the diet of ballplayers. They get in their work, shower, and either skedaddle to snap up the nearest available tee time or hang in the clubhouse, obsessing over a backgammon game. Robinson had seen it over the years. The routines of spring training don't change. Only the players do.

And because of the latter, over the course of February and March, Robinson would have to learn his new players. In their final year in Montreal, the Expos lost ninety-five games, second most in the National League. Several players from that roster were gone, with new ones taking their lockers, their uniforms, their numbers, their roles. Vinny Castilla, a smiling veteran from Mexico with hair both slicked back and jet-black, took over at third base for Tony Batista, who hit thirty-two home runs the year before but wanted more money, and left to play in the Japanese league. Cristian Guzman, a quiet Dominican who played six successful seasons with the Minnesota Twins, was the new shortstop, replacing Orlando Cabrera, who was traded in a monumental deal the previous July. Cabrera ended up with the Boston Red Sox, whom he helped win the World Series, and then signed a lucrative contract with the Anaheim Angels, just another former Expo the organization could no longer afford. Jose Guillen, the tempestuous and talented outfielder also from the Dominican Republic, arrived to become the power hitter to whom everyone would turn when a big hit was needed, but would have to answer the constant questions about his behavior that had dogged him from team to team, from city to city, during a meandering major league career. The most recent misstep was the most recent memory of Guillen's career, the season-ending suspension that resulted from a tirade at his manager in Anaheim and, ultimately, led to his trade to the Nationals.

The characters who filtered through the doors of the home clubhouse at Space Coast Stadium were, in some ways, like the cast of *Bull Durham,* with everyone there to fill a role as if typecast by Hollywood. Guillen, the Latin hothead trying to get a handle on his teammates just as they tried to get one on him. Reliever Joey Eischen, the crazy left-hander, rolling putts across the carpeted floor of the clubhouse, dropping F-bombs if they didn't hit the tobacco tin he used as a hole. Jamey Carroll, the infielder from the heartland community of Newburgh, Indiana, who quietly organized the team's chapel sessions, whose close-cropped hair helped him look the part of choirboy, who would play whatever position whenever he was asked, who was always front and center during stretching drills because if he wasn't, who knows, he might be cut, and his career might be over. Livan Hernandez, the overweight ace from Cuba with the indefatigable right arm who drove his Mercedes to work and pumped Latin music through the clubhouse. Brad Wilkerson, the outfielder from Kentucky and a new father. Jeffrey Hammonds, the Stanford-educated former first-round pick, trying one last time at age thirty-four. First baseman Nick Johnson from Sacramento, a baseball man's baseball man if there was one in the clubhouse, the nephew of former Phillies shortstop and manager Larry Bowa, but one toughened by his time spent with the New York Yankees. There, opening up with opinions was frowned upon. Media members with unfamiliar faces could approach Johnson, and he would always oblige, as long as he wasn't heading to the batting cage or the massage table. But he would oblige as if he had been taught by Kevin Costner's Crash Davis himself, selecting from among his favorite answers: "Keep grinding; just try to hit the ball hard," and "If I stay healthy . . ." If Johnson didn't know you, he could play the man of few words with the best of them, giving whatever time you needed, filling your notebook with nothing.

Robinson knew some of these guys, didn't know others. Nearly all of them, though, lit up at the idea of playing in Washington. "With what we've been through," Eischen said one day, sitting at his locker, wearing a brand-new red jersey bearing an interlocking "DC" logo over the heart, "you better fucking believe we're excited about it." Never mind that many of them had never been to the city, and even fewer knew where they would live, where they would shop, where they would eat, what the city felt like. It didn't matter. "Just to have someplace to sleep," second baseman Jose Vidro said, "a place we know that when we come home, our clothes will be in the closet, that's what we want."

The previous year, Vidro, a thirty-year-old Puerto Rican who spent his entire career in the Expos organization, signed a contract extension—four years, $30 million—to remain with the franchise, even though he knew not where he would play. "These people," he said, "they're my home. They're who I feel comfortable with."

Robinson thought that one move sent a signal to others in the clubhouse: *The situation will get better. Hang in there. We're not going to be nomads and misfits forever.*

But written into the contract was a clause: If the franchise's situation wasn't resolved by the end of 2004, Vidro could become a free agent. Livan Hernandez, the big right-hander from Cuba, signed a similar deal. The message from the players was clear: *We're willing to stay with you, even want to stay with you, but you have to take care of us. No more three-week road trips. No more indecision about the franchise's future. This mess will be taken care of, or we will leave. We'll sign someplace else. We need a home.*

"We understood," said Tony Siegle, the assistant general manager under Bowden who had served the same role under former GM Omar Minaya. "What were we supposed to do? It was only fair."

There was perhaps no player more looking forward to playing in Washington than Vidro. Not because he knew the upper Connecticut Avenue neighborhood in which he would live. Not because he had any affinity for the city at all. No, for thirteen seasons, he had

toiled as an Expo, first as a teenage farmhand, then as a major leaguer, finally as a star. He considered the franchise, not any one city,
his home. In that uniform, with those people, that's where he felt
most comfortable. "I love Montreal," he said. "It's a great city.
There's not too many cities like that. But we're there to play baseball. We're not there on vacation. And the way things were, we
didn't feel like people appreciated the job we were trying to do."

The job Vidro was trying to do when he arrived at spring training was one far more complicated than he imagined. The previous
September, he'd undergone surgery on his right knee, shutting down
his season early. He came to Viera nearly a month before any of his
teammates, all with the goal of returning to the form that made him,
quietly, one of baseball's best offensive second basemen. Robinson
paid Vidro what, for him, is the ultimate compliment. "He is what I
call a professional hitter," and Robinson didn't say that about every
man that is paid to hit baseballs. Vidro swung the bat from both
sides of the plate, hit the ball to all parts of the field, was a threat to
hit one out of the yard, and with two outs and a runner on second in
a tie ballgame was unafraid to, as Robinson said, "stick his nose in
there and get the tough hit."

Vidro was born in Mayaguez, Puerto Rico, and raised in nearby
Sabana Grande, playing baseball with tennis balls, trying to figure
out a way to make it to the major leagues. He knew about hard work
when he was small. But the previous winter had reminded him of
diligence and difficulty at age thirty. He tried to stay in shape while
overcoming the knee surgery, but it wasn't easy. He couldn't run until
he arrived in Viera. When he showed up, Robinson looked him over.
He knew his star player wasn't in game shape. The next month was
crucial. "I have to get my legs ready," Vidro said, knowing it might
be an impossible task. He needed his legs to make plays in the field,
to drive the ball at the plate, to endear himself to the new fans he
just knew would fill the stands at the stadium he had never seen in
the town where he had never lived.

Yet Vidro, a quiet man, thought quietly: *This is going to be my year.*

Why wouldn't they all think that way? As they gathered, feeling each other out and pulling on their new jerseys, it mattered little to the players that their new home would be Washington, D.C., capital of the free world. It mattered only that it wasn't some combination of the empty stadium in Montreal and the run-down facility in Puerto Rico, that they wouldn't play home games while living out of a suitcase. Anything, they thought, would be better than that.

"It's hard to say exactly what it'll mean," catcher Brian Schneider said. "You just know it'll mean something. New uniforms, new fans, new team, new city. I feel like I got traded. It's all for the best—for everybody in here."

•   •   •

Kᴀʀᴀᴏᴋᴇᴇᴇᴇᴇᴇ! ᴄᴀᴍᴇ ᴛʜᴇ ᴄʀʏ, for the first time, on the morning of February 17. The call to stretch would be bellowed, in the exact same cadence, for the next seven months from strength and conditioning coordinator Kazuhiko Tomooka, a former football player from Japan known simply as Kazoo. *Karaoke*, in the baseball world, is the term for the odd-looking stretches and arm motions that begin each workout, different from those in almost any sport. The pitchers and catchers on hand for the first workout as Washington Nationals gathered in the Florida sun, nearly 900 miles south of the nation's capital. They trekked to the fields down Stadium Parkway from Space Coast Stadium and began rotating their creaky arms, bending at the waist, loosely following Tomooka's instructions while ripping on each other, perhaps the most important preseason ritual. A breeze blew across the flat nothingness of central Florida's Atlantic Coast. In any other setting, all this would be a strange sight, grown men flailing their arms in unison, spitting tobacco at each other's feet, laughing at each other's expense. Here, in the fields of Viera, it was overwhelmingly normal.

The idea that the Nationals would have a new home, would have new players, would have a new identity, was draped over everything during spring training, an undeniable theme, because the players talked about it themselves, and because they were asked about it constantly. Yet in a baseball sense, there were more important matters with which to deal, and none was more important than two numbers: 67 wins, 95 losses, the Expos' record from a year earlier. Any team with such a mark reports to spring training the following season with serious baseball issues, questions that must be answered during seven weeks of spring training, when responding to the call of "Karaokeeeeee!" grows old, when the routines become redundant, but when major plot lines develop.

So in that sense, the Nationals were like any other team in baseball. "We have issues," Bowden said early in spring training. On paper, they were easy to identify. The health of second baseman Jose Vidro was one, probably the most important. There were several established starting pitchers on hand, led by Livan Hernandez, but also including free agent Esteban Loaiza, trying to rebound from a miserable experience with the New York Yankees, one in which he wilted in the pressure of a pennant race in Gotham. Tony Armas Jr. arrived in Viera needing to prove himself yet again, because he hadn't fully recovered from shoulder surgery nearly two years earlier. Tomo Ohka, another right-hander, was coming off a broken arm, shattered by a shot off the bat of Kansas City outfielder Carlos Beltran. Doctors inserted a plate into the arm, and a jagged scar served to remind him of the injury. Yet with the way this team was constructed, with spare parts from some scrap heap, he, too, would be relied upon.

And along the right-hand wall in the clubhouse, folding his lean, 6-foot-5-inch frame onto a stool in front of his locker, a baseball glove bearing a stitched rendering of the Texas flag perched on his left hand, sat John Patterson, in some ways a typical member of the Nationals, but very much an atypical personality in baseball. In a clubhouse in which many of the members had the shared experience of being an Expo and all the tangential story lines that went along with it, something of a badge of honor, Patterson seemed isolated, withdrawn. He moved with the slow, easy gait of a Texan, as if he were a rancher or a cowboy, but in a way he was a diva of a pitcher, the young man who spent time getting fitted for custom suits in a room down the hall at Space Coast Stadium, whose jeans were faded and ripped in all the right places. Before he pitched, he pumped techno music through the clubhouse, sending his teammates scurrying for their iPods or for the relative quiet of the back rooms. "What is this shit?" they would ask while Patterson's techno blared. And Patterson knew. "It drives these guys crazy," he said.

Behind Patterson's style, though, was determination. A former first-round draft pick, a bonus baby from the mid-1990s, Patterson arrived at spring training with his mind made up: He was through with the injuries, the ailments, and the unsettling environment that had derailed his career for the better part of a decade. Forget that people thought he was fragile, that they questioned his ability. He, and only he, knew what he had been through to arrive at this point. He, and only he, knew that he would leave spring training not only on the team, but as an important part.

Patterson first told his father he wanted to be a major league pitcher when he was all of nine or ten years old. Every decision, from there on out, was made to reach that goal. Growing up in the little town of Orange, Texas, just west of the Louisiana border and just more than a hundred miles east of Houston, Doug Patterson and his son pushed together to develop John into a stud of an athlete. The father, a former minor-league pitcher, and the son, a major leaguer to be, developed a plan. John would pitch in Orange with his buddies when it was convenient, when it made sense for his development. But he would also branch out, throwing for teams in Houston that played at a higher level, spending one summer in Dallas living with an aunt so that he could face the best competition. More than anything else, he wanted to pitch. But in a way, that dream ate into his childhood and made him into the adult who sat in the Nationals' clubhouse.

"I became a real recluse," Patterson said. "I just focused on what I had to focus on, and knew where I was going. But I think that hurt me in the long run, because I wasn't a kid. I became an adult at a very young age."

In little Orange, where Doug had grown up, too, the Pattersons heard the whispers about what John was doing, going off and playing with faraway teams, whispers that sometimes turned into questions asked aloud. "There's a mentality, sometimes, when you start stepping out and doing something different, everybody wants everybody to be the same," Doug said. "You especially get that in a small town. 'Who does he think he is? Why doesn't he want to play with us?'

"It was not always his decision. It was more *my* decision. Game after game he'd pitch in Orange, he'd strike out thirteen or fourteen or fifteen guys. I didn't see the growth that I thought he should have. The opportunities I saw in Houston, in Dallas, it was a more challenging thing for him. So we took those opportunities."

Doug and John would work out together, Doug doing the coaching, John doing the listening, learning what Doug had learned in the Orioles' system, where Cal Ripken Sr. was once his manager, where he was teammates with Eddie Murray, who ended up being a Hall of Famer. People were always questioning them both. When John was 16, a coach asked him incredulously, "Do you really think you're going to be drafted?" One high school math teacher would stand alongside the field, watching the father and son work on technique, on mechanics, on pitching—essentially, on John's career. The teacher worried about it all. She called John's mother, Cheryl, to check in. "What are they doing?" the teacher asked. "Is that John's choice?"

So, in some ways, it became the Pattersons vs. the 20,000 people of Orange. John had very clear goals. He wanted to be a first-round pick out of high school. Moreover, he wanted to be the first high school player taken. At some level, the Pattersons' response was:

Who cares what they think? He was taken by, of all teams, the Montreal Expos, with the fifth pick in the 1996 draft. Yet after he was drafted, he never signed with Montreal. "The people that were in charge then," Patterson said, "they were just so unfair."

Kris Benson, a pitcher from Clemson, was the top pick in the draft that year, and he signed for a bonus of $1.9 million with the Pittsburgh Pirates. The Pattersons felt like that entitled John to a larger bonus than the Expos were offering. The Expos disagreed. The negotiations, such as they were, went through the summer, though the sides rarely talked. Patterson had a scholarship offer to Louisiana State, a college baseball power. Classes would start in September. If he enrolled, the rules stated he wouldn't be able to play pro ball until after his junior year.

Finally, one afternoon, John dismissed the Expos' offer, saying, "This is not right." He decided he would go to junior college, where he would be eligible to play pro ball sooner than if he enrolled at a four-year school such as LSU.

The situation quickly grew even more complicated, though. In a legendary Expos story, the franchise failed to send Patterson a formal contract offer within fifteen days of the draft. They weren't the only team that managed that particular gaffe that particular year. Minnesota, the Chicago White Sox, and San Francisco all did the same thing. Later in September, Major League Baseball ruled that all four players could be free agents, a loophole that had never before been exploited. Patterson was free. But finding loopholes and making waves wasn't on that list of goals. Patterson, just eighteen years old, was thrown into tumult. "He was becoming a man in a hurry," Doug said.

Arizona, which was starting its expansion organization and hadn't yet played a game, signed Patterson for $6 million. The following spring he found himself in his first major league training camp. Fellow prospects wondered why he already made big money. Veterans were wary of the millionaire teenager. He had become something of a curiosity.

"It's hard enough to be a first-round pick," Patterson said. "But when you do something that's unprecedented, it makes it even harder. It makes expectations even higher."

The stay with the Diamondbacks was rough, marked by injury and ineffectiveness. After Patterson missed nearly all of the 2001 and '02 seasons following elbow surgery, the Diamondbacks essentially gave up on him. During spring training of 2004, Arizona sent him to Montreal for a left-handed reliever named Randy Choate. And so, stationed at his locker at Space Coast Stadium in Viera, nearly a decade after he was drafted, John Patterson, who had started only thirty-two major league games, carried with him an obsession to start for the Washington Nationals.

"I'm not coming here to say, 'Oh well, if I don't make the rotation, I'll make the bullpen,'" Patterson said one day early in the spring. He said it calmly and politely, but there was nothing matter-of-fact about it. Behind his eyes was determination. *Are you crazy? Pitch out of the bullpen?* "I'm coming here to make the rotation."

Just two lockers down from Patterson sat the other contender for the final spot in the rotation, a floppy-eared right-hander with mussed-up hair, Zach Day. If Patterson represented isolated determination, Day—nicknamed Harry Potter—was the low-key alternative, seemingly always with a broad, soft, somewhat goofy smile. Like Patterson, he'd started for the Expos the previous year. Like Patterson, he'd spent time on the disabled list—Patterson was out with a pulled groin, while Day missed time first with shoulder tendinitis, then with a broken finger suffered while trying to lay down a bunt.

Of the two, Day was presumed to be the front-runner for that last spot in the starting rotation. He'd received precious few runs from the Expos the previous year, fewer runs than any other starter in baseball, and thus lost ten of his fifteen decisions. But he appeared to be a fixture of the club's future, because he was just twenty-six and possessed a heavy sinkerball that dropped at a hitter's feet, inducing grounders. And, not least, he had already been deemed the face of the pitching staff, invited to Washington over the winter to help unveil the team's uniforms. Day grew up in Cincinnati and still lived there, not far from his grandparents, within a few miles of some of his fifty cousins. That kind of family environment fostered a giving spirit, and Day spent some of spring training talking about how he wanted to help kids in the Washington area, where he had not yet moved, by setting up something called the Z Foundation.

In the hardened environment of a baseball clubhouse, where players spit tobacco into trash cans or empty soda bottles, where cursing is rote and testosterone pumps, it is hard to embrace a softer side. Yet Day did. He is an artist by nature, not just some kid who sketches in his spare time. He is talented enough that when *ESPN: The Magazine* profiled former Expos star Vladimir Guerrero, they included Day's pencil-and-paper profile of Guerrero, considered a masterpiece in the relatively obscure world of baseball art drawn by baseball players. He drew other sketches for teammates, including a drawing of Jose Vidro's favorite car, a souped-up 1997 Toyota Supra, that hung in Vidro's garage. He sketched the three sons of bullpen coach Bob Natal, a drawing that hung in Natal's home. He sketched Robinson, though the manager said, "He won't give me one. Probably thinks he'll make me mad." And he branched out into watercolors and acrylics, abstracts on canvas painted in the off-season, "just to tie the colors in our house all together," he said. He is most likely the only major leaguer who relished trips to Philadelphia not for the cheesesteaks but because he loved to visit the Philadelphia Museum of Art. He used his art, too, for the benefit of others, auctioning off one of his Guerrero drawings for $1,500, turning that into eight baseball gloves and a protective screen—so a coach could pitch batting practice without risking decapitation—for an inner-city Cincinnati high school that was trying, without many resources, to revive a baseball program.

Just as Patterson's experience was shaped by his family, so was Day's. Growing up in Cincinnati, he was a fan of the Cincinnati Reds that won the 1990 World Series behind a Dominican-born right-hander named Jose Rijo, a man who now served as a special assistant to Nationals General Manager Jim Bowden. Day's family was still there. It's where he met his wife, back in high school, where they were sweethearts. It was home, where he was raised with the idea that family should come first. "That's how he was raised," said his mom, Bonnie. "He always had people around, always had family. And I think that made him kind of a giving person by nature."

Day and Patterson were decidedly different. But they represented an excellent example of the competition within the Nationals, two men fighting for one job. One day, as the sun shone down on Space Coast Stadium, Day walked by Bowden, who didn't know what to expect from his young right-hander. "Come on, Zach," Bowden said. "Come on, dawg." It was a way of telling if Bowden was in a good mood, how frequently he addressed people by "dawg." The more "dawgs," the better the mood. "You got fifteen wins in that right arm? Do you?" he asked Day. "I think you do."

"I hope so," Day responded, almost sheepishly. Later that day, he stood by his locker. Robinson had considered sending Day to the bullpen, in part because, with his sinker inducing those ground balls, he might be helpful in situations when he could relieve a starter who'd left men on base and perhaps draw a double-play ball. That line of thinking was fine and all that, but just as Patterson wanted no part of the bullpen, Day intended to make the rotation, too.

"I like the challenge of starting right now," Day said. "I'm sure things get knocked around. It's their job to try and find different pieces to the puzzle. I've kind of made my point that I'd rather start, but I'm not the one up top making the decisions."

•   •   •

THE TWO MEN who would make the decisions about who would make up the Nationals, about who would fit where, were Frank Robinson, the old-school Hall of Famer, and Jim Bowden, the flashy general manager. As they assembled the team, they spent much of the time learning about each other. Bowden's style, it became apparent over the course of the spring, was different from that of any other general manager in baseball. What other executive strutted onto the practice fields down the road from Space Coast Stadium, where most of the workouts took place, in velour Sean John sweat-suits and Chanel sunglasses, the outfits that had players quietly call-ing him "Eminem"? What other general manager greeted his players by saying, "Wilky, what up, dawg?" and then offering his fist to bump? Bowden had a special manner of doing this, one in which, just after his fist touched the other, he pulled it back quickly, recoil-ing, then spread his five fingers out. It was something of a fist explo-sion, often followed by a broad smile and a loud cackle of a laugh.

Unlike Robinson, who had managed the Expos for three years, Bowden knew virtually none of the new Nationals. He needed to know what he had and, more importantly, what he didn't. So he watched bat-ting practice closely, sending messages to his players through the net-ting of the cage. When Jose Guillen, the new right fielder, arrived in Viera, Bowden leaned against the cage as Guillen sprayed line drives. "Beautiful to my eyes, Jose," Bowden said. "Beautiful to my eyes." When Tyrell Godwin, a minor league outfielder with some speed, stepped into the cage one day, Bowden watched Godwin shoot a line drive over the shortstop's head. "That's a single and a stolen base right there," Bowden said. Another liner down the line. "That's a double and a stolen base right there. Come on, Dave Roberts!" Bowden called, invoking the name of the speedy outfielder who'd helped the Boston Red Sox win the World Series by pinch-running and swiping a key base in the American League Championship Series.

Robinson, after watching Godwin for most of the spring, arched his eyebrows when Godwin's name came up. *"Dave Roberts?"* he asked incredulously, scoffing at the comparison.

Bowden, the players and Robinson quickly learned, was a char-acter to be dealt with differently. "I'm just trying to win ballgames, dawg," he would say, and he meant it. His mind was much quicker than most of those around him. He didn't sleep much, sometimes four hours a night, sometimes only two, obsessed with one problem or another he saw on the team. He was a presence, one that couldn't be ignored. Occasionally, his fiancée, Joy, would appear on the fields at spring training, always with a stunning outfit over her stunning figure, a woman who made baseball players, quite used to the presence of beautiful women, turn their heads as she stepped across the grass in high heels. Bowden was aware that as seriously as he took baseball, it was still entertainment, and while he analyzed a hitter's ability to adapt to the breaking ball or a pitcher's command of his slider—serious baseball matters in March—he seemed to be hyperaware of the fact that the Washington Nationals would be putting on a show, not for themselves, and not just for the people of Washington, but for the entire country, because no one else was running a team in the nation's capital. On the morning of the Nationals' first exhibition game—a cool, brilliantly sunny day on which Bowden said he had goose bumps—he watched a groundskeeper walk across the Space Coast Stadium field, wearing a jacket against the cold. It was a blue satin jacket emblazoned with the logo of the Montreal Expos. "Hey," Bowden said. "What's that? Come on." He instructed the crew to find some Nationals gear, to change immediately. "That's embarrassing," he muttered to the side.

ESPN was in town to broadcast the game, and Bowden thought about that, too. This was his team, and how his team played would serve as his audition for the Nationals' job permanently. Whenever Major League Baseball sold the Nationals, Bowden wanted to stick around. His case for doing so would be far better if his troops performed, if they came off as a polished crew. Robinson, a day before the opener, said he was only going to play four or five regulars, because that's how he had always done it, easing the veterans into the spring. No reason to rush it. But Bowden had a different perspective. ESPN? A national audience? The first organized baseball game for professional players from Washington in a generation? *No*, Bowden thought. *We should play the regular lineup. Play them all. This is entertainment.* And Robinson did.

Even with the quirky personality and the sideshow aspect, it was clear in spring training that Bowden was passionate about making the Nationals better, about being Washington's first general manager in a generation. "What an honor," Bowden said about his job, and his mind sped off, full of the team's myriad deficiencies. He looked at the Nationals' lineup over and over again and wondered where the offense would come from.

• • •

JIM BOWDEN'S DESK in his office on the third floor at Space Coast Stadium, the one with the Louisville Slugger affixed to the door, was flanked by two greaseboards, one with the names of every player in the Nationals major league spring training camp, another with the lineups of every major league team, because trades involved finding a fit, and how could you know where a player might fit if you didn't have those players in front of you?

Bowden would sit and look at the names for hours, a gigantic puzzle involving every major league player. But one day he leapt to his feet—he had come to a conclusion about one of his own.

"Chavez," Bowden declared. "He's not going to do it."

Of all the baseball issues that dominated Washington's first spring training in thirty-four years, even the shaky rotation paled in comparison to who would hit leadoff for this club. Endy Chavez, a slight Venezuelan with scant success in the big leagues, was the one who had to come through. One day, fellow outfielder Jose Guillen watched Chavez in the batting cage. He had never played with the kid, didn't really know him that well. But as he assessed the team's chances, it was clear he understood his new team's makeup.

"That's the key, right there," Guillen said quietly, nodding toward Chavez. "He's the key to us surprising people."

That Chavez was a key said a great deal about the Nationals' prospects for success, which were not good. No one who filtered through Viera during the spring, be he scout or baseball writer or fan, was able to look at the team's roster—at names such as Day and

Chavez and Patterson—and predict it could overtake the talented Florida Marlins or the perennial champions, the Atlanta Braves, in the National League East. To attach such a surprise to the narrow back of Chavez seemed absurd. But the pressure on Chavez was more than about just his spot in center and at the top of the lineup. If Chavez could produce, Brad Wilkerson, the versatile outfielder and first baseman, could hit lower in the order, perhaps fifth, where he figured to drive in more than the sixty-seven runs he had the year before, when Chavez failed as a leadoff man and Wilkerson—stocky, not swift—had to take the spot. If Chavez could win the job everyone wanted him to win, Wilkerson could move to left field from center, and there would be less strain on his body.

With all that in mind, Bowden held meetings with each of his new players at the start of spring training. He laid out what he expected and felt them out in return. None was more important than his meeting with Chavez. There would be, Bowden said, no more of this free-swinging bullshit. If Chavez, a sublime defensive center fielder, wanted to make this team, he had to draw some walks. He had to have the mind-set that he was there to score runs, not to drive them in. He had to bunt for base hits. He had to shoot the ball to the opposite field. He had to, as Robinson said, "stop swinging from his ass." He had to be a catalyst, or he wouldn't have a job.

Robinson reiterated Bowden's points in another meeting with Chavez. Hitting coach Tom McCraw tried to drive it home on a daily basis. Barry Larkin, the twelve-time all-star shortstop for the Cincinnati Reds who was serving as an assistant to Bowden, spoke to him. Jose Cardenal, an eighteen-year major leaguer who also served as a Bowden advisor, went over the points with Chavez as well.

"Leading off is a mentality," McCraw said. "You have to understand it. You have to tailor your thinking to each and every situation. When you get to the point where you can enjoy creating havoc, where you can think in terms of scoring a hundred runs—not in terms of driving in seventy-five or eighty—then you've done as good a job as Vidro's done or as good a job as Wilkerson's done, because you've done your job. That's all we want him to do—to do his job."

All the information seemed to frustrate Chavez, who was twenty-seven and quiet. "I've heard it," he said impatiently one day. "I know." The year before, feeling overloaded with advice, he'd told the coaching staff exactly that. *Leave me alone,* he said, *and I'll carry out your orders.* After all the meetings of the spring, he asked for the same thing. The coaching staff obliged.

"Sometimes, there comes a time where you're talked out," Robinson said. "You know what you're saying is not getting through. The individual is tired of hearing it, so leave him alone. It's not that you're not interested in [his] well-being. It's just that you're saying, 'I'm going to leave you alone and let you go, and if you need me, I'm here. We're here. We're not abandoning you.'"

So Chavez was left to his own devices. In the pastures of Viera, where wildfires sprang up occasionally, the battles of spring began. Patterson pursued his spot in the starting rotation. Day did the same. And Chavez, clearly expecting to be the leadoff hitter and the center fielder, followed suit.

•   •   •

THE GRIND OF SPRING TRAINING is just that, a grind. Games are played in the heat of the Florida sun, and the results generally don't mean a thing. So it was a bit odd, following a 9-4 loss to the New York Mets on a Sunday afternoon in Port St. Lucie, an hour south down I-95 from Viera, that the doors to the visitors' clubhouse remained closed. Instead of gathering their belongings quickly and either piling on the bus or shooting off in their cars, the players sat in front of their lockers and listened to Frank Robinson.

Robinson was disgusted. He had watched Jose Guillen let a ball sail over his head in right field. He had watched Endy Chavez hit a ball to the gap that should have been a triple, only to see Chavez trot in lazily with a double. In March, losses don't matter unless they come like this. It was the team's fourth in a row, and, as Robinson said later, "They didn't act like they cared." Things started poorly against the Mets when Tony Armas Jr., whom Robinson at one point called "the key to the rotation," pulled a groin muscle. Armas tried to dismiss it afterward. No big deal. He called his early exit, after the first inning, "precautionary." The next day, though, he would go on the disabled list, a development Jim Bowden called "extremely disappointing." Expected to be the number two starter behind Livan Hernandez, Armas would travel north with the Nationals to visit RFK Stadium for an exhibition game with the Mets, stay long enough to see the place, and then head south to start the season in the minors, with the team's Class AAA club in New Orleans. When baseball returned to Washington, one of the key pieces would be far away. Armas wouldn't return until May.

The problems in the clubhouse in Port St. Lucie, however, were more immediate, for the extent of Armas's problem wasn't yet known. Opening Day in Philadelphia was a week away. And this? This was how the team responded? Robinson let his team have it. He questioned their effort, their focus, their commitment.

"We got to show him that we're ready for the season," Guillen said in a quiet clubhouse afterward. "If you don't show him *now* that you're ready for the season, then when are you going to show him? I know spring training doesn't mean anything to a lot of people, but when it's late in the spring, you really got to go."

John Patterson came in to pitch that day after Armas left, and gave up four runs on seven hits in just three innings. Asked about the effectiveness of his outing, Patterson said defiantly, "I wouldn't change a thing." He recoiled at the suggestion that he was "hit hard."

"Hard?" he responded. "Were you watching?" For the first time in the relaxed spring environment, there was tension in the air.

"I've had enough negative in my career," Patterson would say later in the season, reflecting back on that moment in spring training when he hadn't won a spot in the rotation. "Nobody understands what I've gone through. Nobody understands what it was like to be me through the whole draft process. Guys have had elbow injuries, but maybe not under the same circumstances. I've had negative stuff happen to me. I don't want to go back to being a negative person. I want to be positive and look forward, not backward."

Four runs? Seven hits? Patterson preferred to talk about the eight strikeouts. "I had the best stuff I had all spring," he said. "I didn't know how I gave up four runs with the kind of stuff I had." But when Robinson was asked if Patterson had improved over the previous year, he said, "Not really, to tell you the truth."

On this Sunday, all the new hope and revitalization that was supposed to come with the move to Washington was gone. This team very much felt like the Montreal Expos, just wearing different uniforms. It all contributed to the gloom in the clubhouse. Down a row of lockers, Ryan Church, a rookie outfielder, sensed the same thing. "The intensity sucked today," Church said. "It's time to get going. This is a wake-up call."

Church couldn't know it, but right at that moment the wheels were turning to make sure he was part of the wake-up call. Church understood that baseball, more than anything, is a business, and part of the business was that, because the team had an option to send him to the minors without the risk of losing him to another team, he would likely wind up going. When one of his teammates pulled out a new cell phone one day, Church looked at him. "Cool," he said. "Do you know the area code for New Orleans?" It was a joke at his own expense, because that's where Church was certain he would begin the year, back in Class AAA despite the fact that he had been the organization's minor league hitter of the year in 2004.

But Bowden, too, had sensed what Robinson had sensed, that the team was sputtering, that there was no energy, no life. Was this a product you could bring to the people of Washington? Were these guys destined to match the low expectations of others?

The following night, the Nationals played the Los Angeles Dodgers in Vero Beach, another town with a small stadium tucked along I-95. Armas went on the disabled list, and Bowden arrived at Dodgertown, perhaps the quaintest of spring training parks, heavy of heart because his pitching staff was crumbling. Armas was hurt. Day had been hit hard, and though the coaching staff kept telling Bowden, "He'll get there," Bowden didn't see it. Patterson was happy with how he was throwing, but the coaching staff wasn't convinced.

Bowden had fire in his eyes as he walked through a back gate beyond right field at Dodgertown. In his ten and a half years as the general manager of the Cincinnati Reds, Bowden had made more than a hundred trades. One day, in between games of a double-header, Bowden sent five Reds to the minor leagues because he was so distraught over the team's play. He was unafraid to shake things up. And that day, the sense of an impending shakeup was palpable.

"Something's going to happen," Guillen said.

"They've been very lethargic for a week," Bowden said. "It's been a long spring. It's hot. We've had rainouts. It's frustrating. We understand that. But you know what? Frank aired them out after the game yesterday, and rightfully so. It's time for them to step up and get going."

It didn't happen that night. The Nationals lost to the Dodgers, 3-2. The men scheduled to be in the starting lineup when the season opened managed just four hits. Chavez flailed away, going 0 for 3. His batting average for the spring dropped to .212. His on-base percentage fell to .257. In thirty-seven plate appearances, he had drawn two walks. Robinson, alone in the small manager's office inside the visiting clubhouse, muttered to himself afterward, "He's the same fucking player he's always been. Hasn't changed a thing."

•   •   •

THE NEXT MORNING, the Nationals brass met in a third-floor conference room at Space Coast Stadium. It was Tuesday, March 29. On

Saturday, the Nationals would leave Florida after an exhibition in St. Petersburg and fly north to Washington, the first appearance in their new home. That Sunday, they would face the Mets at RFK Stadium for one final spring training game, then take the train north to Philadelphia, where they would open Washington's first baseball season since 1971 with a road game against the Phillies. In Washington, the team was scrambling to get prepared. The stadium wasn't ready, the batting tunnel the Nationals were supposed to use for practice had flooded, and there was no hot water in the locker room showers. The field wasn't ready because the rails that were supposed to be used to move a section of stands from along the left-field line into the outfield, so the stadium could be converted from baseball to soccer and back again, hadn't been tested. The mound, which weighed 18,000 pounds, wasn't ready, not packed tightly enough with clay, and the pitchers would arrive and kick at it, pick over it, complain about it, blame it.

But more importantly, in Viera, the team wasn't ready.

At that moment, the Nationals appeared to be in disarray. Jim Bowden felt as if he knew at least one reason for this, and at least one potential solution. He had challenged Endy Chavez to improve. Frank Robinson had challenged Endy Chavez to improve. And he hadn't improved.

So Bowden went around the room—to his special assistant, Bob Boone; to his assistant general manager, Tony Siegle; to Robinson himself. Should they solve this problem by sending Chavez to the minors? Should they shake up the team in this fundamental way? There was some dissension. Robinson had had enough of Chavez. Bowden's mind, too, was made up. They discussed it. Siegle, who had recommended Chavez to former Expos general manager Omar Minaya, tried to stick up for him. The support around the table was split. But Bowden knew what he would do.

"At some point," Bowden said, "potential has to become production. It's not working. It's not going to work." The Nationals, as currently constructed, weren't going to score very many runs anyway, and they certainly couldn't give away outs at the top of the lineup. So the meeting ended, and the decision was made: Chavez would go to the minors.

As the front office staff met, Tom McCraw sat two floors below, in the coaches' office, where Robinson's staff held daily meetings prior to games and workouts. Dressed in street clothes, McCraw took a moment to pay some bills, to deal with life away from baseball. Unaware of the decision made two floors above him, he considered the Chavez predicament.

"Endy's looked like Endy," McCraw said. It was not a compliment. "Yeah, there's some things that I like, but he still hasn't got there. As long as he's working on it, you can't ask for more from the man. But when it comes to fruition, I can't tell you. He just doesn't seem comfortable taking what we work on into a game."

Siegle, in these cases, was the bearer of bad news. Moments after McCraw expressed his frustration, Siegle was sent to the training room to find Chavez, bring him into Robinson's office, sit him down, and tell him about the move. "There's nothing worse," Siegle said, "than having to do that."

Chavez had no idea this was coming. He would be the leadoff hitter for this team. That's what he was told, right? "I was working on some things," he said later in the season.

The work, whatever he intended it to be, hadn't paid off. That day, as Bowden played Wiffle ball with four of his sons in the grass near the parking lots outside Space Coast Stadium, Chavez met with Siegle and Robinson in Robinson's office. They told him the plan: He would start the season at Class AAA New Orleans. He was not only no longer the starting center fielder and the leadoff man. He was no longer a major leaguer.

"I was totally shocked," Chavez said later in the season. "Once they called me into the office, I knew. But before that, no. No."

Chavez took the slip of paper, the one bearing the notice of his reassignment, and walked like a zombie back to the clubhouse, where the long task of cleaning out his locker began. Church saw Chavez slump into the clubhouse that day, saw the paper in his hand, saw the look on his face. The gears started to turn, and Church looked away.

Wait a minute. Church's mind started linking things together quickly, just as he had when he'd thought he would be sent to the minors. *If Chavez is out, then . . . Okay, think it through again. Count the out-fielders remaining in camp. Five will go north. Jose Guillen, Brad Wilkerson, J. J. Davis, Terrmel Sledge . . . and me?*

Holy shit, Church thought. *Holy shit! I just made the team.*

The odd dynamic of the spring was apparent in the locker room, with Church trying to contain himself, waiting to call his fiancée and his parents to tell them the news, with Chavez, not more than fifteen feet away, trying to contain himself as well. Chavez was despondent and angry. "I don't know what I would have said," he said later. But the Nationals offered counsel. Eddie Rodriguez, the bench coach, whispered in Chavez's ear. And Cardenal, Bowden's special advisor who'd spent those eighteen years in the major leagues, pulled up a chair and sat alongside Chavez, who stared into the clubhouse blankly, oblivious to his teammates around him, his eyes watering. "I wanted to say so much," Chavez said.

Cardenal whispered to Chavez. *Don't do it. Don't say a word.*

"He was ready to say things that he wasn't supposed to say," Cardenal said. "He was ready to talk bad about Frank and Jim."

So Cardenal, in quiet Spanish, sat mere inches from Chavez and explained. "Don't burn no bridge" was how Cardenal phrased it. *If you rip this general manager, this manager, then others around the league will see it, too. They will call you a troublemaker. They will call you a problem. You will have a harder time finding work.*

A half dozen media members, well aware by now that Chavez had been cut, gathered near his locker, hoping to talk to him. Cardenal kept whispering. The writers stayed away.

"You want to talk, that's fine," Cardenal said. "But no ripping people. You can't rip the GM, the manager, the coaches, the players. Because the only guy that's going to be hurt by that is you."

So Chavez, raging inside, kept quiet. Church let things cool down as well. Later he called his fiancée. "Guess what," he said. "I made the team." And she cried.

·   ·   ·

IN THE THIRTY-FOUR YEARS since Washington last had a baseball team, football's Redskins had countless quarterback controversies. Basketball's Bullets, later the Wizards, had hired and fired coaches and butchered draft picks. But the nation's capital hadn't had a spring like this in more than a generation. In less than a week, the Nationals' players and coaches would be heading north. They didn't know what kind of stadium awaited. They didn't know what the reception would be. They didn't know the town, how to get around, where to live, what to do.

Most of all, though, they didn't know who would play where, who would hit in which spot. Without Endy Chavez, the lineup was a mess. He was supposed to take the first at-bat in Washington Nationals' history. He was supposed to cut down balls in the alleys, to make triples die in his glove.

Frank Robinson stewed over it all. He was supposed to go to Washington, bringing back the city's first team in a generation, with this situation?

"It is very frustrating, as a matter of fact," Robinson said. "This is the first time I've gone this long in spring training, or this close to Opening Day, and not had a clear-cut feel for my lineup or the team that I was going to have Opening Day. It's not a good feeling, really."

The last few spots in the rotation weren't much better. Zach Day, by virtue of a few solid starts toward the end of the spring, won a starter's job, so it would be Livan Hernandez, followed by Day, Esteban Loaiza, Tomo Ohka, and John Patterson, who slid in as a starter only because of the groin pull suffered by Tony Armas Jr. Patterson, though, wasn't concerned about how others thought he got the job.

"I never had any intention," he said, "of being anything other than a starter, and one of the best starters we have."

Over the final week of spring training, Robinson wrote down lineups on napkins and little scraps of paper, trying to figure out what might work. But the only realistic solution was apparent to everyone in the clubhouse. Before one of the last exhibition games of spring training, Brad Wilkerson walked up to the lineup sheet taped to the wall of the clubhouse. "You're hitting fifth," he was told. "Yeah," he said as he turned away and walked back to his locker, "until Monday."

Thus Wilkerson headed north, knowing that it didn't matter that he had prepared the entire off-season to hit fifth, to drive in runs. The Nationals made a charade of the final few exhibitions, hitting Cristian Guzman first, hitting Nick Johnson first, hitting Church first. But Wilkerson knew: He would be the leadoff man.

Jose Vidro flew into Washington for the first time, his right knee feeling good, full of optimism. Day, too, headed north, trying to feel secure with his spot in the rotation, hoping for his breakout year. And Patterson made the trip lurking on the back side of the rotation, ready to pounce on the slightest misstep. Baseball's first season in Washington would begin with the anticipation and angst that comes when men are unsure not only of where they fit and how they should feel, but also of what they should think of their new surroundings. At that point, Washington, to the Nationals, was just a new house. They didn't know where to find the kitchen, the bathroom, the closets. It wasn't close to being a home.

★ ★ ★ ★ ★ ★ ★ ★ ★ ★ ★ ★ ★ ★ ★ ★ ★ ★

Chapter 6

The American, the Cuban, and Baseball Returns

Brian Schneider stood under the cover of the third base dugout at RFK Stadium, out of sight, down a wooden step or two toward the damp hallway that led to the Washington Nationals' clubhouse, and looked out at the crowd still filtering in through metal detectors and bag searches as the spring sun fell down and a cool Thursday evening set in. He had on other occasions worn his bright red shin guards, put on his red hat emblazoned with a white *W*, had even sat in the rudimentary dugout of his new home stadium. He was a big leaguer and a catcher, and there is a calm and cool that comes with both, something that indicates that—no matter what the situation—you are in control, unfazed. Take a foul tip off the inside of your thigh, and crouch right back down. Take a spike in your calf, tag the guy, absorb the collision, hold the ball anyway. Why should it be tough to focus in this situation? Never mind the crowd. *You* run the game.

But peering out from underneath the dugout roof, thinking about what lay ahead in the next few minutes, Schneider was nearly overwhelmed.

"Are you serious?" he said, half out loud, half to himself. No one else could hear as he muttered. Maybe he didn't mutter it at all. Maybe he just thought it. "Am I really doing this?"

Schneider was so distracted by the moment that obvious aspects of his immediate surroundings were something of a blur. The Nationals had already opened the season with a nine-game road trip, a trek on which, surprisingly, they won five games. But this night truly was baseball's return to the nation's capital, the first regular-season major league game in Washington in thirty-four years. In the bullpen, the starting pitcher, Livan Hernandez of Cuba, warmed up his rubbery right arm, and somewhere in the back of his mind Schneider knew, eventually, he would have to join him, for the Arizona Diamondbacks awaited, and a game was supposed to be played, and it counted in the standings. The optimism born by the move from Montreal was about to become a reality, and Schneider and his teammates could feel it, an energy in the clubhouse, even before their new home had become . . . well, before it had become home. But as important as all that was, Schneider was more powerfully aware of the presence to his left, the middle-aged man with the graying hair, dressed in a red satin Nationals jacket that looked bulky, as if he had put on weight in the last year, or maybe as if it were disguising a bulletproof vest. Schneider, by now, was nervous. The man made small-talk to reassure him.

"Oops. Looks like the press photographers noticed we're here," the man said.

"What do you mean?" Schneider said.

"Look to your right."

Schneider complied. It seemed at that moment that a hundred lenses obscured a hundred faces, all pointed at Schneider.

Are you serious? Schneider thought.

And then the President of the United States turned to Schneider—who would receive the ceremonial first pitch, the pitch that ushered baseball back to Washington, D.C., in front of more than 44,000 fans—and said simply, "Here we go. Just catch it."

•   •   •

JUST CATCH IT. It might have been what Pete Schneider told his son, Brian, years earlier in their backyard in Northampton, Pennsylvania, in the Lehigh Valley on the outskirts of Allentown, the old steel town in that Billy Joel song. For all the diversity in the dugout the night baseball returned to the American capital—there were men born in Mexico, in Japan, in California, in the Dominican Republic, in Venezuela, in Indiana, in Texas, in Puerto Rico, and in Cuba—there was no more American kid than this dark-haired, occasionally goateed Pennsylvanian who, when asked how to describe himself and his moment, searched a bit before settling on "patriotic."

And why wouldn't he be? Schneider's father, Pete, grew up in Northampton, went to the U.S. Naval Academy, played baseball there, turned down a contract offer from the Chicago Cubs, and became, for a time, a Navy man, flying P-3 antisubmarine aircraft during the Cold War days. *His* father, Pete Sr., was in the Army and the Air Force, a military man himself. While at the Academy, Pete Jr. met a girl from Annapolis, Karen Laudenslager, and wouldn't you know her father was a military man, too? John Laudenslager, better known as "Schultz" or "Pop," retired as a Navy captain, a minesweeper in World War II who still lives in Annapolis.

Just catch it. Brian might have been four—no, probably three—when he first heard those words coming from Pete's mouth. They have the pictures to prove it, Brian standing with one of those fat orange plastic bats, the ones toddlers use when they somehow figure out how to take a mighty cut at a Wiffle ball, launching it off a wall or under the couch or into the trees lining the backyard, much to everyone's delight. Brian's youth was filled with those moments, and it was no wonder. Pete's own family "grew up sports," as he said, and every sibling and cousin and uncle had some athletic success on his or her resume. Even in that environment, Brian stood out. Just catch it? He almost always did. When major leaguers grow up in places like Northampton, where the population is less than 10,000 and everywhere he turned folks were related as kin or teammate, they tend to stand out. Brian played soccer. He played basketball. He played baseball. Said Mike Schneider, his uncle, who served as the baseball coach at Northampton High, "You could hand Brian a badminton racquet or a bowling ball, and he would excel at it."

But even with eye-catching natural ability, athletic success was groomed and nurtured in him as well. While Brian and his sister, Missy, were growing up, Pete worked in human resources for a couple of energy companies more than an hour away. The rules were simple. Brian had to get in his fifty to a hundred swings a day. And when Pete finally came through the door, "I'd have to pitch till my arm fell off."

"Dad, throw to me."

"It's dark."

"Turn on the lights."

The family moved to a house on the outskirts of town. Pete and Brian used tennis balls because, should they careen into the house, they would cause less damage. They bought a machine that would pitch to Brian when Pete wasn't around. When Brian was young, not even knowing he'd be a catcher, he would lie on the ground and scramble to catch balls his dad would fire high in the air. It was the perfect pop-up drill, the reason Brian, as a major leaguer, would consider it a cardinal sin to drop a pop fly. "He didn't make me do it," Brian said of his father. "I wanted to." This was the way it would be done in the Schneider household, in Northampton, the way it should be done in America, really, the game passed from one generation to the next.

"With my own father," Pete said, "sports was always back to the basics. We learned the fundamentals. You really *learned* the sports, inside and out."

When Brian was about ten, father and son started a new hobby, card collecting. Over the years, they got all the ones you would want,

Crews began transforming the playing surface at Robert F. Kennedy Memorial Stadium in January 2005, part of an $18 million renovation that had the stadium, which hadn't hosted a baseball game since 1971, ready by April. © *2005 The Washington Post. Photograph by Preston Keres. Reprinted with Permission.*

General Manager Jim Bowden leads the cheers at Union Station, where the Montreal Expos are officially renamed the Washington Nationals. The ceremony marks the first appearance in Washington for Bowden, hired in November 2004 to put together Washington's team. *Reuters*

Nationals President Tony Tavares assembled a front-office staff that did much of its work out of trailers at RFK Stadium. © *2005 The Washington Post. Photograph by Katherine Frey. Reprinted with Permission.*

Frank Robinson took a job with the Montreal Expos expecting to manage just one more year. But by the time the Expos moved to Washington, Robinson, who turned seventy during the season, was in his fourth year at the helm. © 2005 *The Washington Post. Photograph by Jonathan Newton. Reprinted with Permission.*

Jim Bowden and Frank Robinson spent spring training in Viera, Florida, learning not only about their team but about each other. Bowden, the flamboyant GM, and Robinson, the old-school manager, had contrasting styles, but agreed on most personnel decisions. © 2005 *The Washington Post. Photograph by John McDonnell. Reprinted with Permission.*

No two figures were more closely associated with the controversy surrounding baseball's return to Washington than Linda Cropp, the chairman of the District Council, and Anthony Williams, the mayor of Washington, D.C. With their battles over, they were able to stand together at the Nationals' home opener in April 2005. © 2005 *The Washington Post. Photograph by Jonathan Newton. Reprinted with Permission.*

On April 14, 2005, Livan Hernandez delivered the first pitch in a regular-season major league game in Washington in thirty-four years, a strike to Arizona's Craig Counsell in front of a sellout crowd at RFK Stadium. © *2005 The Washington Post. Photograph by Preston Keres. Reprinted with Permission.*

Nationals catcher Brian Schneider shakes hands with President George W. Bush after Bush threw out the first pitch at the Nationals' home opener. Schneider, a baseball memorabilia collector from a military family, considered catching Bush's pitch the highest honor of his life. © *2005 The Washington Post. Photograph by Jonathan Newton. Reprinted with Permission.*

Nationals second baseman Jose Vidro (3) congratulates teammates after he hit a home run in extra innings to beat Philadelphia in April. Vidro, the Nationals' best clutch hitter, expected 2005 to be one of his best years, but injuries dogged him all season. © 2005 The Washington Post. Photograph by Jonathan Newton. Reprinted with Permission.

Jose Guillen arrived in Washington with a reputation for being a problem in the clubhouse, but his aggressive nature set the tone for the surprising Nationals early in the season. © 2005 The Washington Post. Photograph by Toni L. Sandys. Reprinted with Permission.

Brad Wilkerson was one of the Nationals' most versatile players, one expected to have a breakout season. But when Endy Chavez failed as a center fielder, Wilkerson had to play center and lead off, roles which he had hoped to avoid in 2005. © 2005 The Washington Post. Photograph by Jonathan Newton. Reprinted with Permission.

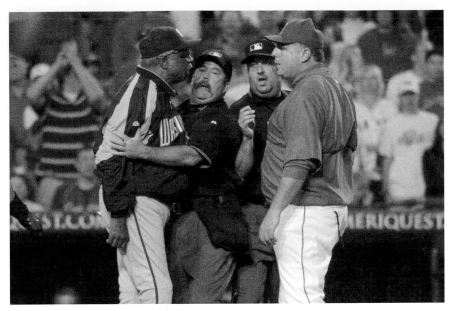

Umpire Tim Tschida holds Nationals Manager Frank Robinson back after Robinson was confronted by Angels Manager Mike Scioscia on June 14. The confrontation, which led to the benches clearing, was a seminal moment for the Nationals in the first half of the season. *Matt Brown / Orange County Register*

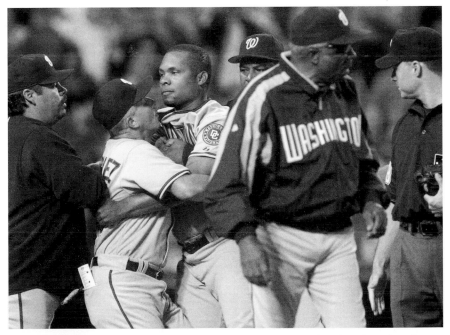

Bench coach Eddie Rodriguez holds back Jose Guillen after the benches cleared against the Angels. Guillen, suspended while a member of the Angels in 2004, admitted afterward he still held a grudge against Scioscia, calling him a "piece of garbage." *AP*

No member of the Nationals was more surprising, or more important, during the run to first place in the first half of the season than twenty-three-year-old closer Chad Cordero, who converted twenty-six save opportunities in a row and became an All-Star. © *2005 The Washington Post. Photograph by Jonathan Newton. Reprinted with Permission.*

One reason the Nationals' chemistry was flawless in the first half of the season was the early relationship between Jose Guillen and Frank Robinson. *Jamie Squire/Getty Images*

When John Patterson arrived at spring training, the only person who was certain he would be a stalwart member of the Nationals' rotation was John Patterson. © *2005 The Washington Post. Photograph by Jonathan Newton. Reprinted with Permission.*

No National came to the United States in the same fashion as Livan Hernandez, who defected from his native Cuba and became a hero with the Florida Marlins, the World Series MVP in 1997. Eight years later, he was Washington's first ace since 1971. © *2005 The Washington Post. Photograph by Jonathan Newton. Reprinted with Permission.*

A huge slump overcame the Nationals beginning in July, when Jose Guillen had a meltdown in the dugout, and then began to battle injuries. *AP*

As the summer wore on, the chemistry in the Nationals' clubhouse slipped away, with players such as Jose Guillen and Brad Wilkerson bickering in team meetings. But just when it looked like the Nationals were coming apart, even Wilkerson and Guillen could embrace after a big win, such as this one in the 12th inning against the Phillies in September. © *2005 The Washington Post. Photograph by Joel Richardson. Reprinted with Permission.*

When the Nationals' first season in Washington came to a close, Frank Robinson paid tribute to the more than 2.7 million fans who supported them at RFK Stadium. But as they headed into the off-season, the Nationals still didn't have an owner, and Robinson didn't know if he would be back for another year — a season in which he would turn seventy-one. © *2005 The Washington Post. Photograph by John McDonnell. Reprinted with Permission.*

the ones collectors dream of. Mickey Mantle. Ted Williams. Ernie Banks. But it was a card bearing the likeness of none other than Burt Reynolds that provided Brian with a nickname. Reynolds played a stuntman in the 1978 movie *Hooper*, and, since Brian spent much of that time climbing on couches or falling over the table or climbing in a tree, Pete thought "Hoops" was appropriate. Northampton's own little stuntman.

So Pete and Hoops began seriously gathering cards and other memorabilia, starting with a small collection Pete bought from a neighbor. Do kids still do that, memorizing the statistics of their heroes, familiarizing themselves with players long since retired, mulling over the tiny information on the back side while chomping on the flavorless, dusty pink stick of bubble gum? Hoops did. He knew Willie Mays and Roy Campanella and players other kids of the 1980s had never heard of. To this day, Brian Schneider might be the only major leaguer with a collection of 200 autographed baseballs, proudly displayed in his house, as if he were headed to the next memorabilia show on a Saturday at a flea market just off some interstate.

This was the path, the route by which a baseball-obsessed small-town kid turns into a big leaguer, the kind of young man who wears a chain bearing a small medallion, one made of the melted-down gold from his dead grandmother's jewelry. Before every at-bat, he kisses the necklace, and his dad's eyes water, the memory of his mother on a major league field with his son. "We always tried to instill in him," Pete said, "not to be a jerk." Hoops followed orders. His uncle Mike decided, when Brian was going into his junior year, that Brian should move from third base to catcher. So Brian caught. He hit better than .400. He threw out base stealers all over the place. He was named the Lehigh Valley's Player of the Year, which, Pete remembers, is a big deal up there.

The next spring, the scouts began to arrive. Brian had a scholarship offer from the University of Central Florida. He could have gone there and had the fallback of an education, because so few minor leaguers make it to the majors. But the Montreal Expos chose him in the fifth round of the draft. The debate was on. College or pro, pro or college. The goal, though, was always the same. Brian wanted to play in the major leagues.

"Dad," he said finally, after the issue had been tossed around and turned upside down, "I want to give this a shot."

So at eighteen, he quit his American Legion team, he skipped the graduation ceremonies at Northampton High, he signed a contract, and he reported to the Gulf Coast League Expos, rookie ball in the oppressive heat of the Florida sun. More than five years later, he would make his major league debut. Nearly five years after that, he would stand in the dugout with the President of the United States, ready to bring baseball back to Washington.

•   •   •

THE NATIONALS PLAYER whose upbringing was probably the most different from Brian Schneider's was Livan Hernandez, the starting pitcher the night baseball returned to Washington. Forget his experience in the big leagues as one of the few men on the roster who had been on the field in situations far greater, with stakes far higher, than an April game against the Arizona Diamondbacks. Schneider had never ridden his bike to the market to wait through the interminable lines just to pick up the two loaves of bread allotted his family each day, a pair of machetes strapped to his side as protection, because when your supply of bread is monitored, there's no telling who will fight you for what. Schneider had never packed a bag at home knowing he would never return, had never snuck out of a hotel room in the middle of the night, leaving his brother behind and running across a street to a waiting car, sweating and shaking because he couldn't be sure what lay ahead, with his mother and father and brother and sister back in Cuba.

"People no know what I go through," Hernandez said. "They no know."

Back as a rookie, they knew pieces of it, for following the 1997 season, Hernandez was *the* story, the twenty-two-year-old Cuban with the indefatigable right arm who belied his age and the situation to be the MVP of both the National League Championship Series *and* the World Series. He brought a cartoonish curveball that didn't snap so much as arc, something like the one thrown by Bugs Bunny, maddeningly slow. Hitters couldn't figure it out, flailing away, walking back to the dugout hanging their heads as if they had just swung and missed at three lobs in a slow-pitch softball game.

His story became familiar that fall. Growing up on Isla de la Juventud—the Isle of Youth—off the mainland of Cuba, he could always pitch. His mother, Miriam Carreras, was a typist for the Communist government. Livan learned his craft from his older half-brother Orlando, something of a legend in Cuba, the man they called "El Duque." At nineteen, Livan joined the Cuban national team. His father, Arnaldo, had pitched for the team before him. That would seem to be the logical dream for Livan, to pitch for Cuba. But no. At a young age, Livan Hernandez knew that would not be enough.

"I'm tired of all the things that happened there," he said. "I no got no life. I no got a dream. I'm the best younger pitcher in Cuba, nineteen years old. I throw harder than anybody, ninety-seven, ninety-six, good curveball. I want to be free. I want to be free. That is what was important."

That singular thought in the mind of a teenager: *I want to be free!* As a member of Cuba's junior national team, he had been to the United States before, had seen how people lived, had thought about cars and clothes and Big Macs. He came back when he was older, with the national team. He traveled to Japan, bought stereo equipment and VCRs and Huffy bikes, all to put on a boat and send back to his family. Wouldn't it be nice to live in a place where you could do all that? Wouldn't it be better for his family if he got out?

"I got a plan," he said. "And when I got something in my mind, I'm going to do it. It was important."

So in September 1995, seven months after he turned twenty, he packed his bag at his home in Isla de la Juventud, the four-room apartment he shared with his mother, knowing what would happen when he landed in Monterrey, Mexico, for baseball's World Cup. He told no one. His coach that season said to him, "You know, we have a good team this year." Livan nodded politely, all the while thinking, *Yeah, right. You're never going to see me again.*

When he arrived in Monterrey, he called Joe Cubas, an agent who had been working to try to help players defect. It was time, Livan told him. The next night, while El Duque and other teammates slept in their hotel rooms, Livan Hernandez quietly slipped from his room, shutting the door on his brother, on Cuba, on his life as he knew it. Cubas and an associate waited in a car across the street, covered in darkness. As he walked, Hernandez could feel the sweat on his forehead, down his back. He stepped across the street, his mind muddled, his heart pounding, and a car raced by, without its headlights on, nearly taking him out. Livan stopped, startled. His heart halted. He blinked. His heart started again—another obstacle sidestepped, and barely.

The next day, Hernandez flew from Mexico to Miami. *This is where I start over,* Livan thought. In January, he signed as a free agent with the Marlins, a deal worth as much as $6 million. He had no idea how to handle it. For two months, he carried a check for $2.5 million in his back pocket. "I didn't know how to use it," he said. Eventually, though, the whole idea of American excess suited him just fine. He bought cars as if they were hamburgers, ate hamburgers as if they were air, put on weight, purchased clothes every week, yet worried about how to get by in this new country without his mother, without El Duque. "That was the hardest part," he said.

At night, with the silence around him, his eyes would stay open. In Portland, Maine, where he was sent in 1996 to join Florida's Class AA team, the struggle was particularly acute. He felt uncomfortable anywhere but the stadium, wanting, he said, to spend twelve or fourteen hours there every day. He couldn't read the street signs, couldn't order food. He seemed withdrawn from his teammates. He loved his curveball and refused to throw his fastball. He gave off vibes that he wouldn't work, halfheartedly stabbing at grounders hit by a coach in a fielding drill, looking every bit like he would prefer to be back on Isla de la Juventud, staving off fights for those loaves of bread. Coaches and catchers implored him to listen, and either he couldn't or he wouldn't. He was ill equipped to deal with it all.

"I don't got no family here when I come," he said. "It's like you blind. You don't see nothing. You don't know what you're going to do. The Marlins gave me a lot of money, and I don't know what I want to do with that money."

Gradually, he became more comfortable, both on the mound and in the States. He went to movies and watched television, hoping to improve his English. By 1997, the Marlins, in just their fifth year of existence, were unexpectedly strong. They called on their Cuban exile to help them toward the playoffs. He was twenty-two, a rookie. He pitched like a veteran. He won his first nine decisions, and the Marlins took the National League's wild-card berth in the playoffs. Over those four weeks in October, he became a hero, striking out fifteen Atlanta Braves in one game during the National League Championship Series, then beating the Cleveland Indians twice in the World Series, including in Game 5, giving the Marlins a lead, three games to two. Three days later, just prior to Game 7, he burst into Suite 251 at Pro Player Stadium, the nondescript edifice in the Florida plains off Interstate 95 and Florida's Turnpike, where the Series was about to be decided. Marlins officials had told him there were fans there, fans who wanted his autograph.

And there, across the room, stood Miriam Carreras, his mother. Hernandez, a grown man of 245 pounds, was knocked backward just at the sight. Shock, he said. Utter shock.

"I think," he said, "it is one of my best moments."

The two embraced, a long, hard hug that started to make up for the more than two years since Livan had packed his bag, never to return. "I cried," he said. The Marlins had worked to get the Cuban government to allow Livan's mother to visit the United States. All of the Marlins players signed a letter, sent to Castro's government. And here she was, hugging her son. That night, after Livan returned to the dugout, blowing kisses to his mother in the luxury box, the Marlins won the Series. Livan was the MVP. His mother was in America. His sister would follow. Nephews, too. He owned Miami, screaming, "I love you" to the city.

He stayed at the stadium after the victory, celebrating till four or five in the morning, driving home with the MVP trophy. The next day, he went to the Aventura Mall, with his mother at his side. He handed the keys to a valet. "Livan!" the man yelled. "Livan!" And the crowds descended. Livan wanted to go into Mayor's Jewelers. He wanted to buy things for his mother, to share his riches with her. So police closed the doors, and mother and son shopped. A watch. Some earrings. But they had to leave. The people were too much, waiting to get into the store clamoring to see their hero. Livan's Mercedes was pulled around to a hidden location, and mother and son slipped out a back door. Not like in Monterrey, when Livan had snuck away, about to be alone for the first time in his life. This time, Livan and Miriam slipped away together.

But the ride couldn't, and didn't, last. The next summer, Hernandez won ten games and lost twelve. Whispers started. He had become too enthralled with life in America. He didn't work. He ate too much. He wasn't prepared. In the middle of the 1999 season, having won only five of fourteen decisions, he was shipped to San Francisco for a pair of pitching prospects. The Marlins of 1999 were nothing like the Marlins of his rookie year, a group that had been dismantled in the name of saving money. When Hernandez found out about the trade, he cried. "I was no used to the West Coast." Yet he had the chance for more glory. In 2002, Hernandez found himself on the mound for Game 7 of the World Series. There is no bigger stage, and, for Giants fans, there are few greater collapses than that of Hernandez, who couldn't even get one out in the third inning before he was removed. The Giants lost the game and the Series. Hernandez, a star five years earlier, was a scapegoat. In two World Series starts that year, he lasted just five and two-thirds innings and allowed nine earned runs.

So the following March, late in spring training, he was closer to being a has-been than a hero. The Giants, scarred by his ineffectiveness in the World Series, wanted desperately to unload him. Montreal Expos GM Omar Minaya was a willing taker. "Why?" wondered Frank Robinson, the manager. "What for?" wondered Tony Siegle, Minaya's assistant.

"I thought we needed better at the time," Robinson said.

When Hernandez reported to the Expos for that last week of spring training in 2003, the pitching coach, Randy St. Claire, sat him down. "I don't know you," St. Claire told Hernandez. "I've never known you. But I've heard bad things about you. Lazy. Dog. Showman."

By the end of that season, though, St. Claire had drawn other conclusions. "I couldn't have been more wrong," St. Claire said.

The Hernandez the Expos got turned out to be an ace. In each of his first two seasons with the franchise, he led the major leagues in complete games and innings pitched. Something about growing up in Cuba had instilled in him a mentality that when he took the ball, he did not want to give it up until the game was over. Forget that Hernandez's body was not that of an elite athlete, chiseled and sculpted, but more like one belonging to a refrigerator repairman, his pants hanging low on his backside, a visible paunch resting over his belt, the John Belushi of pitchers.

It was that journey that led him to this moment, the moment a Cuban-born right-hander would throw the first pitch for a team representing Washington, D.C., the American capital. It was that journey he thought about while in the bullpen beyond the left-field wall, warming up at RFK Stadium, just more than twenty blocks east of the U.S. Capitol. There was no more American setting.

"It make me proud," Hernandez said.

•   •   •

THAT MORNING, in the Foggy Bottom neighborhood outside of downtown Washington, Alan Alper woke up, a kid on Christmas morn. His present couldn't be unwrapped until that night at RFK Stadium, where he had last been for a regular-season baseball game . . . well, when they'd last played regular-season baseball there, in 1971. That night, he had cried. This morning, he wanted nothing more than to climb to the top of his townhouse, to get on the roof, to scream, "I have a baseball team again!" His eyes welled up, even at the mention of the moment. He resisted the urge to get on the roof. But he got to the stadium—three hours early.

•   •   •

ON THE NIGHT baseball returned to Washington, the Nationals were told to be in their home uniforms—their dress whites, really—far earlier than normal, for they would have a pregame visitor. So it was that while the Diamondbacks dressed down the hall, the Nationals stood in a ring around the tan carpet, cramped in the small space in front of their red lockers, joined by a Secret Service man wearing a Nationals uniform, and President Bush walked in.

Bush's connection to baseball was deep. Not only had his father, former President George H. W. Bush, played the game at Yale, but Bush himself had been a partner in the Texas Rangers, a member of the most elite of old-boy networks, a major league baseball owner. When Bush walked in, the team was quiet, hardly knowing what to say or do. The President walked up to each player, shaking his hand, looking him in the eye.

"That's the biggest thing I learned about the President," Brian Schneider said. "He looks you right in the eye. He gets eye contact with you, and then he talks to you. It's kind of intimidating in a way, you know?"

Bush asked Nick Johnson, the first baseman who had spent so much time on the disabled list, how he was feeling. He remembered, back in 1991, when the Rangers traded a minor league left-hander named Joey Eischen, who now stood in front of him wearing a Nationals uniform, a plug of tobacco spilling out over his lip, President be damned. And he approached Livan Hernandez, who had struggled through traffic that night just to find his way to the ball-park, arriving a half hour later than he would have preferred. It didn't matter now.

"*Buena suerte,*" the President said.

Buena suerte? For real? The President of the United States was speaking to Hernandez in Spanish. *Good luck. You represent Washington, D.C., now. Good luck. Buena suerte.*

"It's something amazing for me," Hernandez said. "Amazing."

Schneider, though, had the most amazing job. President Bush was to throw out the ceremonial first pitch. To perform such a task, he had to warm up. How many pitchers had little Hoops helped get ready in his lifetime, back in Little League in Northampton, back in rookie ball, up into the majors? Too many to count, but no one like this.

What do you talk about? Schneider, so willing to label himself a patriot, was just learning what it would mean to play in Washington, to have so many avenues to the power structure that runs the country. In the off-season, with the team having relocated from Montreal, Schneider started tapping into the community. Given his family's ties to the military, he was something of a buff, rattling off names of fighter jets and Navy ships. A connection got him out to the Coronado San Diego Naval Base, where he went on a jet ride. And not just any ride—the controlled crash of a landing put him on the deck of the U.S.S. *Carl Vinson,* an aircraft carrier. He spent the night, hung out with the sailors, and grappled with what they were doing.

"What year did you graduate from high school?" Schneider would ask, signing autographs in the mess hall. The answer, it seemed, was always 2003 or 2004. Schneider, at twenty-eight, considered himself young. "*I'm* signing autographs for *them*?" he said. He befriended the commanding officer, or perhaps the commanding officer befriended Schneider. He doled out Nationals hats, and it occurred to him that lids representing Washington would mean just a tad more to these guys, these nineteen- or twenty-year-olds, than those from, say, Montreal.

Was this the kind of stuff he should talk to the President about? Or should he just shut up? The pair headed out the clubhouse door, around the corner to the right, down the stairs toward the dugout, then hung a left into the batting tunnel, where the Nationals could take hitting practice in inclement weather. RFK Stadium, still undergoing slipshod renovations, was a near disaster that night, and the tunnel had been flooded only a day before. But in those moments before the game, underneath the stands, when he and the President were alone to warm up—save for two Secret Service agents in the hallway and the White House photographer in the tunnel—Schneider could have been completely under water and he wouldn't have cared.

Bush asked where Schneider was from. Northampton, Pennsylvania, he said, the Allentown area. Of course, Bush replied. He had campaigned there. Schneider told him about his dad going to the Naval Academy, his grandfathers both serving their country. Schneider was amazed, because Bush was completely engaged, two guys trading stories and playing catch. "He was really talking to you," Schneider said. "He wasn't just blowing you off, like, 'Uh-huh. Uh-huh,' nodding his head.

"I just got comfortable. If I thought about what I was doing, who I was with, I'd start to get nervous. But I didn't expect it to be that easy. A couple of times, I caught myself." He was almost too relaxed. *It's the President, Brian. Easy now.* "I didn't want to be too nonchalant with him, and sound like I was being . . . well, maybe not cocky, but I wanted to make sure I was giving him the proper respect. Whatever you think of him, whether you voted for him or not, he's the President of the United States. He's our leader. I just have so much respect for him. But it was a little weird that way, because I caught myself being too comfortable with the President."

They warmed up and talked for perhaps fifteen minutes, with Bush saying from the beginning that his pitch would likely be high. "I'm not going to bounce it," he said, and Schneider was reassured. And then, suddenly, the President turned to him.

"I'm ready. Are you ready?"

What do you say when the President of the United States asks about your level of preparedness?

"I'm ready," Schneider said.

Outside the stadium, as the crowds gathered—walking from the Stadium-Armory Metro stop on the orange and blue lines, learning the path back to baseball—Pete Schneider, his wife, Kari, their daughter Missy, two of Brian's uncles and an aunt, and Brian's new bride, Jordan, went to the will-call window to pick up the tickets Brian had left there. They got the tickets and started for the gate, then noticed they had the wrong tickets. What? How could this be? They were for Diamondbacks family members.

They marched back to the will-call window.

I'm going to miss the President's first pitch—to my son, Pete thought.

Do you have the tickets? Does anyone have the right ones? Here they are. Here they are. My son, you know, is going to catch the President. We have to hurry.

And then . . . the lines. Because of Bush's presence, each and every fan, concessionaire, media member, security guard, usher, and player had to go through metal detectors. Snipers paced the top ring of the stadium. And the Schneider clan nearly panicked. They worked their way to the front, and pushed through, into the stadium, racing to their seats, tucked under the upper deck, just behind home plate. The Ballou High School Majestic Marching Knights, from a high school in one of the District's poorest and most violent neighborhoods, had long since taken the field, performed, and marched off. Anthony Williams, the bow-tied mayor who knew little about baseball other than that he wanted it in his city, had been introduced, and evaporated into the crowd. Had the team already been introduced? Oh, God, it must have been, because someone (the Navy Band Sea Chanters) had just belted out "God Bless America," and someone else (opera star Renée Fleming) was just being introduced to sing the national anthem.

Here they were, finally. Their seats. *Okay. You sit there. You sit here.*

Where was Brian?

And then it hit Pete.

He's with the President, he thought.

That he was, standing underneath the dugout. The grandson of Pete Schneider Sr. and Schultz Laudenslager, military men, the son of Pete Schneider, military man, was standing next to President Bush, just chatting.

"Are you nervous at all?" Brian asked the President, mostly as a means to calm down, and also as something of a way to pass the time.

"No, I'm not nervous. Are you nervous?" Bush asked.

"Yeah, I'm nervous," Brian admitted. "It's not too often I get to do this."

"Don't be," Bush said.

Standing next to them in the dugout, a sixty-seven-year-old man named Joe Grzenda held a baseball. Grzenda, a journeyman of a pitcher who was once a reliever for the old Washington Senators, had kept this baseball for thirty-four years in his home in Goldsboro, Pennsylvania, not too far from Northampton. On September 30, 1971, Grzenda had sat in the upper deck at RFK Stadium, thirty-four years old, pondering the future in the hours before the Senators' final game. He was a reliever for the Senators, and he wanted to stay in Washington. The team, though, was moving to Texas. That night, they would host the New York Yankees in their final game in the District. And Joe Grzenda threw the last pitch.

In the ninth inning, with the Senators leading by two runs, Bobby Murcer hit that pitch back to Grzenda, who threw it to first. Two outs. Grzenda got the ball back, and needed only to retire Horace Clark to end it. But then, the fans streamed over the walls. They were on the field. The game was forfeited. And Grzenda took the ball to the clubhouse.

But here it was again, back in Washington, back in RFK. Standing near the dugout steps, Grzenda told Schneider about the ball. "I'd really like it back," he said. No problem, Brian said. Grzenda didn't know it, but he was speaking to a kid with 200 baseballs, all kept for their historical significance. Brian Schneider knew the meaning of a keepsake. He would bring the ball back.

And it was time, 6:52 P.M. "Here we go," Bush said. "Just catch it."

"Ladies and gentlemen," the public address announcer boomed, "please direct your attention to home plate, and welcome Nationals' starting catcher, number twenty-three, Brian Schneider."

Brian ran onto the field. Grzenda followed. Then there was Bush. Grzenda handed him the ball, Washington's baseball past becoming part of a present that people had awaited for a generation.

"And here, to throw out that same ball, to mark a new era of Washington baseball, the President of the United States."

Bush was true to his word. He hurled the ball confidently, and, had a right-handed hitter stood at the plate, it would have been high and inside. Schneider caught it. Flashbulbs popped everywhere.

Holy shit, Schneider thought. *There it was.*

He'd thought it would take forever, but it was over just like that.

And from Alan Alper's seat in Section 514, the thought was the same. Baseball had been away forever. Now, in an instant, it was back.

•   •   •

LIVAN HERNANDEZ, the Cuban, and Brian Schneider, the Pennsylvanian, worked that night to usher baseball back into Washington as if they were Tom Seaver and Johnny Bench. In the top of the fourth inning, Arizona left fielder Luis Gonzalez hit a ground ball up the middle, past Hernandez, one that shortstop Cristian Guzman, ranging well to his left, couldn't quite corral. It was a single. And for eight innings, it was the only hit Hernandez allowed.

When Nationals third baseman Vinny Castilla unloaded a triple in the bottom of the fourth, Jose Vidro and Jose Guillen scampered home, the first runs in Washington since 1971. The upper deck at RFK Stadium, packed now, shook more than a little. "Holy shit," said Tony Tavares, the Nationals president. "What's going on?"

It was that kind of night, newcomers learning from the old-timers that this is what it used to be like, that the seats swayed during the glory days of football's Redskins, when the eastern edge of Capitol Hill was *the* place to be. Glory days? This was one glorious day indeed. Castilla, who had doubled in his first at-bat and hit the two-run triple, later added a two-run homer. When he came to the plate in the eighth, all he needed was a single to complete the cycle, a single, double, triple, and home run, all in one game. A Diamondbacks reliever named Lance Cormier unleashed a two-seam fastball that thwacked Castilla right in the shoulder.

Then came perhaps the most beautiful sound of the night. Those 44,000 who had waited for baseball, who had waited through political haggling and impasses and arguments, they got together on one thing. They booed. They booed loud. They booed hard. They booed long. Castilla just needed a single for the cycle, one of baseball's most difficult achievements. But when Cormier plunked him in what was sure to be his final at-bat, he no longer had a shot. So the boos came down, and the Nationals smiled.

"That was the most impressive thing," outfielder Brad Wilkerson said later. "They knew the game. They knew he was going for the cycle. They started booing, and they wouldn't stop. That felt good."

Hernandez, tiring now, finally wore down in the ninth, allowing a three-run home run that cut the Nationals' lead to 5-3. But the young closer Chad Cordero finished the job, and the final out settled into the glove of rookie Ryan Church in center.

In the next few hours, Brian Schneider would gather with his family at the Mandarin Oriental Hotel, maybe two miles from the stadium on the Potomac River, across from the Jefferson Memorial, and he would tell the story of his evening with the President five, ten, fifteen times. And Livan Hernandez, the winning pitcher, would celebrate with his mother.

"How can I not be happy?" Hernandez said afterward, speaking for himself and for thousands of others. "It's baseball."

Chapter 7

★ ★ ★ ★ ★ ★ ★ ★ ★ ★ ★ ★ ★ ★ ★ ★ ★

Jose Guillen, Outcast or Leader?

*T*he sky was brilliantly blue over San Francisco that Saturday morning. SBC Park, nestled next to McCovey Cove, seemed the perfect setting for a ballgame. The Nationals had arrived in the Bay Area having taken two of three in Los Angeles from the Dodgers, then beat the Giants in the first of three on a Friday night. Yet Saturday, three hours before game time, Jose Guillen sat curled up on a couch in the visitors' clubhouse, athletic shorts around his waist, a blue towel over his head, barely hiding his heavy eyelids.

No big deal. Some days, Guillen's presence sparkled in the clubhouse, his white teeth showing at every turn as he pounded fists with other players or clubhouse attendants or reporters, joking in high-speed Spanish or his slightly broken but always intelligible English. When the switch was on, he bubbled and would talk about anything and everything, always mixing in the phrase, "I tell you the truth." You never knew whether, in fact, he was telling you the truth, but the way Guillen said it—staring straight at you, making you believe others would lie but he would not—was, in that moment, convincing.

Then, there were the other days—like this Saturday in San Francisco—when Guillen would do little more than stare straight ahead.

He moved through the clubhouse silently, as if stalking prey. Few people spoke to him on those days.

The night before, San Francisco pitcher Tyler Walker plunked Guillen in the left elbow with a pitch. He was replaced by pinch runner Ryan Church, and Church hit a three-run double in his next at-bat, helping the Nationals to a win. Ten hours later, Guillen's elbow was still throbbing. He took pain relievers to help control the swelling on his elbow, because he couldn't flex his arm to swing a bat. The pills floored him. He moved only slightly on the couch. Music thumped around him. Teammates laughed, played video games on the gigantic TV just a few feet away. He lay still, paralyzed, it seemed. For a time, no one approached.

So for the first time all season, Frank Robinson made out a lineup card without the name "Guillen" marked in the third or fourth position. And, naturally, the ribbing began. Vinny Castilla shouted to Guillen: "Sissy!"

"Jose!" general manager Jim Bowden said, barely stirring Guillen on the couch. "I thought you were going to play 162. What's going on, dawg?"

Bowden was smiling, joking with Guillen about playing time. It seemed like an indication that, as Guillen had said time and again in spring training, "the past is the past."

Or, it could be argued, the tip-off that the past was the past, that Guillen was a new person, had come the night before. After Guillen had doubled on Friday night, Church jogged onto the field as a pinch runner. Guillen jogged off the field, removed his batting helmet, stepped into the dugout.

Nothing else happened. He was taken out of the game, yet the fury remained inside.

•   •   •

It's hard to pinpoint exactly where Guillen's attitude—combustible, competitive, contrarian—comes from, but the place to start is San Cristóbal, the sprawling city of 120,000 or so on the southern shore of the Dominican Republic. The city, founded in the late 1500s, was where the first Dominican constitution was signed. Rafael Trujillo, the ruthless dictator who brought order to the country after U.S. occupation, was born there. So were major leaguers. Raul Mondesi, the temperamental journeyman outfielder who during the 2005 season completed his career with a failed run for the Atlanta Braves, grew up in San Cristobal. So did Jose Rijo, the charismatic pitcher who led the Cincinnati Reds to the 1990 World Series title, retired after surgery in 1995, returned at age thirty-six in 2001, retired again, and took a job with the Nationals as an assistant to Bowden in the off-season. "We don't got shit there," Rijo said. "No McDonald's. No hotel. Nothing." When Guillen was growing up, the townspeople grew sugarcane. They grew plantains. And they grew baseball players.

"I grow up in the poor family," Guillen said one day, sitting at his locker at RFK Stadium, tucked in the back right corner of the clubhouse, where he can be seen when he wants to be seen, where he can hide when he wants to hide. "We don't have the stuff, the money, like a rich family has."

No different from many Dominican players. "That's what it's like there," said Rijo, who's known Guillen most of his life. "Dominicans, we have more needs. We're more hungry. We live in reality."

It is this world into which Guillen was born on May 17, 1976. His father worked on the assembly line at the local glass bottle manufacturer. His mother sold fruit from the front of their house. Jose—skinny, just 135 pounds hanging from his bones when he was sixteen—played baseball.

From a young age, he was pulled in two directions. His father, whom he describes as tough, a disciplinarian, wasn't enamored of the idea that he would play baseball. A pipe dream. Forget the arm that would regularly unfurl throws from right field that stayed seven or eight feet off the ground, with no arc to them, just straight lines to second or third base, even home plate, tight as guitar strings. To his father, no matter. Is it realistic to take that skill overseas, to make millions? No, his father said. Jose weighed just 135 pounds. Why not get a job?

"Work, work, work," Guillen said. "That's all I heard from him."

His mother, though, was different. She encouraged him. Jose and his five siblings—three older brothers, a younger brother, and a younger sister—all helped around the fruit stand, scurrying in and out, watching her work. But his mother liked the fact that Jose played baseball, that he wanted to get out of the Dominican Republic. *Go play*, she said.

Yet in 1994, he arrived in the United States, just seventeen, not ready for all that lay ahead. The Pittsburgh Pirates discovered him, brought him over, threw him to the wild world of American baseball. He got a signing bonus of $2,000, and he sent it to his mother, so she could come over, too. She worked in a restaurant in a Dominican neighborhood in New York. He began his minor league tour, through Bradenton, Florida; Erie, Pennsylvania; Augusta, Georgia; Lynchburg, Virginia. He was a teenager who had known only San Cristobal, who played in the Little League Rijo established there, who arrived without a glove. Now he was busing through the backroads of the East Coast of the United States, sleeping in unfamiliar beds, eating unfamiliar food, confronted by unfamiliar people.

Guillen was combative even then. He established himself quickly as a player. But off the field, he was difficult. His managers in those early days in the minors had a tough time getting him to fit in, to do what his teammates did, show up on time and go through the drills and understand that his talent might be special, but he wouldn't be treated like he was. He became guarded. He didn't trust his coaches. And it affected his teams. Managers would tell him that there is a time to steal a base, there is a time to try to throw a runner out, yet he would steal bases when he wanted, throw to third when he should have gone to second. His manager his first three years was Jeff Bannister, a coach's son from Texas who wanted things done a certain way, and expressed those thoughts to Guillen. Guillen, though, was so in love with his talents, his strong arm and powerful bat, that he would frequently ignore the advice, throwing farther than he should just to prove he could, trying to pull pitches out of the park that he should have taken the other way for singles.

"He thought I was trying to hold him back," Bannister said.

So conversations that Bannister describes as "colorful" would ensue regularly. The reality: They would scream at each other. Guillen never wanted to come out of a game. He never wanted a day off. He was competitive to a fault, almost more so with his teammates. If one, say, hit a single, then Guillen was going to damn well hit a double. If one hit a homer 390 feet, Guillen's sole mission would be to hit one 410. "He always compared himself to everybody else," Bannister said.

So he didn't act like everyone else. In his first year in the United States, he played hard for Bannister in the Pirates' extended spring training program in Bradenton, Florida. Bannister was going to take the best from that program to Welland, Ontario, to play Class A ball in the New York–Penn League. He wanted Guillen to go along, against the advice of some of the Pirates front office members who wanted him to stay in Florida and play in the less-advanced Gulf Coast League. Their hesitance wasn't based on ability. Rather, it was attitude. "I can handle him," Bannister said. Bannister won the argument, and he told Guillen that he was invited north. Bannister then held a mandatory team meeting, laying out the ground rules for everyone, all these kids, whether they were staying in Bradenton or heading to Canada. He was getting worked up during the speech, fire-and-brimstone Texas stuff, but his eyes scanned the room. He kept speaking, but his eyes moved more quickly, searching.

Where the hell was Jose?

The meeting broke up. In Bradenton, the Pirates complex is known as Pirate City, and the young players are all housed in dormitories. Bannister headed to Guillen's room, knocked on the door. There he was.

"I already had the team made," Guillen said. "I didn't need to go to the meeting."

"Guess what?" Bannister said. "You get to stay here."

That would be screaming match number one.

Still, Guillen didn't learn. Two summers later, Guillen was en route to becoming the MVP of the Class-A Carolina League, playing for the team in Lynchburg, Virginia. Bannister, the manager, got to the ballpark—the Durham Athletic Park, the one Kevin Costner and Susan Sarandon had made famous only a few years before—early, then watched the team bus roll in. Players filed off. Guillen didn't. An hour or so later, when some of the opposing Durham Bulls showed up, Guillen was with them. Bannister allowed him to walk into the clubhouse, where he informed Guillen that he would no longer be playing that night.

Guillen bellowed at him, "What do you mean?"

But Bannister insisted. Guillen wasn't the superstar he thought he was.

"I was a kid," Guillen said, thinking back.

He was a kid, though, whose self-image was fortified because he could do things others couldn't. One night in Wilmington, Delaware, he turned to chase a ball hit over his head in right field. The runner on first took off, rounding second confidently. There was no play. Except for Guillen. He scooped up the ball off the wall and threw it toward third. Not *over* the cutoff man, on an arc, but *through* the cutoff man, on a line. When the runner arrived at third, the third baseman was already holding the ball, as if he had just pulled the hidden-ball trick. He had not. Bannister turned to the players and coaches on the bench. "If you blinked," he said, "and you didn't see that, you missed one of the most amazing things you'll see in baseball."

Yet even as Guillen went through those difficult times in the minors, he realized something, almost immediately.

"This is," he said, "an American game."

The Nationals club that broke camp at spring training and

headed to Washington had more foreign-born players than any other major league club to open the season. Tomo Ohka, a pitcher, hailed from Japan. The rest of the foreign-born players were Hispanic. Guillen and shortstop Cristian Guzman were Dominican. Pitchers Esteban Loaiza, Luis Ayala, and Antonio Osuna, along with third baseman Vinny Castilla, were Mexican. Second baseman Jose Vidro and backup first baseman Wil Cordero grew up in Puerto Rico. Pitcher Tony Armas Jr., son of former big league slugger Tony Armas, was Venezuelan. And pitcher Livan Hernandez came from Cuba. On a road trip later in the season, Hernandez purchased T-shirts and foam-and-mesh trucker-style baseball hats for his teammates, a celebration of diversity. Each one was imprinted with a personalized saying.

Huego en Mexico
Huego en Dominicana
Huego en USA
Huego en Puerto Rico
Made in . . . insert country here

At times in the Nationals clubhouse—with rapid-fire Spanish bouncing from corner to corner, with the Latin hit "Gasolina" by Daddy Yankee pumping from speakers—baseball seemed anything but an American game. *"A ella le gusta la gasolina (dame mas gasolina),"* the lyrics exclaimed—"She likes the gasoline (give me more gasoline)."

It was a comfortable environment for a man from Latin America. Yet in those early years of his career, in hardscrabble American towns such as Lynchburg and Erie, it had been unclear to Guillen whether he would ever be in a clubhouse such as this.

"When I came, I heard people talking," he said. "I had no idea. This being my first time in the States, and I'm just like, 'What are they saying? What am I thinking about, being over here?'"

What became clear to him, he said, was that "I got to learn this language. Being a rookie, you don't know if they're making fun of you. They're saying this, this, and that, you have no idea. You want to know why they're laughing at you, and sometimes, some of the guys come up and laugh, and I don't know what they're saying, and sometimes it was bothering me. I just put in my mind: I got to learn this language."

So he did.

"A lot of guys, they don't care about it," Guillen said of Latin teammates who relied on Spanish, who had a difficult time communicating with some people in their organizations, with the almost exclusively white American media. Take Vladimir Guerrero, the former Montreal Expo who won the American League Most Valuable Player award in 2004, the year Guillen hit behind him in Anaheim. Guerrero spent much of his time in Montreal using Manny Acta, then the Expos' third base coach, as a translator.

"I said, 'Vladdy, why don't you speak English?'" Guillen said. "He just said, 'Nah, I don't need to.' He's not interested. He comes ready to play, to play baseball, and that's it.

"But this is an American game, and that's what I keep telling everyone. You got to learn *their* language. They don't got to learn *our* language. We're getting paid by American people. That's the truth. Like it or you don't like it, but I don't think American people should be forced to speak Spanish. To me, if you come to the States and you don't try to learn the language, you're stupid, because you're not getting paid by Latin people, and you got to learn what they're saying."

That kind of stance actually put Guillen at odds with his countrymen, with other players from Latin America. Major League Baseball ratcheted up its steroid testing policy prior to the 2005 season. The lasting image of the hardened stance on steroids became Mark McGwire, under questioning from a House panel, repeatedly saying he was there "to talk about the future," not about what he might have done in the past. Rafael Palmeiro, the Baltimore Orioles' first baseman who appeared headed for the Hall of Fame, pointed his finger at the panel, saying he had "never" used steroids. Yet he tested positive during the season and was suspended in early August. The reality, once the season began, was that a disproportionate number of Latin American players, both major and minor leaguers, were caught and suspended.

David Ortiz, the slugging Dominican designated hitter who has never been linked to steriods, said in an interview with the *Boston Herald* in early May that Latin players weren't being properly educated on the subject, that the language barrier presented a problem, that they were more prone to taking steroids unwittingly because the guidelines were in English. Guillen, a week later, standing by his locker in the visiting clubhouse in Arizona, had a simple response.

"Bullshit!" he said. "To me, there's no excuses. I came from the Dominican. I speak no English. No English. None. *Zero!* We get paid good money to come here and play this game, and to me, it's no excuse to be making."

He was talking, stream-of-consciousness style now, his voice rising. When the team arrived in Arizona, a huge two-locker stall at the far end of the clubhouse had a placard bearing the name Mike Wallace affixed to the top. Wallace, known to everyone in baseball as "Wally," is the team's clubhouse manager. The Nationals hadn't been in Phoenix for thirty minutes when Wallace's name was taken down and replaced by Guillen's—an indication of Guillen's rising position in the clubhouse. As he talked, he stood in front of that locker, bigger than any of his teammates'.

"I'm a good friend of David Ortiz," he continued. "But to me, it's no excuse for those guys that they've been catching with steroids, or whatever they put in their body. They need to learn. It's been in the Dominican all over the TV. It's been all over the place. They know what's going on. Trust me. They know what they're putting in their body.

"I'm Dominican. I should defend my people. I'm Latin. I should defend all Latin players. But to me, it's no excuse. *It's no excuse.* They're getting caught. They've been cheating. Unfortunately, this has been on some Latin players. But what can you do about that?"

•   •   •

LYING ON THAT COUCH in the clubhouse at SBC Park on that May day, however, Guillen appeared unable to do anything about anything. So Robinson filled out his lineup. Nick Johnson, the first baseman, would hit third. Vinny Castilla, the third baseman, would hit fourth. Never before had the Washington Nationals played without Guillen in one of those two positions.

Guillen's absence seemed to be the most jarring aspect of the lineup that day. But Jose Vidro, the stalwart second baseman, sat out for the second straight game with what was being described as a high sprain of his left ankle. Vidro had sustained the injury three days earlier in Los Angeles, when he sprinted all the way from first base to score on a double by Castilla in a win over the Dodgers. After that game, in the clubhouse, Vidro had cut off approaching reporters before they could reach his locker stall. "I'm fine. I'm fine. I'm fine! *I'm fine!*" he'd said defiantly.

"That's the way I was before, the way I always used to be when I got hurt," Vidro said later in the season. "I'd probably take one day off, two days off, and I'd heal and heal fast. I really thought I'd be fine."

He wasn't fine. Thirty minutes after making that declaration in the visitors' clubhouse at Dodger Stadium, Vidro had walked across the perfectly manicured outfield, the stadium lights turned low, toward the team bus. Teammates, even those who sauntered aimlessly, blew past him. Vidro could only hobble. It had taken him nearly ten minutes to reach the bus. By the time the Nationals reached San Francisco, it was clear that the injury might be major.

"I'm nervous," general manager Jim Bowden said, standing on the field during batting practice. "I'm worried. I'm praying it's not serious, and he says he feels better today, but we'll see. We're going to have an MRI taken, but I'm just not sure."

By the end of the day, the Nationals knew that Vidro's problem was worse than just a sprained ankle. By the end of the road trip, he was on the disabled list, out with tendon damage in his ankle. The 2004 season had ended prematurely for Vidro because of knee surgery, something he should have had done earlier, really, because problems had slowed him for two years. But now the man who perhaps more than any National had wanted to come to Washington, to have a baseball home, wouldn't be a part of the story for two months, the two most difficult months of an otherwise stellar career.

Man, he thought, *I went through this last year. I tried to do the surgery so I wouldn't come up with a knee injury again, and then I work hard on my knee, and then all of a sudden I get this other thing?*

"It was depressing," Vidro said later in the season. "I couldn't really understand what was going on. This is the year I was looking forward to for so long, to be part of a good team, to be part of a good city."

He wasn't part of it. He would go to rehabilitation just over the Potomac River in Virginia. He would return to his family's apartment in Northwest Washington. But he couldn't bring himself to go to RFK Stadium, to enter the clubhouse, to be with his teammates. "That would have killed me," he said. It nearly killed him anyway. He couldn't escape the thoughts going through his head, over and over. He would try to convince himself that injuries are just part of baseball.

"But what I didn't understand is: Why does this keep happening, over and over, for a year or two years?" he said. "This is not me. This is not the baseball player I am."

The only solace Vidro could find was in his wife, Annette. No one knows Vidro better. They met in 1990 as teenagers in their native Puerto Rico. They grew up together, really, lived through the years in the minor leagues, had a son, Jose Junior, and a daughter, Anais.

Annette knew how much baseball meant to her husband. More than that, she knew how much this season, the season with stability provided by the city of Washington, meant to him. So when Jose grew depressed, he knew where to turn. While the Nationals were playing, Jose and Annette would talk and talk and talk some more. Annette kept the rules simple: Don't bring up baseball.

"I don't know what I would have done without her," Jose said later in the season. "She knew how important this was for me. She understood how much I love this game. She understood what I was going through inside. There were times when I tried not to talk to her about it. But that was the only time when I felt really relaxed, when I expressed myself about it. And she always listened."

•   •   •

WHILE JIM BOWDEN FRETTED about the injury to Jose Vidro, Jose Guillen appeared on the field, headed to the left side of the batting cage, where he grabbed a fungo bat. He picked up some baseballs and hit grounders toward first base, lazily, hazily, as if he was partly there, partly somewhere else. The technical assessment of his injury was a bruised left triceps, sustained when that pitch hit him the night before. But that didn't seem to be what bugged Guillen on the field.

"I was just so dizzy," he would say later. "It was just one of the weirdest days in baseball."

And it didn't figure to be a day when the Nationals would have much success, not with the lineup they rolled onto the field, not with Giants right-hander Jason Schmidt, San Francisco's best pitcher, on the mound against them, and especially not after Nationals right-hander John Patterson threw an ill-advised 3-1 fastball to Giants right fielder Moises Alou with the bases loaded in the third. Alou, the son of Giants manager Felipe Alou, tore into the pitch, sending it into the left field seats, where frantic Giants fans, bathing in the sun, battled for it. It was a grand slam. It put the Giants up 4-0. And with Vidro and Guillen both out, it figured to end the Nationals' day.

"He got hurt," Robinson said of Patterson afterward. "One big swing of the bat. You could tell he just didn't have his good stuff today."

That was the thought that entered Robinson's mind the following inning, the top of the fourth, with the Nationals down those four runs. Patterson didn't have his good stuff. He had a 1.60 ERA entering the game and in some ways had been the Nationals' best pitcher to date delivering on the promise he made to himself in spring training. Yet Robinson couldn't escape the thought: *He doesn't have his good stuff.*

As it turned out, neither did Schmidt. He walked Brian Schneider to lead off the fourth, an unforgivable sin for a pitcher who had just been handed a four-run lead, particularly an eleven-year veteran who, frankly, should have known better. Shortstop Cristian Guzman followed with a single, putting runners on first and second. And then, the unthinkable: Endy Chavez walked. Yes, that Endy Chavez.

Chavez had been called up earlier in the week, a desperation move after outfielder Terrmel Sledge was lost for the season with a hamstring injury. He hadn't really proven himself in the minors, hitting .269, posting an on-base percentage of .352. In his first week with the major league team, he had two hits in five at-bats. Yet Nationals officials—chief among them Bowden and Robinson— didn't see much of a difference. "He's the same," Robinson said. "Hasn't changed a thing."

Earlier in the day, as they stood around the cage during batting practice, Bowden, rarely subtle, decided to try to send Chavez a message. Castilla and pitcher Esteban Loaiza were around the cage as well. With Chavez taking cuts, Bowden spoke loudly to Castilla and Loaiza.

"Have you guys ever seen someone with a chance to be in the big leagues just refuse to change their approach?" Bowden had barked rhetorically to Loaiza and Castilla. The two players laughed. No, they said, they hadn't.

"I mean, it's not that hard," Bowden had said. "Learn to take pitches. Learn to be more selective. Learn to be a leadoff hitter. And just refuse?"

Chavez, a quiet man, had finished batting practice and was in the lineup that day in center field. Maybe the words had hit home. He walked in his first at-bat of the day, a walk due in large part to the fact there were two outs and the pitcher, Patterson, was hitting behind him. But then, in the fourth, there were men on first and second, with no one out, and he walked again, this time on five pitches.

So the bases were loaded, and Patterson's spot was up. Guillen didn't think much of it. During the first few innings, he'd slept on the couch that had become his pregame home. When he woke, he carried himself to the batting tunnels tucked under the stands behind the Nationals' dugout along the first base line. He took one, two, three, maybe ten swings total. He returned to the dugout, still not wearing the belt to his uniform, no batting gloves, not really prepared. He spoke to Eddie Rodriguez, the bench coach.

"I think I can pinch-hit for you," he said.

And here it was, just the fourth inning. Robinson couldn't shake his thought about Patterson, that his good stuff wasn't there. The Nationals' offense, particularly as currently constructed, wasn't equipped to win shootouts. So when Chavez unexpectedly walked, the call went to Guillen. Pinch-hit for Patterson, he was told.

A scramble ensued. "Get my belt! Get my belt!" He found some batting gloves, got himself together, and strode from the shadow of the dugout into the bright San Francisco sunshine. Schmidt toed the rubber. He threw his first pitch, and Guillen took it, a ball. When Schmidt reared back for his second pitch, Guillen lifted his bat and swung through it. Strike one.

And here it came, the 1-1 pitch from Schmidt. Guillen swung and stung a line drive to right field. Schneider scored from third. Guzman scored from second. Chavez scooted around to third. The Nationals trailed, 4-2.

"How does that *not* fire you up?" said Jamey Carroll, filling in for Vidro at second base.

There were, arguably, more significant hits in the first half of the

Nationals' season. There were, arguably, more significant hits in that very game against the Giants. The Nationals went on to score seven runs in that inning, six against Schmidt. Guillen remained in the game, doubled in his next at-bat, made a pair of fine catches in right field. Ryan Church came through with the biggest hit of his young career, a bases-loaded double in the top of the ninth that gave the Nationals the lead.

But the day belonged to Guillen. In the ninth, with the Nationals trailing 8-7, he came up with Jeffrey Hammonds on first base, representing the tying run. He took one pitch for a strike, then unleashed a mighty cut against Giants reliever Jeremy Accardo, missing. Clearly, he was trying to win the game with a homer. But Accardo's next pitch sailed past catcher Mike Matheny. Wild pitch. Hammonds scooted to second.

At the plate, Guillen's thoughts changed. Forget the fact that he had the ability to hit a game-winning home run. Forget the fact that a single would tie the game. His job was clear. With no outs, he had to, at the very least, move Hammonds to third, where he could score on a sacrifice fly, a wild pitch, a well-placed ground ball, a single.

"I'm a winner," Guillen said, "and a team player."

So on the next pitch, Guillen took an inside-out swing and fisted a ball toward second base. It went as a groundout and worked against Guillen's average, his statistics. But Hammonds took third. And when Guillen returned to the dugout, he received fist bumps from every single teammate.

"It changed the ballgame," Robinson said. "It changed the way *they* approached the game. It changed the way *we* approached the game."

Guillen had given himself up for the team. Would he have done that in Erie, in Lynchburg? Most certainly not. Wilkerson followed with a sacrifice fly that scored Hammonds, tying the game. Church later ripped his double, scoring three runs, putting the Nationals up 11-8, the final score.

"Look at us," Robinson said afterward. "We're a bunch of misfits, troublemakers. We come from all over. Can't do much. We're just going to do the best we can, and sometimes they might throw us a crumb and we'll win a ballgame. We'll appreciate that, and continue to take that approach, and hope we get enough crumbs thrown our way."

No win in the first two months of the Nationals' existence was more stirring. After the game, sitting in his office tucked around the corner from the visitors' clubhouse, Robinson made pronouncements no one could have foreseen in spring training, when the talk had centered around the baggage Guillen carried to Viera, the baggage he would bring with him to Washington.

"I don't know if too many hitters would've done that, hitters of his stature," Robinson said, thinking back to that ground ball. "He did it, and everybody on this ballclub responded to it and appreciated what he did, and told him when he came into the dugout. And he was rewarded for it, because we capitalized on it."

Robinson got to thinking now. The victory gave Washington four wins in the first five games of a long West Coast road trip. The Nationals were just two games out of first. Guillen's impact got to Robinson.

"Those types of things, they're little things, but they help you win ballgames," he said. "They see a big guy doing it, other guys will start doing it. It'll rub off on the ballclub.

"I tell you, he is slowly becoming the leader of this ballclub. This ballclub is taking, really, on his attitude. Hard-nosed. Let's go out and play nine innings of baseball, and play it hard. That's what he brings to this ballclub."

When the sun set in San Francisco that Saturday night, the Nationals, and Guillen, could smile. The clouds hadn't yet gathered, but they would. The storm would come later. The season is just too long to go without a burst of thunder from Guillen.

★ ★ ★ ★ ★ ★ ★ ★ ★ ★ ★ ★ ★ ★ ★ ★ ★ ★

Chapter 8

The Chief, the Winning Streak, and First Place

*B*aseball was a staple in Washington from the early 1900s through the '40s and '50s. Even after the original Senators departed in 1961, taking off to Minnesota, they were replaced swiftly by the expansion Senators, not missing a season. But for most of those years, Washington wasn't a baseball town, not in the truest, purest sense. Not like Cincinnati, a founding member of the National League, which for decades traditionally staged the first game of the season, because people breathed baseball there, and it was their right to kick things off. Not like St. Louis, in the heart of the heartland, where attending a Cardinals game without wearing some sort of Cardinals gear is considered heresy, and talk of the next season begins moments after the conclusion of the current one, rarely slowing down even as winter sets in. Not like Boston, where the Red Sox can be a sick obsession. Not like New York, where the off-season maneuvering is frequently more compelling than the in-season games. Washington had its football, its Redskins. It had its politics. And for those thirty-three years, it had no baseball.

So on a glorious Sunday afternoon in 2005, the moment kind of snuck up on the nation's capital. The Florida Marlins, infinitely more talented than the hometown Nationals, played at RFK Stadium. The supremely gifted A. J. Burnett took the mound to face Washington, throwing tiny little fastballs that tipped the radar gun at 97 mph, darting away from the Nationals' batters, unhittable stuff. And where, exactly, were the Nationals coming into this game? Hmmmm. They'd beaten the Marlins on Saturday night, a 7-3 thumping in which the hometown team looked pretty good. Come to think of it, they'd beaten the Marlins on Friday, too, when Livan Hernandez threw an unthinkable 150 pitches, when a rookie outfielder named Ryan Church lifted a sacrifice fly in the eleventh to win it. So that made one, two, three . . . well, it made six wins in the last seven games, including three against the Atlanta Braves and two against the Marlins, the two clubs that were supposed to provide the chief competition in the National League East. Check the standings, then check them again. A win on this particular Sunday could put the Nationals—"a bunch of misfits and outcasts," according to their manager, Frank Robinson—in first place.

"Pretty cool, huh?" closer Chad Cordero said.

Washington, a baseball town at least for a few days—for that to happen, even for a small stretch, the unexpected had to become reality. And by the end of that afternoon, when the crowd of 40,995 leapt to its feet, they looked down to celebrate that moment—*first place!*—to perhaps the most unexpected element of all, the pudgy kid with the flat-brimmed cap standing in the middle of the diamond, watching the final out recorded on a quickly sinking fly ball to left, bumping fists with his catcher. They looked at Chad Cordero and cheered. Another save in the books, so many more to come.

·   ·   ·

TONY SIEGLE DIDN'T KNOW what to expect when he drove through the streets of Chino, California, on that day in the early summer of 2003. He had flown in from Toronto that morning, met one of the

Montreal Expos' scouts, Tony Arango, at the airport, and headed for the Cordero household, a modest home befitting the modest family that lived there. Siegle, the Expos' assistant general manager, carried with him a folder that outlined a presentation and, in the end, contained a contract, with a line that awaited the signature of one Chad Cordero.

Siegle had been through this kind of thing before, trying to woo a first-round draft pick, only to be frustrated that the player demanded more from whatever club Siegle worked for, and Siegle had worked for plenty, from Houston to Philadelphia to Milwaukee to San Francisco to Colorado to Montreal. Now, as the car wove through the streets of Chino, a working-class community of about 70,000 southeast of Los Angeles, he would be entering the home of a pitcher so physically unremarkable that most baseball experts had predicted him to be selected in the third round, not the first. He didn't throw 95 mph, didn't stand 6 feet 6 inches tall, didn't have an overhand hammer of a curveball. But the Expos, at the time, were different from most clubs, so they thought differently than most clubs. Arango watched Cordero pitch at Cal State Fullerton, watched his fastball tail a bit as it reached the plate, watched him work quickly, confidently. Dana Brown, the scouting director, came in and watched as well, and the two men came up with a mission: Convince Omar Minaya, the Expos' general manager, to take this kid he'd never seen in the first round, with the twentieth pick overall. "I liked the way he reacted to the situation, the way he responded," Brown said. "There was something about him that wasn't measurable. It was makeup."

Baseball scouts have their own language, and they cast it about as if everyone understands it. A kid has a "plus arm" or "plus speed," meaning, quite simply, that he throws better or runs more swiftly than an average player. They talk about "ceilings" and "upside," different terms for potential. And they talk about "makeup," the most nebulous of these terms. Makeup includes attitude, upbringing, demeanor, work ethic. It includes, really, whatever you want. Scouts such as Brown, a young man but an old-school evaluator, are taught to look at prospects, read their body language, and fill out reports projecting how a young man's physical ability and mental makeup might contribute to his potential to become a productive major leaguer. Arango and Brown looked at Cordero and considered his situation. They thought he would sign quickly. They thought he would rise to the majors quickly. They thought, given that their franchise was owned by Major League Baseball and couldn't afford to get into a protracted contract squabble, Cordero was a nice, safe, solid choice, not as much because of his physical attributes as because of his attitude, his makeup.

All this was rooted, naturally, in Cordero's upbringing. Chad wasn't much more than two years old when he discovered he might want to play baseball. He would scurry around the house, picking up anything—"a broom, a flyswatter," said his mother, Patti—and make it into a bat. At ten, he would hop the fence behind his grandparents' house to join the rest of the family in games on Sunday afternoon, and there were plenty of family members to join in. Patti had four sisters, and they all played softball. Chad had ten cousins, and they would play baseball together, waiting for their grandmother to pass the juice and the ice over the fence, something to suck down between innings. At that same age, Chad began pitching against the older kids, eleven- and twelve-year-olds. It is a time when a one-year difference in age can mean a significant difference in size, in strength. So in one game, little Chad faced the opposing team's best hitter with the bases loaded. The outcome, of course, was predictable: grand slam. But Edward Cordero saw something in his son that day, something that would resurface years later as he worked his way through Don Lugo High, as he went on to close games at Cal State Fullerton. The kid came up again, and Chad was still on the mound. "It didn't faze him," Edward said. Chad struck him out. His makeup was taking shape.

His is, at its best, a ferocious attitude, yet anyone who came into contact with Cordero off the field during the 2005 season would be hard pressed to find him ferocious. He wore a soft, almost goofy smile, and his heavy eyelids portrayed what seemed like a detachment, a mellowness that sent out the vibe that he could not, would not, be disturbed. Approach him in the clubhouse, ask him, "What's goin' on?" and his response was usually, "Just chillin'." He wore, almost exclusively, short-sleeved button-down shirts, untucked, no fancy suits or designer jeans. Occasionally, Patti would ask him if he wanted her to buy him some new clothes. "Come on, Mom," he'd say. "I don't need that." He spent his money on CDs and video games. He bought a house back in Fullerton and let his former teammates and his younger brother use it, paying some rent. Really, it was a place to hang, an off-season home where Chad could feel comfortable. He took to his college nickname, "Chief," easily, and it came not because of his commanding presence, but because of the small amount of Native American in his ancestry. "I don't really leave there in the off-season," he said.

"He's just so mellow," said his mother.

So how to account for his on-field demeanor?

"He'd become a different person when he got into a game," said George Horton, Cordero's coach at Cal State Fullerton. "He had a different makeup," and there's that word again, unsolicited. "I don't want to exaggerate, but I'd say it all the time. He'd get that adrenaline rush, and it's like he went from Clark Kent to Superman. He'd take his glasses off, and he'd just take over."

These are the qualities the Expos saw. These are the qualities they hoped would remain. But in the car on his way to Cordero's house, all Tony Siegle could do was hope the kid would put his name on the contract.

When Siegle and Arango arrived, they were greeted by Edward, Patti, and Chad himself. Patti offered drinks. Siegle politely declined. Arango accepted some ice water. These negotiations wouldn't involve a swanky dinner, which was just as well. Siegle was a kind man in such situations, but hardly a schmoozer. In the Corderos' kitchen, he began to lay out his case. As he was doing so, he was overcome by a thought: *Man, I hope they take all this money, because these are just really nice people.* The presentation was under way.

The Expos, Siegle explained, were unlike any other franchise. They were so bereft of talent, they provided premature opportunities to those players who were even halfway decent. Go through the farm system. What other closers were there? The entire organizational depth chart appeared on the Corderos' kitchen table. Rocky Biddle was the closer at the major league level, and he was hardly established. This was an opportunity, Siegle said. If Cordero signed quickly with the Expos, they'd get him to the minors, they'd work with him, and—who knows?—he might be in the major leagues by the end of the year. No, the money might not be what he'd get if he haggled with another club, one that might give him $10,000 or $20,000 or $50,000 more as a signing bonus. But the sooner Cordero advanced to the major leagues, the sooner the clock would start ticking toward the time when he'd be eligible for arbitration, the sooner he'd become a free agent, the sooner he'd make the really significant money. "That's what matters," Siegle said. "Some of these kids get shortsighted about that kind of thing."

Cordero, twenty-one at the time, sat quietly and listened. In the preceding days, Edward had been straightforward with his son. Edward drove a truck for Wonder Bread, traveling all over southern California, a blue-collar man leading a blue-collar life, providing for his family. But when it came to the draft, he had done his research. The Expos, Edward explained to Chad, were unlikely to offer any more than "slot" money, meaning Chad would be fairly compensated for the slot in which he was chosen, but no more. Because he was the twentieth pick overall, he should expect to get more than pick twenty-one but less than pick nineteen.

"It's your choice," Edward said. "If you're comfortable, do it. If you're not, don't."

As Siegle continued his presentation, he wasn't sure how to feel. He had been told the kid was itching to begin his pro career, that money wasn't going to be an issue. He had been told the family was reasonable and down-to-earth. "But you never know how they're going to react," he said. "You hear kids are ready to sign, but when you get into the living room, that can all change."

Yet in this situation, in the little house in Chino, an absence hung in the kitchen of Edward and Patti Cordero. Patti was there. Edward sat by Chad's side. And that was it. There were no other outsiders, no one whispering in Chad's ear. A first-round pick mulling over his first contract *without an agent*.

"A couple of people called us and told us we could have gotten more money," Chad said. "But I didn't want it. I didn't want more."

This is a story, two years later, that Siegle can't recount without tears welling in the corners of his eyes, without the hairs on his arm standing straight up. Siegle began his career in the game in 1965 as a scoreboard operator with the Houston Astros. He had worked under twenty-three general managers, known countless players, been involved in negotiations good and bad, made friends and enemies. But he stayed in baseball because of moments like this with the Corderos. He stuck with the game for the love of it. Too few times, he felt the love back. This was one of them.

The Expos' offer was for a bonus of $1.35 million and an assurance that Chad would be invited to spring training with the major league club the following year. Edward Cordero looked at his son.

"Chad, what do you think?"

"Dad," Chad said, "that's more money than I ever thought I was going to get." He looked at Siegle. "Where do I sign?"

Siegle showed him the line.

"It was," Siegle said, "one of the most electrifying experiences for me to hear a young kid say that. I knew we had something."

Cordero scribbled his name. He was a professional ballplayer. He was an Expo. "If nothing else," Siegle said, "we had a quality human being here."

Quality human beings, though, don't always make good pitchers.

And the Expos needed a good pitcher. Heck, they needed five of them. They flew Cordero to New York, where Montreal was playing the Mets, so he could have a bullpen session in front of the club's brass before reporting to rookie ball in the Gulf Coast League. Edward, who used to trek across California to take in baseball games in Los Angeles or San Francisco—"He used to drive eight hours just so he could boo the Giants," Chad said—came along for the ride, as did Chad's brothers, Matthew and Alan. They got to sit in the dugout at Shea Stadium, got to walk on the big-league grass, got to see a big-league clubhouse, got to witness big-league batting practice up close.

Chad, though, had to throw, and so he headed out to left field, to the visitors' bullpen beyond the blue fence, underneath the jetliners landing and taking off at LaGuardia. Minaya was there. Frank Robinson, the Expos' manager, was there as well. They all headed out to the bullpen in left field to watch the kid they had taken with their first pick in the draft throw strike after strike.

Here came Cordero's first pitch. It bounced. Here came the second pitch, and it bounced. One pitch sailed way high, another darted way low. Pitches all over the place. Cordero's heart pounded, thumped, like it never had before. Robinson said to no one in particular, "This is our first-round draft pick?"

"I don't think I've ever been that nervous," Cordero said. "I realized where I was. I realized there was a Hall of Famer standing right behind me. It was a little overwhelming. I finished, and I was like, 'Holy cow!' I still couldn't believe where I was. I mean, you got *Frank Robinson* right behind you, watching."

•   •   •

ON MAY 30, 2005, Alan Alper turned fifty-two years old. It was Memorial Day. The Nationals hosted the Braves. Was Alan going? "Are you kidding?"

As a kid, he used to go to RFK Stadium on his birthday, because the Senators seemed always to be home on that day, yet they always seemed to lose. Maybe this team was different. He could always hope, even if in the days leading up to birthday number fifty-two it didn't seem so. The Nationals were swept in Cincinnati by a mediocre Reds team, then dropped the first two in St. Louis to fall to 24-25 on the year, the first time they were below the .500 mark since they were 3-4 just a week into the season, before they had even played a game in Washington. *Dear God*, Alper thought, *just let them be .500 on my birthday.*

So on the Sunday before they returned home for Memorial Day, Brad Wilkerson delivered three doubles in St. Louis, Livan Hernandez pitched seven strong innings, and Chad Cordero pitched a one-two-three ninth for his eleventh save in thirteen chances, and they arrived at RFK for the holiday with twenty-five wins and twenty-five losses. There was no way of telling what would happen in the ensuing weeks, no way of telling what that one win, at the time, might provide. But Alper had sensed something over the previous month or so. From the time the team was christened the Nationals during that naming ceremony back in November at Union Station, Alper hadn't gone a day without wearing some sort of clothing pertaining to Washington baseball: a T-shirt, a hat, a sweatshirt, a golf shirt. His wife, Marina, would joke—it was a joke, right?—that there was no point for anyone to go to the Nationals' team store, for they could find anything they needed in the Alpers' townhouse, the one with the Nationals flag flying outside in the Foggy Bottom section of Washington, near George Washington University. Alan had the blue road jacket *and* he had the red home jacket, because in Washington, at the height of the red-versus-blue debate, "you have to be politically correct," he said. His main decisions each day went something like this: *Should I wear my Senators Historical Society shirt or my red Nationals golf shirt?*

"Literally, I feel naked if I don't have something Nationals-related on," he said. "*Naked.* There's such a sense of pride. *We have a team!*" and he puffed out his chest in an exaggerated manner, his voice rising. Then it would soften and he would come back to earth, because he is an educated man and knows how such emotional outbursts must sound coming from the mouth of a fifty-something . . . well, a fifty-something kid.

"I know it's silly," he said. "I know it's totally silly for a grown person. But I don't care."

So he went to the game on that Monday, Memorial Day, his fifty-second birthday. He took the Metro, the orange line or the blue line—either worked—to the Stadium-Armory stop. And he noticed them, the people in the Nationals hats and the Nationals jackets. It wasn't just on the Metro going to games, though. The Nationals, by that point, had overtaken the Boston Red Sox as the baseball franchise that sold the most merchandise. They sold red caps and blue caps, caps with the *W* for Washington and an interlocking *DC* for the District of Columbia. They sold flags and pennants and T-shirts and clocks. They sold towels and blankets and glasses and mugs. And, apparently, they didn't sell it all to Alan Alper.

"When I was a kid and watching the Senators, the only people who wore the hats were kids," Alan said. "You didn't sell the jerseys that the players got. The public didn't wear them. It was something the players had. Just to see so many people with the hats, it's like a sense of community. I can't tell you how many conversations I have that I wouldn't have had otherwise, just because someone is wearing a Nats cap.

"I mean, there's women, young women in their twenties or thirties or their teens, wearing the hats, going to games! I knew, as a screwed-up teenager with raging hormones who was scared to death of girls, that I wasn't going to get a girlfriend going to baseball games. Any girls that went to games were already with somebody. They weren't alone. That's not the case now."

He looked around and couldn't find a common demographic that stitched together all the people who wore Nationals hats. All these people from all over the D.C. metropolitan area simply loved the team, *their* team. They would talk to him about how the team was doing. "Cordero looks good. What's wrong with Guzman? Is he overpaid? Patterson has some potential. Did you go the other day when . . . ?"

"I don't know if it's pride to the level that I have it," Alper said. He was crazy, but he recognized it, and how crazy does that actually make someone? "But they identify with it. They're happy that they can wear the home team hat. It just fills me with pride."

• • •

On HIS BIRTHDAY, Alan and Marina sat in the 500-level seats behind home plate, the yellow seats that were as high as you could get, and looked down upon the action against the Atlanta Braves, who were swiftly becoming the hated Atlanta Braves, because if you have a new team, you need to forge a new rivalry, and the Braves had won their division every year since 1991 (save '94, the year of the strike). Tomo Ohka pitched for Washington that day; Alan had read about him, had watched him pitch before. Earlier in the month, when the team was on a road trip to the West Coast, Ohka asked to be traded. He no longer liked Frank Robinson, the manager. He no longer felt like the coaching staff had confidence in him.

But on this day, Ohka wore a Nationals uniform, and he decided to throw a gem. It is the kind of thing that happens when a team is about to begin a charmed run, though no one—not Alan Alper, not anyone in the announced crowd of 39,705—could know it at the time. In the seventh inning, Ohka held a 2-1 lead, and he faced Braves right fielder Brian Jordan. With the count 1-1, Jordan lofted a long fly ball down the left field line, high, on an arc, not a shot, but still a threat. Jordan trotted halfway down the first base line, but didn't have much hope. The ball, he thought, was sure to be foul, well left of the tall yellow pole marked with a few feet of black at the bottom. The Nationals left fielder that day was a man named Marlon Byrd, and he raced over to give it a look. The wind gusted, pushing the ball away from the seats, back toward fair territory. *Cool,*

Jordan thought as he walked down the line. *Keep blowing. Keep blowing.*
It did. Byrd jumped, but the ball eluded his glove. It hit the foul pole,
right on the black portion, and fell over the fence. Jordan, a bit
stunned, went into his home run trot, because a ball that hits the foul
pole is a home run, and the game was tied, 2-2.

Out of the dugout came Frank Robinson. He couldn't charge
out, because he was sixty-nine, but he came anyway. The ensuing
five minutes presented the kind of scenario that happens to winning
teams. Robinson asked Byrd what he had seen. "It was foul," Byrd
said confidently. So Robinson took up his case with the third base
umpire, Jerry Layne. Robinson, who'd spent three years in the commissioner's office as the vice president of on-field operations, reading umpires' reports about confrontations, learning how they dealt
with things, appealed to his calmer senses, which was rare, for him,
in a case of confrontation. He knew he wasn't going to flat-out
change Layne's mind. "Let's get another opinion," Robinson asked.
So Layne called to the crew chief, Ed Montague, who was calling
plays at second base and who had run to the outfield to look at the
flight of the ball. The umpires conferred in short center field. Jordan
was long since in the dugout. The tying run had long since been
posted on the scoreboard.

And then Montague emerged from the huddle. He extended his
arms flat, parallel to the ground. No home run. Foul ball.

Robinson headed back to the dugout. Braves manager Bobby
Cox took his turn arguing, to no avail. Disgusted, Jordan grabbed his
helmet, grabbed his bat. Ohka threw one more pitch. Jordan
grounded it back to Ohka, then flung his bat in disgust. The home
run turned into an out. The Nationals held the lead.

The win wasn't secure, though, until the Nationals had extended
the advantage to 3-1 on Jose Guillen's two-out RBI single in the seventh, and Chad Cordero came in to pitch the ninth. Robinson had
talked, during spring training, of keeping the closer's job open, but
he had no intention of doing so. The closer's job was Cordero's now,
no questions asked, and in a tight game, Robinson gave him the ball.

Cordero, more than anyone in the Nationals' bullpen, could handle the pressure. And here he did, recording the first two outs of the inning, and the Memorial Day crowd, including birthday boy Alan Alper, came to its feet, pressing Cordero for a strikeout of the Braves' center fielder, Andruw Jones. Cordero missed with his first two pitches, then threw a strike, a fastball that blew right by Jones.

So the next step was simple. Cordero unleashed one more fastball. But Jones swung, the kind of mighty swing that would allow him to lead all of baseball in homers at the end of the season. He crushed it to left field, a solo home run that brought the Braves to within one run. Here was Cordero, twenty-three years old, allowing a home run to one of the game's best hitters. He hadn't given up a home run since the fifth game of the season. How do you shake that kind of thing off?

Remember back to when he was ten, and that big kid hit a grand slam. "I really think he can do that better than other people," said Edward Cordero, who had watched his son pitch more games than almost anyone. "He just forgets stuff. He makes himself forget stuff."

"Things don't bother him, not outwardly, anyway," Frank Robinson said. "If he gives up a big home run, he still has the same demeanor as if he struck somebody out in a tough situation."

The Nationals could not know what would happen with the next hitter, Braves catcher Johnny Estrada. But they had a sense that if they were going to have problems winning games, Cordero wasn't going to be the reason. In college, back at Cal State Fullerton, Cordero had taken a class called "Mental Skills for Sports." He didn't ask questions, didn't seem particularly inquisitive on the subject. But the professor, Ken Ravizza, noticed Cordero "soaking it up," he said. And he watched Chad take the lessons taught in the classroom onto the field. Keep things in a rhythm. Breathe in the same way. Be consistent in your mannerisms. Home run or strikeout, take precisely the same approach.

Sitting on the bench in the dugout along the first base line at RFK Stadium that day, Randy St. Claire, the Nationals pitching coach, sensed what he had in Cordero, too. Never mind what the kid looked like. Talk about who he is. Talk about . . . well, for lack of a better term, his makeup.

"His fastball is deceiving," St. Claire said. "It's where it comes from. He's a short-armer. Short-arm guys, they have that deception. It comes from behind the head, so the hitter doesn't see it till real late. When you get a long-arm guy, hitters see it for a long time. With Chad, you don't see it till the last minute.

"But you know what? I think what's even more important for Chad is that it takes a special demeanor to be a closer. They don't get too high, too low. It doesn't matter who's coming to the plate. They pitch their plan. And he's got that special demeanor."

"I'll go out there to talk to him," catcher Brian Schneider said, "and it's like he has no idea what the situation is. Not that he doesn't know, because he does. But if I didn't know, I couldn't tell by looking at his face or talking to him. He just wants to know what we're going to try to do to the next hitter, and then wants to pitch. It's pretty cool, really. He acts the same way with a ten-run lead and nobody on as he does with a one-run lead and the bases loaded."

So with Jones's homer still rattling around beyond the left field wall, Cordero cleared his head and faced Estrada. He missed with his first pitch, ball one. But his second was in the lower part of the strike zone, and Estrada lifted it to center field.

There it was, what would become the formula: A late hit, this one from Guillen. The ninth inning from Cordero, recording yet another save. And a one-run victory.

The next day, the Nationals would beat the Braves again. They would trail 3-0, get key hits from Guillen and Nick Johnson to take a two-run lead, turn the game over to Cordero, watch him give up a solo homer to Julio Franco, then put two men on. Again, Schneider looked to his man. "He seemed fine," Schneider said. "Other people would freak out. Not Chad."

Cordero was maturing, right there at RFK, before spring turned to summer, before anyone had any idea he would make the all-star team. "Man, my heart was racing," he said. Racing? Who could tell? "I'm sure it was," Robinson said. "But he doesn't show it. He seems to have a knack for knowing when he needs to turn it up a notch."

With that, he did. He struck out Brayan Pena, a rookie catcher. He struck out Rafael Furcal, a veteran shortstop. And thus, the final: Nationals 5, Braves 4, another one-run win.

That night Robinson said "I have faith in this ballclub."

"I think," Wilkerson said, "our best baseball's ahead of us."

•   •   •

MAYBE THIS HAD HAPPENED BEFORE, back when Joe Cronin was both the shortstop and the manager and he drove in 118 runs. Maybe it felt like this when Joe Kuhel, not Nick Johnson, was the first baseman and hit .322. Maybe Earl Whitehill could become Livan Hernandez, and Alvin Crowder could turn into Esteban Loaiza.

That's what was happening on that Sunday, June 5, at RFK Stadium, with the Florida Marlins about to be swept out of Washington. This first year with baseball back in the nation's capital was turning into, of all times, 1933. That was the last year Washington's baseball team was in first place as late as June. Then, the nation's capital had a truly dominant team, for the Senators won the American League pennant by seven games over the New York Yankees behind the hitting of Cronin and the pitching of men like Whitehill and Crowder. That year, the Senators' batters hit for a higher average than any team in the league; their pitchers posted a lower ERA than anyone they faced. There was no way anyone living in Washington seventy-eight years ago could know that a drought was about to begin, the drought that would spawn the most familiar phrase associated with baseball in Washington: "First in war, first in peace, last in the American League." Never again, from that point on, would a baseball team from Washington settle into first place for the heat of a summer in the District.

Yet by the time Cordero took the mound that afternoon, the Nationals had picked up a feeling about themselves. Before games the clubhouse was a hubbub of smiles, of jokes, of card games and mingling. The veterans in the clubhouse noticed.

"I've been on teams where, not that guys didn't get along, but they didn't really interact as much," third baseman Vinny Castilla said one day, sitting in one of the cushy chairs in front of the wide-screen television, one that rotated from *SportsCenter* to Mexican soap operas to DVDs pumping out music videos. The back row of the clubhouse ran from the left corner, where Livan Hernandez tucked himself, to the right, where Jose Guillen took up residence. In between, Esteban Loaiza, John Patterson, Tony Armas Jr., Carlos Baerga, Wil Cordero, and Cristian Guzman kept their belongings, all but Patterson a Spanish-speaking Latin American. Along the right wall, extending from catcher Brian Schneider just around the corner from the main door, all the way down to Jose Vidro at the far end at the corner next to Guillen's locker, were several of the American players: backup catcher Gary Bennett, outfielder Brad Wilkerson, first baseman Nick Johnson, utility man Jamey Carroll, rookie outfielder Ryan Church, rookie reliever Gary Majewski. Then came young Dominican rookie Tony Blanco and Vidro, from Puerto Rico. Along the left wall were more pitchers, Cordero, the closer, down to Luis Ayala, the skinny Mexican who was Cordero's chief setup man, with the slots for injured relievers T. J. Tucker and Joey Eischen—the "grumpy old men," Eischen called themselves—in between. It was, like most teams, a strange mix, guys from different backgrounds with different beliefs.

"Here, the Latin guys like the American guys, and the American guys get along with the Latin guys," said Castilla, the veteran from Mexico who'd married an American woman and made his home in suburban Denver, where he spent much of his career with the Colorado Rockies. "It's not like that in every clubhouse. But there's no problems here. It's important."

There were other elements that seemed to make things click.

Bennett, for instance, had played for Philadelphia, the New York Mets, Colorado, San Diego, Milwaukee, and now the Nationals, in a low-profile career that spanned ten big-league seasons. He had been on good teams, mediocre teams, bad teams, seen good attitudes, mediocre attitudes, dreadful attitudes. One day, before a game in June, he sat in front of his locker, a crossword puzzle on his knee, and, between spits of tobacco juice deposited neatly into an empty Gatorade bottle, tried to explain what was happening in the Nationals' little clubhouse.

"You can tell by how guys react to situations," Bennett said. "I've been on teams where we might win a game, but if the big gun goes oh-for-four, then he's not happy, and it makes everything uneasy. Here, that's not the case. You see any of our guys—Guillen, Wilky, the guys we count on—if they have a bad game, and we win, that's all that matters."

Yet even for veterans such as Castilla and Bennett, there is no way to quantify chemistry, not the kind that occurs in a clubhouse. When the mix is stirred correctly, and the smiles abound and the wins ensue, you don't talk about it too much, because what if you do and then something goes wrong and it falls apart? Jim Bowden, the Nationals' general manager, had, like Castilla and Bennett, seen chemistry both good and bad, and he thought he knew how to figure it out, too. Even as his team got hot, Bowden was looking for ways to tweak it, but he was wary of disturbing the situation in the clubhouse. With Vidro out because of an injury, and Guzman, the shortstop, off to a horrendous start, hitting below .200, Bowden thought about pursuing D'Angelo Jimenez, an infielder with potential whom Cincinnati had sent to the minors. But Jimenez and Guzman were friends from the Dominican Republic, and Bowden knew, because his entire career had been with the Reds, that Jimenez's work ethic, his attitude, were substandard. Bowden was concerned that if things weren't going well for Jimenez personally, he would complain, sulk, and, in turn, suck Guzman into that abyss.

"I don't want to do anything to upset the mix we have going on," Bowden said. "I know how hard that can be to get. These guys get along. In any move we make, we have to take character into consideration. I'll overlook a guy's tools if he has the kind of character that will upset this clubhouse."

There were small concerns, too. "Chemistry's always good when you're winning," Robinson said. "But what'll test these guys is when things turn." When Tomo Ohka made his next start after Memorial Day, Robinson removed him in the fourth inning of a 3-3 game against the Marlins. As soon as Robinson appeared from the dugout, Ohka turned his back to him. Bowden, watching from his box above the stands behind home plate, saw Ohka's response. "You can't have that on a major league club that's in first place," Bowden said later. "Come on." Robinson fumed on the mound. "Pure selfishness," he called Ohka's actions. Bowden decided to fine Ohka $1,000 for "contempt." Careful of that chemistry.

"It just sets a bad precedent," Robinson said of Ohka's actions. "The chemistry should be sky-high right now on this ballclub—and it is. But one person can damage that chemistry to a point where it hurts the team."

Five days after the fine was levied, Ohka was traded to Milwaukee. Chemistry, driving the team's tweaks. A month earlier, Bowden had made another move with chemistry in mind. On May 14, a Saturday afternoon, Bowden called Philadelphia's general manager, Ed Wade. Back in November, the Phillies had been interested in Endy Chavez, the man who, in spring training, was presumed to be the Nationals' center fielder, but who was now toiling in minor league ball in New Orleans. The Phillies asked again about Chavez in December. Each time, they offered a young outfielder named Marlon Byrd. The Nationals' scouting reports on Byrd, however, were mediocre. Bob Boone, the former major league catcher who managed both Kansas City and Cincinnati, served as one of Bowden's top advisors. He had spent the previous year as a scout with the

Phillies. "I didn't think much of him," Boone admitted. So over the winter, Bowden asked for reliever Ryan Madson in return for Chavez. The Phillies declined, and the teams couldn't complete an off-season trade.

But by this point, Chavez was long an afterthought. The Nationals had called him up, watched him perform the same way he always had, and sent him back down. Bowden had called around to see if he could trade Chavez for more pitching, "but there just wasn't a market for the player," he said. So Bowden took one more shot at Wade. Would he do Chavez for Byrd now? Wade said he would. Before he completed the deal, Bowden said he would have to ask his manager, Frank Robinson.

Bowden marched down to the clubhouse at RFK Stadium, where the Nationals were to face the Chicago Cubs. He went into Robinson's office and explained the situation.

"Frank," he said, "I've got a chance to get Marlon Byrd for Endy Chavez. What do you think?"

Robinson, by this point, was long since done with Chavez, just as Bowden was, and though the two men differed in both style and substance, they agreed on more things than not. Robinson thought about it, though not for long.

"If you can get Byrd for Chavez," Robinson said, "then I'll personally get in my car and drive Chavez to Philadelphia and bring Marlon Byrd back."

So Bowden went back to call Wade. The Nationals would do it. It was three hours between the first phone call and the last, but the trade was done. Bowden went back downstairs to tell Robinson.

"Hey, Frank," he said. "Get your car keys."

Marlon Byrd, musclebound outfielder, was added to that delicate Nationals' chemistry, and Endy Chavez, by now a minor leaguer, was gone. It was a little tweak, but one Bowden thought could potentially be important. It was a time in which everything the Nationals did went right. So when Byrd got his first start, two days after he arrived, he rapped out three hits, drove in three runs, and the Nationals, naturally, won. The chemistry, it seemed, was undisturbed.

•   •   •

CHAD CORDERO, QUIETLY, was part of that chemistry, in large part because he stayed out of the way. By now, he was developing into a bit of a star, having saved fourteen ballgames in sixteen chances, having worked his way out of trouble, having allowed home runs only to strike out the next two hitters. But it hardly changed him. Each day, he and Gary Majewski would drive in from the apartment they shared in Alexandria, Virginia, just across the Potomac River from the District, a quick shot north on I-395, past the Pentagon and the Jefferson Memorial on the left, past the proposed site for the Nationals' new stadium on the right, and on into RFK Stadium. Each day, the two young relievers would stop at 7-Eleven, and Cordero would get a Slurpee, all the flavors mixed together.

"That's my favorite," he said.

"I don't know how he drinks that," Majewski responded.

Cordero's teammates would make fun of the way he walked, with his feet spread out. "Like a duck," pitcher Esteban Loaiza said. "Look at the Chief," Loaiza would yell. "Duck boy!" And Cordero would smile, laugh, and waddle away. He could take it, just as he could take being on the mound in those situations when the Nationals led by a run and the opposing team's best hitter was at the plate.

"My heart races sometimes," Cordero said. "I can feel it. But I guess it doesn't show. I don't know what it is, really. I really don't. I guess maybe I concentrate more."

Look at his face, at the smile, and then the blank stare. He didn't know how to explain it, because it was inexplicable. He was developing into the Nationals' most valuable player, perhaps the single biggest reason they were in first place, and he didn't know exactly how he'd gotten to that point.

On that Sunday, June 5, Ryan Church ripped a three-run homer in the bottom of the eighth inning, and the Nationals took a three-run lead to the ninth. Naturally, Cordero took the mound at RFK, and nearly everyone in the stands expected him to finish the job. But just as he did, along came another development. In Pittsburgh, the Pirates finished off a 5-2 victory over the Braves. If Cordero could protect his three-run lead, Washington would sit atop the National League East in the standings the newspapers across the country would print the following morning. Washington, which had been picked to come in last. Washington, which didn't have a team for thirty-four years. Washington, in first place in June, for the first time since 1933.

And there it was for Cordero, a leadoff single, followed by a strikeout, then another strikeout, then the ball to left off the bat of Juan Encarnacion. Byrd, the new addition, watched it sinking, sinking faster, and he charged. If things were going poorly, if the chemistry wasn't in place, the ball surely would have dropped in and the inning would have been extended. But all was right in Washington at that moment; the ball hung up, and Byrd raced, charged, and caught it. RFK Stadium exploded.

At that moment, Alan Alper listened to it on the radio. "Bang! Zoom!" Charlie Slowes, the play-by-play man, exclaimed, the best Washington could do for a signature call, the one that would be used throughout the summer, the one to which Slowes would add, "Put another cuuurly *W* in the books!" when the Nationals won. The ball settled into Marlon Byrd's glove, Slowes belted out his call, and the realization washed over Alper. It was enough, really, for there to be a baseball team from Washington. "That's all I ever wanted," he said. But to have it be in first place. *First place?* He is an emotional man, so his emotions poured out.

"I just bawled my eyes out," he said. He couldn't talk. "I didn't know what to think. It was beyond words. Oh, God. I was flabbergasted."

Consider, then, what would happen over the ensuing weeks, when the Nationals remained at home for three games against Oakland, three more against Seattle. They won them all, four of them by just one run, each one of those narrow victories saved by Chad Cordero. By the end of the homestand, the Washington Nationals were the best story in baseball, winners of ten straight games, walking on a tightrope but maintaining their balance because Cordero, each time, provided the steadying influence in the end. As they packed their bags to head to the West Coast for a ten-game road trip, their enthusiasm for each other and for their new home couldn't be contained.

"I've never been a part of a club at the major league level that's had as much confidence as this team," Wilkerson said one day. "It seems like nothing fazes us."

At that point, that's exactly what it seemed like.

Chapter 9

* * * * * * * * * * * * * * * * * * *

Frank Robinson: Intimidator

*I*t didn't seem, when the move was made, that there was any reason for Frank Robinson to stand on the first base line at Angel
Stadium. Not from the stands it didn't. Not from Mike Scioscia's
viewpoint from the opposing dugout, where he managed the Los
Angeles Angels. But there was Robinson, out of his dugout and on
the field, all in the name of protecting his team. It had always been
that way. As a player, he'd slide hard, swing hard, fight hard, dust
himself off, do it again. He wasn't playing anymore, hadn't for thirty
years. Yet if there was any advantage Robinson could get, well, he
was going to get it. He would want his manager to do the same, had
he still been playing. Early that morning, Robinson had had surgery
on his right eye, cleaning up the laser procedure he'd first had performed in November, sharpening his vision, his focus. He'd previ-
ously had his hip replaced. His shoulder still ached from his playing
days. He had overcome prostate cancer. By most accounts, he should
have been sitting in an easy chair in his Los Angeles home, maybe
thirty minutes away without traffic, rather than standing on that
baseline, managing a first-place team, looking to virtually everyone

in the sellout crowd of nearly 44,000 like he would be starting trouble in—*tick, tick, tick*—oh, any moment now, really.

So here it came. Angels reliever Brendan Donnelly, in from the bullpen, on to face Nationals pinch hitter Carlos Baerga in the seventh inning of a game Anaheim led, 3-1, with a runner on first base. Donnelly had been one of the most effective relievers in the American League over the previous two years. But at that time, he was struggling, having allowed a game-deciding home run to the New York Mets three nights earlier. The aging Baerga, portly and past his prime, wasn't a fearsome hitter. Donnelly's entrance was just a baseball move, a manager calling on his bullpen to protect a late lead. The moment, though, wasn't about Brendan Donnelly, Anaheim reliever. It was about Frank Robinson, Washington Nationals manager.

Robinson waited for Donnelly to be announced into the game. He then approached home plate umpire Tim Tschida and asked him to check Donnelly's glove.

Donnelly hadn't yet thrown a pitch, and Tschida hesitated. Robinson persisted. Check his glove.

This was, at best, unusual. Players and coaches have suspicions about other players from time to time, about how they make the ball do certain things, about what advantages they might be trying to gain. But before Donnelly threw a pitch? Tschida couldn't have known it then, but Robinson had some ammunition.

"I told him," Jose Guillen said, late in the season. "I knew he had it on there."

If there had been any doubt that Guillen would make a stir upon his return to Anaheim, it ended right there. Guillen's one year with the Angels ended with 104 runs batted in and a suspension that cost him an appearance in the playoffs. Here, on the trip, was a chance for a bit of revenge, and Guillen relayed the information about Donnelly. So on the advice of his occasionally out-of-his-mind right fielder, there Robinson stood.

Tschida and the three other umpires conferred on the infield as Donnelly stretched on the mound. Scioscia emerged from his own dugout, but the umpires asked Donnelly for his glove. Donnelly turned it over. After a little more than a minute, with that sellout crowd wondering what was going on, Tschida called Scioscia over. There was a substantial amount of pine tar on Donnelly's glove, Tschida told Scioscia. Pine tar, a black, sticky goop, is banned by baseball, as is any other "foreign substance," be it saliva or Vaseline, that might be applied to a baseball to help give pitches a sharper break.

The Angels' manager became visibly upset. When the meeting finally broke up nearly two minutes later, Scioscia's lips were easy to read: "This is fucking bullshit," he said. But Donnelly, who hadn't thrown a pitch, was ejected. The umpires took the glove off the field, down a ramp, under the stands. It would be sent to baseball officials, and later Donnelly would be suspended for ten games.

Scioscia, a catcher for the Los Angeles Dodgers for thirteen years, was well aware of the rules of the game. He had been involved in this same situation in the 1988 National League playoffs, when a Dodgers reliever named Jay Howell was caught with the goop on his glove. Howell was suspended for two games. Scioscia was his catcher. "It's been around for years," Scioscia said. "It's common." Now, in his role as the Angels manager, he was livid. He pivoted away from the umpiring crew toward his own dugout and signaled with his right hand for a new reliever, Scot Shields.

Disgusted, Scioscia stalked to the mound and told Donnelly to head to the dugout, but his gaze rarely left Robinson, still standing on the first base line. Before Shields even got to the mound, Scioscia, forty-six, strode directly toward Robinson, sixty-nine. Robinson, wearing wraparound shades to protect that surgically repaired eye even though it was night, awaited his arrival. What would happen? A little chat? A pat on the back for protecting the integrity of the game? Not hardly.

"I'm going to have every one of your pitchers undressed," Scioscia said, pointing directly at Robinson. The implication was clear: *If you're going to use chicken-shit tactics like that, well, then, I'll do the same fucking thing to you.*

Robinson, peering out from behind those shades and from under his blue Nationals cap, was, by his own admission, "taken aback." Robinson had watched Scioscia as a young manager in the instructional Arizona Fall League, watched him develop his craft in stadiums with only a few dozen fans. He had watched Scioscia guide the Angels to the World Series title in 2002. He had, from afar, developed a respect for a man he didn't know well. But here in Anaheim, Scioscia had stirred the inner Frank, the one that didn't come out as often as it had in those days long ago, when he held a bat and swung for the fences. Scioscia turned to head back to his own dugout, along the third base line. Had another man been managing the Nationals, the matter could have ended right then. But Frank Robinson wore that uniform, that title, so it didn't end. It was just beginning. Here we go.

Robinson took a step to follow, shouting, swearing at Scioscia. He still had moments like these, three months from his seventieth birthday. The inner Frank came roaring out. Don't you know who he is? He is Frank Robinson, Hall of Famer, manager of the first-place Washington Nationals!

"Let me tell you this," Robinson said, explaining the incident the next day. "If people let me intimidate them, then I'll intimidate them. But I wasn't going to let him intimidate me. *I am the intimidator.*"

Barbara Robinson, Frank's wife, sat in the stands that night, as did his daughter, Nichelle. As Barbara's husband of forty-four years began to jaw with Scioscia, the benches emptied, men pouring onto the field to tussle with each other. Barbara, who was sixty-four herself but looked much younger, sat in her seat, trying to take it all in. The team was in first place. Frank was not only still managing but screaming. At another manager. In the middle of the game.

"I was just trying to comprehend it all," Barbara said.

It must have been surprising.

"You know, it's true, it should be," she said. "But he's not your typical person."

. . .

A TYPICAL PERSON isn't born in Beaumont, Texas, to a funeral director who splits with his wife, leaving her to move her family of ten to Oakland, California. A typical person doesn't peer into a casket at a young age to see a corpse, his father's macabre work sending a shiver down his spine, then run scared. A typical person doesn't grow up as an exceptional athlete, sneaking into old Oaks Ball Park to see the Pacific Coast League's Oakland Oaks, walking around lower Myrtle Street with peers such as Curt Flood and Vada Pinson, future major leaguers a few years younger, and Bill Russell, the future Boston Celtics Hall of Famer, the man who reshaped professional basketball, as a hoops teammate at McClymonds High.

Anyone who knew, even remotely, the Frank Robinson who walked onto the field at Angel Stadium knew that defining characteristic. He wasn't typical. He was reserved but combative, aggressive yet stoic, mean but compassionate, old but energetic. Maybe more than anything, he was hardened, hardened by his life, hardened by baseball. He was certainly hardened by his forays in the minors, into southern cities where the word *nigger* flew often, where his teammates had to bring him a sandwich on the bus after they were done eating in the restaurant, where he had one thought: *I need to get to the big leagues, because I need to get the hell out of here.* He became a man who, as a player, was regarded as one of the most ornery and angry cusses in baseball, never smiling, never associating with the opponent, never giving in. Knock him down with an inside pitch, and he'd get up, dig his foot into the dirt, and move *closer* to the plate. He was that way at twenty, when he broke into the majors with Cincinnati. And in some ways, as he stood on that field at Angel Stadium, he was that way at sixty-nine. His gait had slowed. He sometimes was stooped over. But somehow, a power remained in his presence, in his hands, with long, strong fingers that looked able to snap a bat in two, still. A force remained in his forearms and wrists, still thick and sturdy as two-by-fours. And in his eyes, in his glare, there remained that, that . . . that what?

"I wasn't *angry* when I played," Robinson said one day later in the season, holed up in his office at RFK Stadium, golf clubs stuck in the corner. Not angry. What's a better word? "Determined," he said. "I played with a determination."

"Frank wouldn't take no shit," said his old friend from Cincinnati, Sonny Webb. "Not on the field. Not off the field." Ask him about being hit by pitches, something that happened 198 times in his career. Angry? At the pitcher? Enough to charge the mound? "No," he said. He would vent in other ways. He would slide like a truck into second base, legs up, ready to take it out on whichever middle infielder was unfortunate enough to be in his way. But to this day, he argues it wasn't out of anger.

"I looked at it like this: If I got on base, my job was to score a run. That's the number one priority. Now, second: If there's a ground ball in that infield, my job was to break up the double play to give my team another out, an extra out. That's the way I approached those things, without hurting someone intentionally. Now, if you happen to get spiked, or I spike you, that's part of the game. I didn't go in there saying, 'I'm going to cut this guy up,' or anything like that. But if you got in the way, that was part of the game. My job was to do my job, and your job was to do your job. If you can't get out of the way, you have to take your punishment."

For Frank Robinson, that is not anger. It is baseball. There is no smiling in baseball. But does that mean he was angry or unfriendly when he played, that he is that way now? With most people, even shy ones, there is the backdrop that with familiarity comes understanding. *Take the time to get to know me,* someone like Robinson might say, and in his case, it would seem to work, because time spent with him reveals pride, determination, hardheadedness, caring, fire, nonchalance, ego, almost everything in between. But don't tell him, even after months or years, that you *know* him.

"No one knows me," he said. "Hell, my wife doesn't really know me. I've got a circle around me, and I decide how close to let you." Over the years, yeah, sure, the circle had gotten smaller, and he has allowed more people to get a bit closer. He admits that much. "But I laugh when I hear someone say, 'Well, I know Frank.' Hell, no, you don't."

No wonder he still bristled at some of the assessments made back in his playing days, made by opponents to whom he never spoke, by teammates with whom he rarely hung out. "I had a chip on my shoulder?" he asked, and he pulled his head back, wrinkled his face from his cheeks to his chin to his brow, and squinted his eyes together, a look of mock surprise and disgust. "Why would I play with a chip on my shoulder? This is the game that allowed me to earn a living. They didn't keep me out, like Jackie Robinson and the guys before him. Why would *I* have a chip on *my* shoulder?"

Maybe because he went through some of those same things, endured some of the same prejudices, that any African-American player in the 1950s endured. Oakland was a black city, and in those days when he played on championship-caliber teams at McClymonds High, he didn't encounter outright racism. But put him in minor league towns like Ogden, Utah, where he spent his first year in pro ball, or Columbia, South Carolina, where he toiled the next two summers, and he grew up to the realities of the rest of the country, to the rest of the times, fast. If some people took him for angry in those ensuing years, if he took himself for determined, they overlooked one of his primary characteristics. He was shy. A momma's boy, really. In Ogden, he had one minority teammate, a Cuban, and the two were thrown together throughout that summer of 1953 because they couldn't eat with their teammates. *"Jamon y juevos"* was all the teammate could say, and Frank Robinson would eat his ham and eggs in silence. He wasn't angry. He was homesick.

The next summer he went to Columbia and made those treks to Macon, to Montgomery, arriving by bus early in the morning, trying to catch a cab from the team hotel, where he wasn't allowed, so that he might find a YMCA where he could sleep for the night. He didn't know what the major leagues would be like, hadn't spent time in Cincinnati, but it had to be better than this, didn't it? Yet his chances of getting to the majors grew dimmer in 1954, when he came up with a lame shoulder. They took him out of the outfield, stuck him at first base, but at times he couldn't even throw the ball around the infield for warm-ups. In those days, diagnoses were sketchy at best, and he went to a dozen doctors only to get a dozen different opinions. One said he should "throw it out," just play catch day after day and it would, as if by magic, go away—a common remedy of the time. Another said he needed surgery, and in those days, cutting open your body wasn't done with tiny scopes stuck through minute incisions. Surgery was a career-ending prospect, and Frank Robinson wanted none of it. Finally, one doctor told him there wasn't anything wrong, that the problem was in his head. "Bullshit," he responded succinctly, and went back to trying to throw it out.

That damn arm. He'd have been in the majors at age nineteen if it had been healthy. He just knew it. In 1955, he and a third baseman named Marv Williams were the only black players on the Columbia team. Robinson tried, as well as he could, to dismiss the comments he heard from the stands, to endure the trips to segregated hotels, to commit himself to getting to the majors, bum shoulder or not. One night, though, it all could have ended. After he made the last out of the game in Columbia, as he ran past the first base bag and down the line into right field, the invective from the stands got personal. They called him a nigger. They told him what they'd do to him. He doesn't care to go into detail, even a half century later. But he was enraged. He nearly went after the guy, nearly jumped into the crowd, but his teammates caught him. He would have popped someone. "Imagine that," he said. "I would've been jailed in Columbia, South Carolina, a black man in 1955. What do you think my chances would've been?"

The whole thing scared him, scarred him. The next day, the team was supposed to leave for Charlotte, North Carolina, for a road trip. "I'm not going," Robinson said. Forget it. That was enough.

He and Williams, his black teammate, stewed about it all that night, mulled over their career paths. Eventually, they decided they'd drive up to Charlotte themselves and rejoin the team. Their chances of getting out of Columbia were better if they stayed with the Columbia team than if they abandoned it. So Robinson dusted himself off, dug in, and moved closer to the plate. It would be Robinson's last year in the minors. The next season, at twenty, he was the National League's Rookie of the Year for the Reds, clubbing thirty-eight home runs. But all through his career, his image was shaped by those experiences, figuring out how to take what he was dealt, and adjust. In the coming years, it might be figuring out a pitcher, dealing with a manager, playing through an injury. Years later, it might be managing the hopeless Baltimore Orioles, who started the 1988 season by losing their first twenty-one games. Or, maybe, being fired by the Orioles just thirty-seven games into the 1991 season and then having to adjust to the fact that, in all likelihood, he'd never work on a baseball field again.

But can a stubborn man make adjustments so readily? When Robinson first came up, Cincinnati was something of an integrated town, as best it could be, but it certainly wasn't without its tensions. Robinson, though, became part of the community, living there year-round. After he met his future wife, Barbara, in the parking lot of the Los Angeles Coliseum one night—the same night he told her he would marry her—he brought her to Cincinnati, and they adopted their son, Kevin, there. Frank made local friends, none closer than Sonny Webb, a blue-collar man who worked at General Electric, a guy with whom Robinson would bowl for hours and hours into the night, then go to an all-night diner for a burger and some fries, or drive across the river to Covington or Newport, Kentucky, to take in a singing act, James Brown or Sam Cooke at the Copa Club or one of the other joints over there.

On one of those nights, after they had finished playing in the six-foot-and-under basketball league at a local church, they headed to one of their favorite diners, one Webb remembered was called the Big 60. Robinson, Webb, and another friend sat, laughing a bit, when three white men came in and sat down at a table nearby. They began staring at the three black men. Rednecks? "More like racist motherfuckers," Webb said, thinking back on that night, back to February 1961. "Just didn't like black." There was an exchange, something of a what-are-you-lookin'-at back-and-forth. Swiftly, a call went to the police, who had a car in the area. The white officers came in. "All right, you boys, what's going on, boys?"

Robinson's back got up. "Boys?" he said. "Who are you calling boys? We're men." Knock him down, and watch him dust himself off again. Here came Robinson.

"You didn't mess with Frank," Webb said. "I mean, I knew him as a fun-loving guy. But he wasn't going to take no shit. None."

The cops ended up arresting Webb; they threw him in the cruiser and charged him with disorderly conduct. Robinson went downtown, paid the fifty bucks to bail his friend out of jail, and they went back out, back out to another of their favorite hangouts, Babe's, to review the events of the evening. But they got to thinking: *Hey, we never got our burgers.* Frank had paid for them, and, well, they were still hungry, so they headed back to the Big 60 and asked for their burgers, only to be told they'd been thrown out.

Disappointed, Robinson and Webb were ready to walk out of there, as they tell it. But in the back, a cook recognized them as the guys from earlier in the night. The cook took a knife, looked at Frank Robinson, and made a slashing motion across his throat. Robinson, stone-faced, pulled up his sweater. There, tucked in his watch pocket, was the .22-caliber Beretta Frank carried in those days. It didn't matter that he had never fired it, that he never intended to fire it, that it was really meant to provide him protection when he walked to his parking spot at his house, which was in a dark area. Just as, years later, he wasn't going to let Scioscia intimidate him, because he is the intimidator, he wasn't going to let some cook threaten him without a response. But it just started more trouble. The cook went outside, found the cops. "He's got a gun. He's got a gun!" And the cops were inside, on Robinson, patting him down. "You got a gun?"

You think Frank Robinson was a no-nonsense, hardened guy before that? How about afterward? He was arrested, thrown in jail, allowed to stew there by Bill DeWitt Sr., the Reds general manager. In those days, such an incident could be swept away by club officials, because athletes were protected, and a phone call or two from DeWitt would have kept it out of the papers. DeWitt never made them.

Robinson never forgave him. It was, really, his first slight in Cincinnati. But he wasn't programmed to forgive and forget. "You step on my toe, it hurts for a while," Robinson said, "and I'm not going to forgive you for stepping on my toe until, maybe, it stops hurting. Then I might think about it."

Talk to Robinson about some of those years in Cincinnati, and you might think his toe still throbbed with pain. The following year, 1961, was his best yet, when he hit .323, when he slugged thirty-seven homers, when he drove in 124 runs, when he won his first MVP award. Yet in his mind, the whispers about him in the Reds organization never stopped. In 1959, Vada Pinson, the kid Robinson knew from the streets of Oakland, from the fields at McClymonds High, became one of the Reds' starting outfielders. The two men roomed together, hung out together. They were of the same background, the same experience. Pinson, though, was three years younger, and Robinson could hear the buzz: *That old Robinson, he's a bad influence on Pinson.* In his autobiography, *Extra Innings*, Robinson said he thought he and Pinson were regarded as a "Negro clique." One of them had to go, and by God if it wasn't Robinson. On

December 9, 1965, a man burst into the bowling alley in Cincinnati where Robinson and Sonny Webb were rolling a few strings, and the news came out: Robinson had been traded. The Baltimore Orioles would send the Reds three players—right-handers Milt Pappas and Jack Baldschun and a reserve outfielder named Dick Simpson—for Robinson.

His initial response was shock, then an attempt at a joke, saying he couldn't possibly wear that damn Orioles hat with the stupid cartoon bird on it. The word, though, came from DeWitt. Robinson was thirty years old, and yeah, sure, he had clubbed thirty-three homers and driven in 113 more runs the year before. But he was an *old* thirty.

Ask Frank Robinson, forty years later, about that one phrase: "old thirty." Might as well slap him across the face. Hell, he's not an old seventy. So the real response didn't come in the days after the trade. No, it came the next year, when Frank Robinson dug back in the box. It was like he was taking on more than the American League pitchers, almost all of them new to him. It was like he was taking on Bill DeWitt. Old thirty? He hit .316 to win the batting title. He hit forty-nine homers, more than anyone else in the league, a career high. He drove in 122 runs, also the most in the league. And there it was, Robinson's adjustment to the situation in which he found himself, his response to DeWitt—the Triple Crown. In the thirty-nine seasons since then, only one man, Boston's Carl Yastrzemski, won the Triple Crown. Oh yeah—the Orioles won the World Series, too, sweeping the Dodgers. Frank Robinson homered in the first game off Don Drysdale, and his solo shot in the fourth game, also off Drysdale, was the only run the Orioles, behind right-hander Jim Palmer, would need, a 1-0 victory that clinched the Series sweep.

Part of Robinson's adjustment upon arriving in Baltimore, he said, was trying to loosen up. He might not have *been* angry. But if he *seemed* angry, that was enough. "I'm not sunny," he said. "I'm a quiet, kind of withdrawn person. I don't mix easily with people. I don't meet new people easily. But I had to adjust. I had to learn how to deal with different situations, and going to Baltimore was one of those."

Taking the managing job in Montreal was another. Getting used to the fact that the players didn't want to take infield practice every day was another. Some things he would bend on. Others he wouldn't.

And at Angel Stadium, with his team in first place, goddammit if Frank Robinson was going to bend on this one, on this night, when Mike Scioscia's pitcher had cheated, and Scioscia was confronting *him?* The inner Frank was bound to surface.

•　　•　　•

FOR THE MOST PART, what ensued that night was a typical baseball fight, one in which bluster reigns over actual blows, one in which shouting and jawing far outweigh actual brawling. The bullpens emptied, and two groups of pitchers sprinted in from left field, side by side, displaying more of an idle show of support than a true intent to pound each other. There was both pushing and shoving. Yet in the middle of the fracas, there was a body flailing wildly. Look more closely, and it wore a gray uniform, one with "Washington" scrawled across the front. And there he was, suddenly being hauled off the field into the dugout by two teammates, indistinguishable because of the storm they were trying to contain.

Oh, no. It's not him, is it? Yep, sure is. Jose Guillen.

Not a week earlier, Guillen had sat at his locker in RFK Stadium and discussed, calmly, his relationship with Mike Scioscia, with the Angels. Though his mantra for much of the early part of the season—when writers would arrive at his locker, looking to pin a story about baseball's return to Washington on the revival of the club's temperamental slugger—was simply, "The past is the past," it clearly wasn't the case, even in those days leading to the trip to Anaheim.

Anaheim was where he'd played with perhaps baseball's best player, Vladimir Guerrero, and complemented him nicely. Anaheim was where he'd driven in a career-high 104 runs. Bob Boone, the former Angels catcher who had managed Guillen in Cincinnati, had recommended the player to his new club, which signed him to a three-year deal prior to the 2004 season. "And I was proud of it," Boone said, "because he had a great season." Yet it was as an Angel when, early in the season, Guillen had become incensed after being hit by a pitch in Toronto, where he publicly challenged his pitching staff to fire back. Anaheim was also where, ultimately, he was determined to be expendable, despite his compact batting stroke, his innate talent, responsible for twenty-seven home runs.

By the time he was dragged off the Angel Stadium field on this night, his travails with the Angels were old news to the writers and fans of both teams. Without that past, the past that was clearly raging into the present, the scuffle might have been just that, a conflict between two teams over one incident. Not so. As much as Guillen said he wanted to move on from his time with the Angels, as much as the Angels clearly wanted to forget about Guillen, this was personal. "I'm not over it," Guillen would say. "I never will be."

On September 25, 2004, with the Angels battling the Oakland Athletics for the American League West championship, Scioscia removed Guillen for a pinch runner in a tie game against the A's. It was as if Guillen were a teenager again, playing in Erie or Lynchburg or some other decidedly minor league town with a decidedly minor league attitude. He threw his hands in the air. He walked slowly toward the dugout. He flipped his batting helmet in the direction of his manager. He slammed his glove against the dugout wall.

None of the actions, by itself, was particularly abhorrent. He didn't fire the helmet hard, in a fit of rage. He didn't throw it *at* Scioscia. Nationals General Manager Jim Bowden, out of baseball at the time, was at the game, watching from the stands.

"I'm telling you," Bowden said. "It wasn't that bad."

But given all Guillen was and had been, given those days in the minor leagues when he seemed to want the rules for him to be different from the rules for others, the message was clear. At a crucial time, in a crucial game, Guillen's inability to spare his own fury over being replaced took precedence over the game itself. The Angels won that day. Afterward, Scioscia, by several accounts, confronted Guillen at his locker after the game. The two screamed at each other, and Guillen, physically threatening now, had to be restrained. In effect, that was it for Guillen with the Angels. He was suspended not for a game, not for two, not just for the rest of the season, but for the playoffs as well. The risk, if there was one, turned out to be well worth it, for the Angels actually got hot without him, won the division title without him, moved on without him. They were eventually swept by the Boston Red Sox in the first round of the playoffs, which Guillen watched on television. "It hurt," he said later. "It was hard. I could have helped them."

They didn't want his help. As it had been in Pittsburgh, in Tampa Bay, in Cincinnati, and in Oakland, it was over. Forget his production. On November 19, Guillen was traded to Washington for an outfielder named Juan Rivera and a backup shortstop named Maicer Izturis.

And to that point, on that night in June, he fit the Nationals' profile. New ballclub, new city, new start—new star? Yet as well as Guillen had played over the season's first two months, his status in Washington wouldn't be confirmed until he got through Anaheim, until he dealt with the questions one final time. Pressed on the subject—why had he gotten so mad?—Guillen claimed it was a matter of Scioscia's style. Confront him in public, and he took it to be a personal attack. Confront him in private, and it's a business issue.

"If you're a manager and you call me into the office, and we talk in the office with a closed door, it's a different story," Guillen said prior to making the trip to Anaheim. "That's why I don't like it when people say I went after Mike. Mike called me and approached me in front of all my teammates right at my locker. He said I was not saying things I'm supposed to be saying. We were screaming face-to-face. As the manager, I believe, you come to me, you ask me to talk in the office, we talk."

Which was the approach Robinson, his new manager, took with Guillen. He couldn't have been sure that was the correct path with this particular player. It was a guess, really. During their first four months together, from spring training through the early part of the season, the old-school manager and his combustible right fielder had come to something of an understanding. Robinson was aware that things might not always be as they seemed where Guillen was concerned. "I read," Robinson said. "I know he's had some problems. But it's not my job to bring them up." When Guillen arrived at spring training, Robinson didn't usher him into his office, sit him down in the first day, and say, "Okay, what the hell happened in Anaheim that you're here now?"

"Why would I do that?" Robinson said. "He's got a clean slate."

Guillen, in turn, appreciated that tactic, though it was more accidental than designed, more Robinson's approach from another era: Let players be players until they cause a problem, *then* address it. Robinson was familiar with labels. Remember how they called him difficult, angry, in Cincinnati? Guillen hadn't caused a problem yet, and was, in fact, leading the team with ten home runs as the Nationals got ready for the road swing through Anaheim and two other cities. There was, at the time, no compelling reason to go through the past.

Guillen, too, subtly let Robinson know how he wanted to be treated. In spring training, Robinson would sit in his golf cart and watch drills on one of the fields in Viera, away from the action, alone. And then, suddenly, almost mysteriously, Guillen would appear at his shoulder. The two men, staring straight ahead through dark wraparound sunglasses, would learn a bit about each other. Guillen would do most of the talking, an odd dynamic given the two men's respective places in the game, one an aging Hall of Famer, one of the best hitters the sport has ever known, the other a journeyman who had never fully realized his potential, joining his seventh major league team in seven years. Each tried to feel the other out, Guillen by talking, Robinson by listening.

But for all his flare-ups in the past, this was a different spot for Guillen, a situation in which he knew, because of the team's makeup, he would be in right field every single day. If he wasn't hitting third, he would hit fourth. If he wasn't hitting fourth, he would hit third. And even when he was struggling—"I'm swinging like a fucking little girl! I should be hitting ninth, behind the pitcher!" he ranted one day during a slump—he would be in the lineup anyway. It was what he had always wanted. It wasn't like in Tampa Bay, where he said he was told he would play every day but was shipped to the minors. It wasn't like in Cincinnati, where the outfield was stocked with talent, and he had to wait for at-bats. Robinson knew that the Nationals didn't have a bat around which the order would turn, someone who the opposition would look to with fear, a singularly dynamic hitter the way it was when the great Guerrero gripped his bat with his bare hands for the Montreal Expos, swinging at pitches at his shoe tops or over his eyes, and hitting them out of the park. Guerrero, though, was gone, perhaps the best Expo ever, never to become a National. So with no one like him, Guillen was Robinson's best hope. He might as well listen to him.

"I learned a little bit about this kid," Robinson said.

He thought, at that time, that he had. He heard one word—*winning*—more than any other. Other managers from Guillen's past might roll their eyes at the thought. Robinson, true to his promise of a clean slate, didn't. Guillen backed up his talks about winning with examples, not only of how he wanted to be treated, but of how he expected his teammates to prepare. At one point in spring training, Guillen sidled up to Robinson. Clearly, something was on his mind, and he let it spill. Sure, these were exhibition games, the time when veterans, in particular, would take their two or three at-bats, shower quickly, and scoot out the door, never mindful of the result or the production of others, concerned only with preparing themselves for the season. Guillen, though, wasn't happy with the environment in his new clubhouse, and he told Robinson. Too much music, he said, too much frivolity in the moments before games—exhibition games.

"There's a time they have to start getting ready for the game," Guillen said. "The music should go off in the clubhouse. The kids, the other players' kids, should go out of the clubhouse."

Robinson thought about it.

"He was right," Robinson said. "That means, here's a guy that's very observant, very sincere, and understands what has to be done to be successful. It kind of opened my eyes a little bit toward him, because I had never heard that kind of thing about him. All I ever heard was this guy wants to play every day, but he's very selfish. You'd hear that you can't take him out of the lineup, but you never heard about this guy, how he felt about the game itself and preparing himself and going about playing the game."

•　　•　　•

AT ANGEL STADIUM that night in June, after Brendan Donnelly was ejected and Mike Scioscia confronted Frank Robinson, it was Jose Guillen who became the focal point of it all. Eddie Rodriguez, the Nationals bench coach who had become as close to Guillen as anyone on the team, tackled him from the front, though Rodriguez was a small man, not as powerful as Guillen, who stood just 5 foot 11 but was a solid 195 pounds. Jose Martinez, the batting practice pitcher who earned a job with the team because of his long-standing friendship with second baseman Jose Vidro, tackled Guillen from behind. Antonio Osuna, a relief pitcher on the disabled list, helped out as well. They all dragged Guillen into the dugout, where the storm was quelled. The inner Jose had come out and was, barely, bottled back up. "I don't know what I do if they not get me," Guillen said. "I probably punch somebody. I probably try to hurt somebody."

When the teams went back to their dugouts and Robinson and Guillen had calmed down, the next hour of activity was perhaps predictable, given Robinson's resolve, Guillen's furor, and the relationship the two had danced around before it formed solidly.

"Evidently," Barbara Robinson said the next day, "him and Jose have something going. I don't know. Maybe he sees a little bit of young Frank in Jose. They're connected."

Come on. Frank Robinson in Jose Guillen? Later in the season, Robinson was asked about whether that could be true. He didn't say anything for several seconds, and he pressed his long, strong fingers against each other, tip to tip.

"Yeah," he finally said. "It's true. I played a lot of times with injuries and stuff that I maybe should have taken some time off. I played with a lot of determination. I don't know if you want to call it fire. I guess they think he's angry, just like they thought I was angry."

So in this situation, with tempers having flared and simmered, the thoughts turned: What would young Frank have done? Why, he would have hit a home run his next time at bat, for spite as much as anything. So what did Jose do? Scot Shields, who had replaced Donnelly, overcame the hubbub and worked out of the seventh uneventfully, then hit Ryan Church with a pitch to lead off the eighth. That brought up Guillen. As the crowd booed, there was no mistaking his feelings as he stepped to the plate. Look at him—not a hint of a smile, not a glance to anyone, anything, other than the pitcher. He ripped at Shields's first pitch, a high fastball, and fouled it off. There was so much in that one cut, fury and venom and competitiveness and, yes, anger, that just settling his body down again took some doing. Shields pitched again, a sidearm slider that is particularly difficult to hit. Guillen swung again. This time, he produced one of his best swings of the season, one in which he drove through the ball with his left hand, a line drive that didn't tower on an arc. Rather, it tore through the air, maybe fifteen feet off the ground the entire way, seemingly leaving Angel Stadium not in seconds but in fractions thereof, a two-run homer. "A missile," center fielder Brad Wilkerson called it. Before it left the yard, Guillen tossed his bat in the air with one swift, violent movement, as if to say to the Angels, *Take that*. The ball bounced off the back of the Angels' bullpen with such force that it hurtled back into left field. Angel Stadium fell quiet. Guillen, rounding third, not more than a hundred feet from Scioscia, let out a guttural roar. He had tied the game.

Four batters later, second baseman Junior Spivey drove in the go-ahead run with a single to the opposite field, and the Nationals went on to a 6-3 victory. The inner Frank appeared and shouted down Scioscia. The inner Jose appeared and was funneled not into a fight but into a homer. The following day, Jim Bowden, the general manager, sat in the dugout. The sun shone on the field. Bowden's face was shaded by the overhang. He glowed anyway.

"Games like that, last night, are games that only are with teams that win pennants," he said. "Not only Frank firing the team up, but the support that Frank got from the players, immediately was shown. And if you studied the eyes of the players after that incident, this place changed. This will be a game that will be very memorable come October. You'll point back to this game because heart, character, passion showed up. And Frank fights for the players, and the players will fight for Frank, and that's one of the reasons why he's going to be the National League Manager of the Year at the end of the season."

Bowden, as much assigned Frank as Frank was assigned him, might have believed all of it at that moment, and he might not have. But it was theater, and he knew it. The game hadn't started until just after 10 P.M. on the East Coast. Very few in Washington were able to watch it from start to finish. Yet the next day, Bowden's cell phone began ringing, calls from back east. The nation's capital was abuzz with Frank and Scioscia and Guillen and the Nationals, who were, my goodness, still in first place. Bowden, staying at his home in Hollywood, bringing Joy to the stadium each night, smiled from ear to ear, all energy and sound bites and, well, pride.

The following night, the Nationals won in perhaps even more dramatic fashion, taking a 1-0 lead into the ninth, courtesy of Brian Schneider's home run off Angels starter Bartolo Colon, then watching as closer Chad Cordero allowed the Angels to load the bases with no outs in their final at-bat. A single would have won the game for the Angels. A sacrifice fly would have tied it. Cordero's response: strikeout, pop-up, strikeout, ballgame.

"Are you kidding?" Schneider said afterward.

They had taken two of three from the Angels. They were in first place. Their new city was agog. And Jose Guillen, sitting in front of his locker, slowly buttoned the buttons on his shirt. He looked at Vinny Castilla, the veteran third baseman, who dressed next to him. "Vinny. Vinny!" Guillen said. "You might not want to leave. You might want to stop me from what I might say." Guillen smiled and let loose. His mantra, "The past is the past," was gone.

"You know what? I want to beat this team so bad. I can never get over about what happened last year. It's something I'm never going to forget. Any time I play that team, Mike Scioscia's managing, it's always going to be personal to me."

He had publicly denied it before. He couldn't any longer.

"If you're a good player, and you get suspended for the reason you just want to play every day and you just want to stay in the lineup, and your manager comes and approaches you in front of everyone, what should you do? I always say that if he approach me differently, it would be a different story. I know it's over, but that is something I will never forget from him. He should've handled that differently.

"He showed no class. No respect. We have to move on. We have to move on. It's over."

But it wasn't, because with Guillen, it rarely is.

"I don't got truly no respect for him anymore, because I'm still hurt from what happened last year. I don't want to make all these comments, but Mike Scioscia to me is like a piece of garbage. I don't really care. I don't care if I get in trouble. He can go to hell. We've got to move on."

And in this way, the Nationals moved on from Anaheim, their sixty-nine-year-old manager still setting the tone, their combustible slugger still responding to his lead. It seemed like a combination, a connection, that might work for an entire summer.

Chapter 10

★ ★ ★ ★ ★ ★ ★ ★ ★ ★ ★ ★ ★ ★ ★ ★ ★ ★ ★

"America's Team" Hits a Bump

*T*he District of Columbia slows to a crawl in the summer, when the heat settles in over the Potomac River basin and, with nowhere else to go and nothing better to do, just hangs out, heavy air that seems immovable for months. Get in the shower, walk outside, wait five seconds, and it's time for another shower. The average high, in July, is nearly ninety degrees, the average low not much below seventy. Once the Fourth of July comes and goes, and the fireworks go off over the Lincoln Memorial and the Washington Monument, and hundreds of thousands pack the National Mall and the Ellipse, where those first baseball games in the nation's capital were played nearly a century and a half ago, the city empties out. The federal government, the engine that makes the town hum, all but shuts down. The light atop the U.S. Capitol, the one that shines only when Congress is in session and at work, stays dark. All that remains are the tourists riding the Metro, waiting in lines, sweating through their T-shirts—all seemingly marked with "FBI" or "ATF" or some such ode to a government agency—enduring the oppressive and unsettling heat.

The Washington Nationals' clubhouse at Robert F. Kennedy Stadium, on days like these, was an unbearable place to be during the summer baseball returned to the city. The air-conditioning didn't always work well—it made things meat-locker cold in some quarters, stuffy and stagnant in others. Joey Eischen, the left-handed reliever who frequently used the time before games to putt golf balls across the tan, carpeted floor, tried several tactics. *Keep the door open. Keep it closed. No, keep it open again. Let's get a fan in here. Let's point it this way, now that.* Flies that appeared to be the size of Black Hawk helicopters jetted through the area where the players' lockers lined the walls before they headed back to the players' lounge and the coaches' locker room, almost on a continuous loop. The flies were so comfortable it was as if they had been there since the glory days of the Redskins, more permanent residents than the Nationals themselves. In the hallway that led to the clubhouse from the dark, dusty concourse on the stadium's bottom level hung a stench that, at its worst, smelled as if a toilet had backed up. It was the Nationals' home, and there was none other like it in the major leagues.

On Washington's biggest day of the summer, the Fourth of July, the Nationals lost to the New York Mets, an afternoon affair that preceded America's most mammoth celebration, down East Capitol Street from RFK Stadium, down Capitol Hill to the Mall, where all those tourists from every part of the country packed in to see the guy who used to play the mayor on *Spin City,* that Michael J. Fox sitcom, introduce performers such as Gloria Estefan and the Beach Boys. The loss that day was no big deal for the Nationals, because it basically resulted from Frank Robinson's desire to give his key relievers a day of rest following a twelve-inning game the day before in Chicago. So Robinson left right-hander Sun Woo Kim in for the ninth inning of a tie game, Kim gave up three runs, and that was it: baseball on Independence Day in the nation's capital, but a loss for the local nine. The sellout crowd of 44,331, even larger than Opening Night, shrugged it off. The Nationals, after all, had won their previous six, including a sweep of the Cubs in Chicago, and first place in the National League East remained secure, at least until the all-star break, which was now only five games away. The heat, not quite ninety that day, was in the stadium, in the city. It wasn't on the Nationals.

The night after Americans celebrated their country's birthday and came to the District to do it, Jose Guillen strode to the plate at RFK Stadium in the bottom of the first inning of a scoreless game against the Mets. It was a lazy, hot Tuesday night in the summer. On the mound for the Mets stood Pedro Martinez, once the best pitcher in baseball, now a master craftsman with a new team, closer to the end of his career than the beginning. So much had gone so well for the Nationals to that point, and the matchup against Martinez was one to anticipate. Esteban Loaiza, no Martinez to be sure, had nevertheless pitched well for Washington, winning four of his previous five starts. And even with the town empty for the holiday week, the Nationals sold 35,087 tickets to people willing to sit and sweat at RFK.

Martinez retired the first two hitters of the inning, Brad Wilkerson on a strikeout, Jose Vidro on a fly ball. For Wilkerson, striking out was nothing new, for he was doing so at an alarming rate for a leadoff hitter, among the league leaders all year. Vidro, though, found pleasure even in a fly ball. This was Vidro's first at-bat in two months. He was finally returning from his ankle injury, and he could hardly wait to be back. He faced Martinez, who'd been the ace of the Montreal Expos' staff in 1997, when Vidro was just a rookie. And as he did so, he was nearly overcome by emotions.

"It's so hard to sit out, man," he said. "But these guys, they do such a great job without me. I'm just so happy to come back at a time when we're in first place, when we're playing so well." Now they just had to continue on that same path.

With Vidro retired, Martinez turned to Guillen, who to that point was having a career year, on pace for a monster season. But

Martinez knew Guillen, knew him from back in the Dominican Republic, their home country, and knew him from facing him over the years. Martinez had a reputation as being someone unafraid to hit a batter with a pitch. He had even been called a headhunter at different points in his career, both with the Expos and, later, with the Boston Red Sox. Four times, when he had faced Guillen in the past, Martinez had hit him with pitches. Rattle Guillen, and that might rattle the Nationals. Guillen's batting stance is such that he leans out nearly over the plate, his left arm and elbow exposed as he lunges into the pitch before he tries to turn and drive it. Over the first three months of the season, Guillen had already been hit nine times.

So here came pitch one, and Guillen fouled it off. Guillen dug back in. And then—*plunk*. Martinez's next pitch landed with a thud in Guillen's back. But it wasn't that fastball whistling toward the plate, more than ninety miles per hour. It was an off-speed pitch. The Nationals had a man on first. Considering how valuable runners are against the likes of Martinez, who doesn't allow many, there was reason to be happy.

Guillen, though, stood at the plate, staring daggers at whatever crossed his gaze. He tossed down his bat, not violently enough to make a scene, but angrily, methodically, purposefully. Slowly, he ripped the Velcro that held on his shin guard, freeing it from his left leg, and he tossed that to the ground, too, right in the batter's box. Gradually, he began a painstakingly slow walk to first base, anger in his eyes, on his face, taking over his head. Here it was, Guillen's rage, about to surface.

The Nationals couldn't know it right then, but their best moments were behind, not ahead. They wouldn't be in first place for long.

•　　•　　•

SUCH THOUGHTS HADN'T seemed possible forty-eight hours earlier. When the Nationals returned from Chicago on the night of Sunday, July 3, things could scarcely have been better. That afternoon marked the halfway point of the season. Eighty-one games down, eighty-one more to go. The weekend at Wrigley Field could have been drawn up by the Chicago Chamber of Commerce, wispy clouds moving across a brilliant blue sky, three day games with temperatures in the mid-seventies, after which the bars of Wrigleyville teemed with revelers just happy to be a part of the scene, even if some team named the Washington Nationals—*Who are these guys?*—was disposing of the Cubs, game after game after game.

That Sunday morning, as Ryan Drese sat on a folding chair in front of a table in the visitors' clubhouse at Wrigley Field, a space in which fitting an entire baseball team is something akin to cramming clowns in a Volkswagen, Frank Robinson walked by. Drese, that day's starting pitcher, was eating breakfast, and Robinson was blunt. "Don't look at the lineup," he said. Drese had been with the Nationals less than a month, a right-hander who'd been released by the Texas Rangers, then claimed by Washington. The Nationals' general manager, Jim Bowden, had traded right-hander Tomo Ohka to Milwaukee in June, and Bowden's hope was that Drese, picked up the day of the trade, could fill that spot. The early results were mixed, with two superb performances and one disaster.

Drese looked up from his cereal, staring blankly at Robinson. He didn't know this man, the Hall of Famer who shuffled through the clubhouse in gray baseball pants, blue socks, and flip-flops. "Don't look at the lineup," Robinson repeated. Drese finally asked why. "I don't want you to get sick," Robinson said.

Nick Johnson, the first baseman who had never made it through a season without getting hurt, had been out a week with a bruised heel, and later in the day the team would place him on the disabled list. Vidro was nearly ready to return, but remained on a rehabilitation assignment in the minor leagues. He wasn't with the club in Chicago, and there was no telling how long he'd be able to last or how well he'd be able to move on his bad ankle, not to mention on his right knee, surgically repaired ten months before, even when he *did* come back. Left fielder Ryan Church, a rookie, had slammed into the outfield wall in Pittsburgh in late June while making a catch that ended a game and secured a win, but he hadn't played since and was on the disabled list, too, the pain in his shoulder and chest and ribs still acute. And shortstop Cristian Guzman, he of the .201 average, was out with a strained hamstring, hardly a blow to the Nationals' offense, but thinning the defensive alignment and the depth nonetheless. It was a wonder, with all the injuries, that this team was anywhere near the top of the division, let alone in first place.

So the lineup Robinson worried might make his pitcher sick included a cleanup hitter, Vinny Castilla, who'd struggled to hit .202 in June and was battling a painful problem in his left knee, one that he said prevented him from driving the ball. It included a first baseman, Carlos Baerga, who had no business playing in the field, who had earned the nickname "Fred Flintstone" during his days in Arizona, because when he started to run, his legs moved up and down like pistons before they finally propelled him forward, just like Fred starting up his car with his bare feet back in Bedrock. It included a pair of outfielders, Brad Wilkerson and Jose Guillen, who trotted onto the field with a different aching body part for each day of the week, neither able to hit as he preferred. It included backups Jamey Carroll and Junior Spivey and Marlon Byrd. Come to think of it, Robinson looked at the lineup and nearly got sick, too.

Yet on the field before the game, Bowden basked in the Wrigley sunshine, in the glory of being the general manager of the team that was, at that moment, the best story in the sport. RFK Stadium regularly rocked, filled nightly with more than 30,000 fans willing to ignore the fact that there was no owner, that precious few games were available on television. Yet they roared, and their presence along with a competitive team would have been enough for Bowden. Baseball was back in Washington, and *the team was in first place.* Bowden understood the magnitude of the story. It was apparent in his mischievous grin, in the glint in his eyes. Sometimes Bowden didn't know what he might say, rambling from point to point, from east to west, from planet to planet. But when he got hold of something he thought the media or the public might grasp on to, he'd use it. He'd use it again and again. And with the Nationals only a few hours from completing the eighty-first game of their first season in Washington, with their Fourth of July game in the District just a day away, Bowden spewed forth his assessment.

"We're witnessing the birth of America's team," Bowden said. He rattled off the places the Nationals hailed from, Mexico and Cuba and Puerto Rico and Korea and the Dominican Republic. He spouted the phrase "melting pot." He said it "with all due respect to Jerry Jones," the owner of the Dallas Cowboys, the franchise that actually *is* America's team. He talked about how hard the players worked and how well they got along. "We are," Bowden said, "what America's all about." And when his roll ended, when he had said all he had to say, he punctuated it the way he punctuated the performances he thought were his best, by singsonging the end of the theme to *SportsCenter*.

"Dah-dah-dah. Dah-dah-dah."

And Jim Bowden smiled even more broadly. The show was over, for now. Later, with the Cubs and Nationals playing a taut affair under the sun at Wrigley, he sat in the back row of the section of seats directly behind home plate. To his right sat Joy Browning, his fiancée, who draped her arm across her man's back while he fidgeted with his BlackBerry, keeping in touch with general managers across the country on trades and waiver moves and rumors and innuendo, his thumb rolling across the little device, which all but pounded with the pulse of baseball. Bowden turned to Joy, and they shared a laugh. It was a good day to be the general manager of the Washington Nationals.

America's team won another game that day, the kind of win that comes only to teams who are touched by something out of their hands, something beyond their comprehension. "Magical," Frank

Robinson would call it later in the season, when the moment had long since passed. They led the Chicago Cubs 2-0 headed into the bottom of the ninth. They handed the ball to Chad Cordero, their twenty-three-year-old closer who had converted the last twenty-six save opportunities with which he was presented, a streak that dated back to April, a kid who, later in the day, would be named to the National League All-Star team. Cordero, as was so predictable by now, got the first two outs. "When we give him the ball," Robinson said, "and we have a lead, that means we have a win."

Except not on this day at Wrigley. Cubs right fielder Jeromy Burnitz managed to fist an 0-2 pitch over the infield for a single, bringing up third baseman Aramis Ramirez. And, finally, what everyone in the Nationals dugout knew had to happen eventually, happened. Cordero threw a fastball for a strike. He missed with two sliders. And then he did it again, going back to the fastball. Ramirez hit it well to left, over the head of Marlon Byrd, over the brick wall, over the ivy, the two-run homer that tied the game, that gave the beleaguered denizens of Wrigleyville something to cheer about as the temperature cooled and the wind picked up a bit.

Cordero, who betrays little emotion on the mound but for the thump of his fist on his chest when he saves a game, headed back to the dugout after the inning, and Robinson was leading the cheers. "Here we go, guys," he said. "Chief's picked us up all year. Let's pick him up." Cordero could hardly hear the encouragement, the spirit, he was so mad. He headed down the tunnel toward the clubhouse and hurled his glove against a wall. "I just thought I blew it," he said later.

The game went to extra innings, and the Nationals scored two in the eleventh on a double by Wilkerson. The Cubs, though, scored two more in the bottom of the inning, and it was tied again. Finally, in the twelfth, at the end of a long weekend, Nationals catcher Brian Schneider, who'd caught the previous eleven innings, came up with two outs to face a left-hander named Sergio Mitre, from whom Schneider had never seen a pitch. All he wanted, after so much baseball, was to find something he could put a halfway decent swing on. Mitre missed with ball one. He threw a fastball on the second pitch, and Schneider hit it to right. It, too, passed over the brick wall, over the ivy, and into the seats, a homer.

It was the winning run, providing the 5-4 victory that both ended the first half of the season and defined it. A solid pitching performance, this one from Drese. A couple of key base hits. Flawless defense. The ability to overcome circumstances that should, by all rights, prevent them from winning. And, in the end, a one-run victory.

"I think it gives you an indication of what they're all about," Robinson said afterward, leaning back in a chair in the manager's office, considering that day's events and the events of the first half. Robinson had already held a team meeting afterward, one in which he congratulated both Cordero and right-hander Livan Hernandez on being named to the All-Star team. Teammates strolled by the two pitchers' lockers, offering congratulations, and they were heartfelt. Bowden went to Nick Johnson, who had just been placed on the disabled list, who was hitting .320 but whose heel still hurt. "Nick," he said, "you're an All-Star in our minds." He went to the locker of Jose Guillen, who was hitting .310 with seventeen homers. "It's crazy you're not an All-Star," Bowden said.

They had played eighty-one games and won fifty of them. Do the quick math. Halfway through the season, they were on pace to win a hundred games. Never had the Montreal Expos won that many. Never had the Washington Senators, in either incarnation, won that many. Even the 1924 Senators, who'd won the District's only World Series championship, won only ninety-two regular-season games.

But here they were, the Washington Nationals, the best story in baseball. When they got back to the District, Robinson had a conversation with Thomas Boswell, the eloquent columnist for the *Washington Post*, on the steps of the home dugout at RFK Stadium. Boswell brought with him on every trip to the ballpark not only more than thirty years of experience covering baseball, but a lifetime spent growing up on Capitol Hill, living and working in Washington, watching Senators games at RFK Stadium, watching the team depart, watching his city sit idle, waiting for another team. Each day, Boswell pulled out a new statistic or theory about why something had happened or would happen, always well thought out, sometimes accompanied by a notebook full of color-coded numbers, research done by hand. His enthusiasm for the sport, and for having baseball back in his hometown, was infectious. Boswell told Robinson that day, "All you have to do is play .500 ball the rest of the way—"

Robinson cut Boswell off. "We're not thinking about .500," he said. "We're thinking better than that."

•   •   •

WHEN JOSE GUILLEN ARRIVED at first base after Pedro Martinez hit him with a pitch, the Nationals had their first base runner of the evening. But Guillen didn't score, and he took his glove to right field after the inning. The crowd couldn't know it, but he was incensed.

From there, he let loose. He yelled in to Jamey Carroll, playing shortstop. He wanted Carroll to tell Esteban Loaiza, the pitcher, to hit the first batter that came up, Mike Piazza. But Loaiza didn't comply, and Piazza grounded out. How about the next guy? Nope. Marlon Anderson walked. Maybe the next? Not a chance. David Wright and Jose Reyes flew out. Nothing. No retaliation from Loaiza.

"It was a tight game, and Pedro was pitching," Loaiza said later. "We can't put runners on base then. It's early. Maybe later. But he said he was yelling, and I didn't hear him. I don't know."

"It wasn't," Frank Robinson said, "the time for that." There were two more games left in the series. Heck, the Nationals would play the Mets later in the season. You can't rush these things.

But Guillen wouldn't have it. When he came back to the dugout from his spot in right field, he confronted Loaiza. He confronted

Brian Schneider, the catcher. "Why the fuck didn't you hit someone? Why the fuck won't you protect me?" He was seething now, and the Nationals were taken aback. They had to know that Guillen had this in him, because he had bounced from team to team to team, never settling into a city, a situation, despite his ample ability. Yet on that night, with things going so well for the Nationals, not to mention for Guillen, it was a surprise.

"He never mentioned anything to me, and then he started going after Schneider," Loaiza said. "And Schneider didn't hear him, either. Everybody was mad. I was mad." Teammates stepped in. They pulled Guillen away. People calmed down. "We still had a lot more game left," Loaiza said.

The atmosphere, throughout the remainder of a tight game, remained tense. Guillen wasn't the same the rest of the night. To Guillen, baseball had a protocol. Pitchers had to protect hitters. He didn't care about the situation. He didn't care about the impact on the game. Follow the protocol. The previous year, during his one-season stint with the Angels, he'd been struck in the ribs by Blue Jays right-hander Justin Miller in the sixth inning of a May game in Toronto. The Angels starter that day, John Lackey, was ejected the following inning for hitting one of the Blue Jays. It would have seemed to be retaliation. Yet afterward, Guillen spewed profanities in assessing the situation, bemoaning the fact that he believed he and Vladimir Guerrero, the Angels' star outfielder, were easy targets.

"I don't know how many times I've been hit, and there's no retaliation," he said at the time. "I don't know how many times Vladdy has been hit, and nobody . . . does anything. I'm giving everything I've got. I'm playing hurt, I'm playing in pain. And I'm not getting any help from nobody."

So here it was again. Same player. Same situation. Different team. Different city. Guillen remained in the game and, seemingly to anyone in the stands, responded admirably. He lined three hard singles off Martinez. The last one, in the seventh, drove in Jose Vidro with the Nationals' third run. And all the elements of yet another moving, improbable story about the return of baseball to Washington and the emotion that went into it were there, because when Vidro slid across the plate, when the crowd cheered his arrival there, he had tears in his eyes, so moved was he by his return to the field, by the response he received in Washington, by the fact that his wife, Annette, had helped him through those two months on the sidelines. "I want to dedicate this to her," he said afterward.

In the ninth, though, came more evidence of Guillen's meltdown. The Mets drove Loaiza from the game in the ninth, and in came Chad Cordero for the save. But a couple of singles followed, the last, by David Wright to Guillen in right. Cliff Floyd was the Mets runner on third base, and he was going to score easily. Yet Guillen, always impressed by his own right arm, threw home anyway. The ball sailed over the cutoff man. It sailed over the catcher. It sailed to the backstop, a ridiculous error that put runners on second and third with just one out in what was now a 3-1 game. It was the ninth inning. He had three hits. The Nationals were winning. Yet Guillen hadn't shaken that first inning slight, hadn't forgotten that Loaiza didn't retaliate.

Cordero eventually secured a 3-2 victory, the Nationals' twenty-third win by one run. But the clubhouse afterward was decidedly tense. The press asked Robinson if he had asked Guillen what he was thinking on the throw home. Robinson said no. "I suggest you guys don't ask him, either," he said. "Not tonight, anyway." When reporters arrived at Guillen's locker, tucked in the back right corner of the clubhouse, Guillen sat, shirtless, and looked up. Just as his behavior had been exemplary in the clubhouse till that moment, he had been accommodating and affable with a doting press, who wanted to recapture his renaissance season with this new team in this new town. But in the moments after this game, no one could reach him. Not Robinson. Not Eddie Rodriguez, the bench coach who had made a mission of connecting with Guillen. Not anybody.

"I don't want to talk to you guys," Guillen snapped, putting the palm of his hand up to reporters. "Okay? *Okay?* Thank you."

The exact fallout from such an episode can't be quantified, and even as the season wore on, there were different views within the Nationals' clubhouse as to whether Guillen's actions that steamy night at RFK Stadium precipitated anything of substance. Robinson, for his part, let his player stew a day. A couple of players approached Robinson. "Are you going to handle this?" they asked. Yes, he assured them, he would. Guillen, the next day, tried to put it past. "Everything's fine," he said, smiling as he had for most of the first half. "I tell you the truth. We got no problems." Yet Robinson brought Guillen into his dim office, where there was barely enough room for four people to sit and have a discussion. Robinson wanted, he said, to find out if Guillen had any sort of history with Martinez. He wanted to find out what could make Guillen lose it like that.

"It couldn't have been just that incident," Robinson said later that week. "It had to be that he had something built up to set him off like that." Robinson tried to talk through scenarios with Guillen, and he played off one fact: Since Guillen's arrival with the Nationals, he'd professed a respect and admiration for Robinson that he'd had for no other manager in his career. So Robinson told him: *Here's how I would've handled it. I would go to first base, and if the next man hit a ground ball, I would make that second baseman, that shortstop, pay for his pitcher's mistake. I would slide hard. Fair, but hard. I would get my revenge, but I would wait for the right time.*

Guillen's appearances in Robinson's office were usually marked by a lot of one-way talk, by Guillen spewing things he felt should be done or should be changed or should remain the same, and Robinson at least giving the impression that he was listening. This time, Robinson lectured him, and Guillen left Robinson's office ready to tell people that he would handle things differently. Robinson watched him go. "It doesn't concern me that it'll happen again," he said a few days later. "I'm aware it might. I understand it could. But the only thing I concern myself with is what's happening right now, the attitude of this ballclub. I don't think about, 'Oooooh, what might happen down a ways.' To me, that's negative energy, and it's wasted energy."

The Nationals lost the final two games of the series against the Mets, then two of three to the Phillies in Philadelphia, one by 1-0 even though John Patterson turned in a stellar pitching perform-ance, one by 5-4 in the bottom of the twelfth. Somehow, in the week since they'd showed resilience and togetherness and guile and gump-tion to sweep the Cubs in Chicago, they had changed as a ballclub, and they went into the All-Star break badly needing just that—a break.

•   •   •

THE SUN SHONE DOWN and a crisp breeze moved off the Atlantic Ocean as Jim Bowden pulled his BlackBerry from the pocket of his gray nylon Nike sweatsuit, the coast of Maine both behind him and in front of him, scarcely different from how he remembered it as a kid. Bowden looked down hopefully as if to plead with the little elec-tronic device, *Please bring forth a message from Dan O'Dowd*. It was July 12, the day of the All-Star Game, the time when most major league players, aside from those assembled in Detroit for the festivities, were supposed to be on a hiatus from baseball. For a general manager, especially one in a pennant race, there were no breaks, whether Bowden was back in his office in Washington, on the road with the Nationals in some other city, or here, on Capitol Island, Maine, where, as he said, "I really grew up." The island was connected to the mainland by a rickety wooden bridge with room enough for only one car to pass. But he was connected, too, by all these electronic devices. This was no vacation, no break. A message from O'Dowd, the Colorado Rockies' general manager, might mean the Nationals were a step closer to acquiring Preston Wilson, the Rockies' center fielder.

But this wasn't it. Not the call he wanted, not the e-mail he needed. The Nationals and the Rockies, by this point, had agreed to the players who would change hands. The Nationals would get Wilson, who was hitting .258 with fifteen home runs and forty-seven runs batted in, run production numbers that would have put him second on the Nationals, trailing only Jose Guillen. The Rockies would get right-hander Zach Day, who was just working his way back in the minor leagues after fracturing his right wrist, and minor-league outfielder J. J. Davis. Yet the deal was wearing Bowden out. Wilson earned $12.5 million, and the Nationals couldn't afford to pay what he was owed over the remainder of the season. Bowden had already convinced Tony Tavares, the team's president, to expand the Nationals' payroll beyond the $50 million they had budgeted at the beginning of the year. Tavares, in turn, had convinced officials from Major League Baseball, which still owned the club, to allow the Nationals, who sat atop the National League East, to pursue Wilson. But they couldn't pay all of his salary. The Rockies would have to eat some of the money.

So back and forth they went. The Nationals were willing to pay $2 million for the rest of the year. The Rockies wanted Washington to pick up $2.5 million. It had taken so long to get even that close. The Nationals, aware their lineup lacked power, began scouting Wilson in spring training. They were concerned about his left knee, which had been surgically repaired the previous year. The scouting reports said he moved okay. They were concerned about his defense. The scouting reports said he could cover center field, which would allow Brad Wilkerson to move to left, a position to which he was better suited, a position that would take less of a toll on Wilkerson's already beat-up body. But in return for Wilson, the Rockies originally asked for more than the Nationals wanted to give. They wanted not only Day but utility man Jamey Carroll and rookie outfielder Ryan Church. Carroll was one of Frank Robinson's favorite players because he did whatever was asked and never complained about anything, and Bowden considered Church, though he was often injured, a true prospect. Finally, the week before the All-Star break, the two teams agreed that Davis, a former first-round pick who was playing for the Nationals' Class AAA team in New Orleans, would join Day as the package.

But the sides couldn't agree on the money. Wilson, too, had to sign off on the deal in order for it to go through. All sides went round and round. "That transaction was the time you woke up till the time you went to bed," Bowden said. "It never stopped. It was exhausting." Yet here, with the deal getting closer and closer, Bowden didn't look exhausted. He looked energized, which belied the circumstances. He had come to Capitol Island not to do business, but not to relax, either. He'd come to put his grandmother, Mildred Smith Bowden, to rest because she had died the previous week at the age of ninety-seven. It was Mildred Bowden who had really defined this place for Jim, for the entire family. It was to Capitol Island that Jim had traveled from the family's winter home in Weston, Massachusetts, where he had learned to sail and played baseball against the children of the lobstermen from nearby Boothbay Harbor. Memories of lobster and steak dinners on Sunday nights, the entire family and assorted friends in attendance, lingered with Bowden that week.

"It was very hard, very emotional," he said. Still, even with the emotions, Bowden couldn't do much reflecting on it all. He wasn't sleeping much. He tried to find distractions in his boys, playing Wiffle ball and taking rides in his power boat, the one he bought after the Cincinnati Reds won the division title in 1995, a little gift to himself for putting that club together, for getting a contract extension from the team's owner, Marge Schott, a boat that he and his boys used to steer down the Ohio River to Riverfront Stadium for games. Yet even those memories seemed long ago. Bowden tried, to an extent, to escape business, but the Wilson deal hung in the air. Bob Boone, one of Bowden's special assistants who had scouted Wilson, called one day, and Bowden was short with him, as he could be with anybody when his mood wasn't right.

"Jim," Boone said, "you're in Maine."

"Bob," Bowden responded, "I've been on the phone all day long."

The energy of an impending deal flowed through the air. But when O'Dowd hadn't called back by late afternoon, Bowden decided to take a ride in the boat. He piled the kids in, Tyler, at fourteen his second-oldest; followed by Chad, a twelve-year-old who never came to RFK Stadium not wearing his Nationals uniform with "C. Bowden" on the back; followed by the twins, Chase and Trey. Together, they set out for a cruise, their father's cell phone and BlackBerry dutifully set to vibrate so he could feel them over the roar of the engine.

"Woooh-hooooooooh!" Bowden screamed as he pushed the accelerator forward, pulling away from the dock, standing in front of the wheel. The kids giggled and laughed, their hair whipping back. "Hold on! Hold on!" Bowden said, looking back, wearing a broad grin, wicked delight apparent in every corner of his red-cheeked face. He turned his blue Nationals hat, the one with the *W* written in script on the front, around so the brim was in the back, out of the way of the breeze. He stuck his smile into the wind and headed out into the Atlantic, zigging and zagging back and forth so the kids had to grip the side of the boat or the seat next to them, everyone having as much fun as can be had on a summer day, trade or no trade. Bowden knew every island, every piece of coastline, and pointed them out. He sped off to a spot where he knew seals congregated, slowed the boat down, then urged his visitors to scoot out onto the bow of the boat. Dozens of seals sunned themselves, slipping into the cold water of the North Atlantic. The Bowden boys had seen it before. And as Bowden pulled the boat back a bit, quietly now, he put his thumb on the air horn, and the blast echoed across the ocean, calm and shimmering. The seals looked up, alert. Bowden smiled again.

His BlackBerry buzzed. It was Brian Cashman, the general manager of the New York Yankees, who had cut veteran pitcher Mike Stanton earlier in the month. But before Stanton became a free agent, the Yankees had ten days to try to trade him. Cashman knew Bowden wanted Stanton, and wanted to make a deal. Bowden didn't bite on giving up something in return. The following day, the Nationals signed Stanton as a free agent, an experienced left-hander Bowden believed could help the team in the midst of a pennant race.

The BlackBerry went back in his pocket, and the boat moved forward, toward Boothbay Harbor, off to a fuel stop. For Tyler and Chad Bowden, this was all they had ever known, their father trying to make deals in all sorts of places at all times of day.

"My dad always trades my favorite players," Chad said, somewhat contemplatively. "Isn't that right, Ty?" Tyler, bigger and older, laughed at his little brother. But Chad was serious. He thought about it some more. "Why is that?" Chad asked. Ty responded quickly, "Because he can."

The boat moved forward. The phone calls and e-mail messages would go on late into the night. And the following day, the day before the Nationals resumed their season in Milwaukee with four games against the Brewers, the Washington Nationals and the Colorado Rockies finally agreed to the trade: Preston Wilson for Zach Day and J. J. Davis. The Nationals would pay $2 million to Wilson for the rest of the year.

"He's going to strike out, and he's going to go one-for-four a lot," Bowden said that night, the deal completed, a mix of fatigue and excitement in his voice. "But hopefully, that one-for-four is with a three-run double or a home run."

The next day, just an hour and forty-five minutes before the Nationals played the Brewers, Preston Wilson walked through the doors of the visitors' clubhouse at Miller Park, a new element added to the Nationals' chemistry. That day, he hit the fifth pitch he saw as a National out to left field for a solo home run, just as Bowden had hoped. But that was it. He went one-for-four, struck out once, and the Nationals lost the first game of the rest of their season. The next night, Stanton made his first appearance for Washington, and before he could throw a pitch in the bottom of the tenth, he was called for a balk that sent the winning run home. The slump was on.

•   •   •

For as long as baseball has been played, players and coaches, owners and managers, GMs and fans have tried to figure out the fickle nature of funks like this. How can a batter such as Nationals third baseman Vinny Castilla hit .347 in April, then hit .202 in June? How can a pitcher such as Nationals right-hander Livan Hernandez win eleven straight decisions before the All-Star break, but then struggle to win even one game after it? How can a shortstop such as Cristian Guzman hit .266 for his six-year career in Minnesota, then sign with Washington and plummet to .095 for the entire month of July, lowering his average to .201 in the three and a half months before the All-Star break?

Switch out the names, the dates, the specific stats, and it could be any baseball team from any era that excels over one period of time, then falls into an abyss, not even closely resembling the team of only a month or two before. The explanation is part physical, part mental, somewhere in the vast expanse of gray that lies between the two, and not even the wisest old baseball sages can quantify it. When the Nationals lost four of their last five games before the All-Star break, when they followed it up with thirteen losses in their first sixteen games after the season resumed, it was apparent that things had changed.

Preston Wilson arrived from Colorado to play center field, but he couldn't play it as well as Brad Wilkerson could—a poor evaluation on the part of the Nationals. Still, after manager Frank Robinson tried him in left and right, Wilson said he preferred center, that it was where he felt more comfortable, so Robinson stuck with him there, even though he played too deep, even though he took poor

paths to balls both in front of him and over his head, frequently looking like a giraffe on ice skates, skidding all over the grass. There were
more problems. Castilla, the veteran who'd hit thirty-five homers the
previous season in Colorado, swung a bat that looked slower by the
day. Worse, he had been a Gold Glove–caliber third baseman during
much of the first half. Yet now, the left knee injury that had nagged
him for much of the season was getting worse and worse, so bad that
when he walked down the dugout steps in Milwaukee, he had to put
his left foot down a step, then bring his right foot quickly to the same
step, then nudge his left foot forward again, all the while clutching the
railing, the stride of an old man, not a major league third baseman.

It went on and on. For most of the first half, Guzman had
remained engaged defensively despite offensive struggles that would
have buried other people. Yet now it was late July. This had long
since become more than a mere "slow start." Guzman didn't get a
hit in his first eighteen at-bats after the All-Star break, and his average plunged to an incomprehensible .180, more than ninety points
lower than he'd hit the year before. And finally his defense lagged. In
the eighty-nine games before the All-Star break, he made six errors.
In the seventy-three thereafter, he made nine. Worse, the number of
balls he had a chance to snare but which instead trickled through to
the outfield increased exponentially.

Wilkerson, the leadoff man, battled a shoulder problem, a hand
problem, a forearm problem, and a thumb problem, all with various
degrees of pain, all at various times. He struck out too much, and his
average, slowly but steadily, slid toward .250 in a year he'd hoped to
hit .300. Nick Johnson, the first baseman, returned from his bruised
heel, but was half the hitter he had been before he went down, and
his defense, sublime before the break, was not quite as tight. Jose
Vidro, the second baseman, virtually creaked when he moved, his
legs bothered him so much. He developed problems in his quadri-
ceps, making the thighs that propelled him both defensively and at
the plate dead and ineffective, a condition that came about mostly
because when he worked himself back into shape following knee

surgery in the off-season, he didn't have enough time for his legs to catch up. Even Brian Schneider, the catcher, eventually succumbed to a shoulder injury that bothered him when he threw, leaving backup Gary Bennett behind the plate for long stretches.

So, gradually, the hits that the Nationals had scooped up and turned into outs during their run to first place turned into singles and errors. And, infuriatingly, night after night, at the moments the Nationals once had come through with key hits, they struck out or grounded out or popped up. Bowden dissected the problems. Robinson tried as well. Each day they arrived at the ballpark hoping things would change. During the early part of July, when things first started to go bad, Robinson virtually bragged about how he was able to leave the struggles at the ballpark, that they didn't bother him when he watched TV or played golf. But as things got worse, he admitted the slump ate at him, that he thought about it as he drove to the ballpark from his apartment in Woodley Park and on the way back home. At the beginning of the season, the streets on his way to RFK baffled him, Florida Avenue starting and disintegrating all at the same time, and it took all his concentration to remember the way. But when the slump hit, he knew them by heart, and, fortunately or not, he was able to place his thoughts on things other than driving. "This ballclub, right now, is taking up all of my thoughts, all of my day," he said in early August. Bowden could rarely leave those losses at the ballpark, because his personality was to be consumed by his job, by each game, each inning, each pitch.

They were opposites, two men thrown together to run a team and bring it to Washington who handled things in far different fashions. Neither of them, though, could stop this slide. It took just eighteen days, the span between July 3 and July 21, for the Nationals' five-and-a-half-game lead in the National League East to evaporate completely as the Atlanta Braves made their annual charge, even with a team full of rookies and a bullpen that wasn't half as good as Washington's.

On July 26, when the Nationals began a three-game series in a flat-footed tie with the Braves atop the division, they entered the ninth inning of the first game with a one-run lead, a chance to regain their footing. Chad Cordero gave up a double to Andruw Jones, a single to Chipper Jones, a sacrifice fly, and it was tied. In the bottom of the tenth, Luis Ayala issued a bases-loaded walk, and the Braves took a victory they shouldn't have had, a lead in the division that might have belonged to the Nationals, and never looked back. Atlanta won each of the next two nights, both times by one run. Washington would never see first place again.

"It looks like we're a team that's coming out to play just to play," Robinson said of his group. "It's not playing with the energy that says, 'We're going to win.' Now, we seem resolved to the fact that we're going to lose this game." The Nationals lost one of those games against the Braves because Cristian Guzman dropped a throw to second, because Nick Johnson and Jose Vidro couldn't see a routine pop-up that fell between them, because Esteban Loaiza made an errant throw, none of them things that would have happened in the first half. Robinson shut the door to the clubhouse afterward and excoriated his team. Where was the focus? Where was the energy? Where was the intensity?

"I've never seen a turn like this," Robinson said one day. "I saw these guys on buses, on planes, in the first half, and the way they interacted, you thought it would last."

"We need some leadership in here," right-hander John Patterson said. Patterson, by this point, had developed into the National's most reliable starter. Yet he didn't have the experience or the standing in the clubhouse to lead. "We need people who have been there before, who know how to handle these situations," he said, finally. So as the questions kept coming—what happened, and why?—the only thing that was clear was that not one but two teams returned baseball to Washington in 2005: a joyous bunch that got along, came up with the big hit, and didn't think any deficit was too large to overcome, and a miserable outfit that disintegrated into factions, where fun was hard to have.

"I don't know, man," Vidro said one day, the silence of the clubhouse providing a backdrop. "Things changed. Things went south. You can't really tell what it is. It's just that when things are going good, everybody gets along. And when things went bad, things came apart."

So the rest of the summer turned into a series of meltdowns and meetings, meetings and meltdowns. After a loss to the miserable Colorado Rockies, Livan Hernandez, for so long the ace of the staff, threatened to have surgery on his ailing right knee, the one that prevented him from pushing off the rubber. He could no longer throw his curveball effectively. Four or five miles per hour had slipped from his fastball. "I don't think there's anyone else," pitching coach Randy St. Claire said, "who would still be going out there." Yet Hernandez's outburst, which simmered for two days, mirrored the deterioration in the clubhouse. "I was frustrated," he said two weeks later. "I let stuff get to me. I no pitch good, and my knee hurt, and it's difficult. It's not easy."

Within two weeks, Hernandez would be removed from another start, another loss. This time, he would toss his glove into the stands, follow it with his hat, step into the dugout, and chuck his jacket over the roof of the dugout, where it, too, floated into the crowd. The following day, Robinson decided to play a card that was, quite obviously, a last-ditch effort to save the season. He rolled his black, cushioned chair out from behind his desk and pushed it down the hallway past the trainers' room and into the clubhouse. He gathered the entire team, the coaching staff, the clubhouse attendants— everybody—and ordered them to sit down and talk. The door to the clubhouse closed at 3:58 P.M. on that Saturday afternoon, August 6, with the San Diego Padres in town, with the Nationals losers in thirteen of their previous sixteen games. The door didn't swing back open until 5:42 P.M.

The meeting started slowly at first, with players afraid to say anything, to step on toes. But at some point, Vidro jumped up and complained to Wilkerson that he had been talking behind Guillen's back too much, muttering that Guillen got star treatment. The fact that Guillen only occasionally stretched with the team before games, that he took batting practice when he felt like it, had bothered some players for much of the summer. "I know what it takes for me to get ready," Guillen said. "I know how to prepare." Guillen complained in the meeting that Wilkerson didn't take charge enough in the outfield. Wilkerson shot back: How was he supposed to take charge when Guillen didn't listen to him? It grew heated, a small issue pointing to larger problems.

On the steps outside the clubhouse, with the door still closed, Bowden ushered his children into the underground batting tunnel. "Are they still in there?" he asked about Robinson and the team, motioning to the clubhouse. Yes, he was told, they were. "Good," he said, and he headed after his kids.

When the meeting finally broke, the Nationals went out and lost to the Padres, 3-2. Earlier in the year, the Nationals had never lost those close games, winning a dozen consecutive one-run decisions. But the loss to San Diego, even after the therapy session, was their thirteenth straight in games decided by one run. Talk about a turnaround. Just a week earlier, Bowden had tried to stoke his team by telling his troops, that as it was currently constructed, they could win. But after the Sunday loss to the Padres, he threatened changes.

"You can't watch these games too much longer, so let's try something different," he said. "It's like sailing a boat. Sometimes, you think you're going the right way. But if your team's losing, at some point, you might as well tack and go the other way and see if that'll work. I'm sick of talking the talk. How many meetings can you have?"

All Bowden could offer, though, was to bring up a minor league outfielder, Brandon Watson, and stick him in the leadoff spot for a few games. There were no overhauls available. There were no options to back up the threats. The Nationals, it seemed, would have to rediscover their own chemistry, and they would have to do so by themselves.

"I've said all along it's easy to look like you're mature, look like the chemistry's going well, when you're winning," Wilkerson said later that night. "But when you're losing, you kind of get the test of time, see how strong you are as a team, and see if you *are* really a team."

The team that brought Washington together was coming apart.

•   •   •

ALAN ALPER HAD LIVED through times worse than this, it would seem, because the Washington Senators of his youth spent entire seasons in last place in the American League, never with a hope of accomplishing much of anything. But Alper and the rest of the Nationals' fan base had been teased through the first part of the summer, teased to believe that this collection of no-names and outcasts could win a division title. Part of the process, then, for Washingtonians as they embraced baseball again was to remember that, far too often, success is offset by pain.

"I would have been happy if they had just *played* here," Alper said one day in July. "I didn't need the winning. Now, every loss kills me." A week later, he came up with a theory. "The ghosts of the Senators are haunting the Nationals," Alper said, and in a way he believed it. "That's what's happening. The ghosts of the Senators wouldn't let the first baseball team back in Washington win the division. They just wouldn't."

In August, with the season's final month approaching, he wondered to himself, and then to others. "Are we out of it?" he asked, hope still in his voice, even if he knew it was foolish. "Can we turn it around?"

★ ★ ★ ★ ★ ★ ★ ★ ★ ★ ★ ★ ★ ★ ★ ★ ★ ★

Chapter 11

Home

*T*here is a corner of the visitors' clubhouse at Turner Field in Atlanta, one with a couple of lockers stuck in a nook, a slice of privacy in the spacious facility which is adorned with a giant flat-screen television that, on most of the Nationals' visits here, showed a movie prior to game time, Adam Sandler or Will Ferrell or some other *Saturday Night Live* alum. On this afternoon, though, the first day of September, there was no privacy anywhere in the clubhouse, and it didn't seem anyone wanted any. Into this environment came Ryan Zimmerman, a rookie out of the University of Virginia who had been the club's first-round draft pick in June. He came from Class AA Harrisburg, a ballyhooed addition set to make his major league debut just a little more than three months out of college. Jim Bowden, the Nationals' general manager, had already said that, defensively, Zimmerman reminded him of the greats who had ever played the position, of Brooks Robinson and Mike Schmidt. When the team, and regular third baseman Vinny Castilla, met the dog days of August and merely continued to slog through the remains of the slump that began in July, Bowden said he thought of Zimmerman "every hour on the hour." Zimmerman arrived at Turner Field, on September 1, still short of his twenty-first birthday, the first player from that year's draft to reach the majors, the first player who would be drafted by and groomed as a Washington National, not a Montreal Expo. Could he inject some life into this team, beat-up and struggling, as the days clicked off the calendar?

The clubhouse into which Zimmerman arrived in his first foray as part of a major league team stretched out before him as a strange scene. Right-hander Esteban Loaiza, who seemed to have friends in the clubhouse on every road trip, sat with three men, laughing. A movie played. Music, from classic rock to hip-hop, thumped through speakers. Joey Eischen and Castilla engaged in a putting contest across a stretch of carpet. The Nationals wore red T-shirts, courtesy of utility man Jamey Carroll, with the words "Carlito's Way" printed across the front, atop a picture of pinch hitter Carlos Baerga's head. Carroll had wanted to pay homage to Baerga in this fashion for more than a month, because it was Baerga, during those good times earlier in the summer, who'd kept the Nationals loose in the dugout. "I've never heard someone that funny," Carroll said, and he printed ten of Baerga's best sayings on the back, including, "Let's get naked" and "Let's hit for an hour" and "This one's for the ladies," the things he would yell under the cover of the dugout, eliciting laughter every time.

"I'm a joker," Baerga said, but in his Puerto Rican accent, it came out as, "I'm a yoker." With a victory the night before in the nightcap of a doubleheader against the Braves, the Nationals appeared in a mood to yoke.

In that back corner of the clubhouse, on the floor in front of two of the lockers, a blanket lay across the floor. A salesman stood over it, and a group of Nationals stood around it, pointing, laughing, joking. There was jewelry. There were sunglasses. It was as if the clubhouse had turned into an open-air street market, and some of the players were more interested in how they would look after the game than how they would perform during it. On the greaseboard visible to everyone who entered the clubhouse were scrawled the words, "Beginning Sept. 1, no wives, fiancées, girlfriends, or kids on the team plane." The message was not only an indication that September call-ups, reinforcements from the minor leagues, were probably on the way, making space a more valuable commodity, but also seemed to set a tone of seriousness. *This is September. There's still a chance we'll make the postseason. Stay focused.*

Except from Frank Robinson's spot back in his office, that focus wasn't anywhere to be found. The movie played. The music thumped. The Nationals, even with all they had been through, were just two games out of the lead in the race for the National League's wild-card playoff berth, the spot that went to the team that didn't win one of the three divisions but had the next-best record. They weren't acting like it, though. Robinson had turned seventy the day before. The season, only two months earlier, had filled him with energy. But now these guys were wearing on him in a way that hadn't seemed possible back then.

That night, the Nationals fell behind the Braves 7-1. They stormed back to tie it in the seventh, and went on to extra innings. But reliever Luis Ayala, who hadn't pitched in ten days because of a bothersome right elbow, came on in the bottom of the tenth to face Braves center fielder Andruw Jones. Over the course of the summer, Jones, it seemed, became a bigger nemesis to Washington baseball than Bob Short ever was, because there seemed to be no pitch the Nationals threw that he couldn't hit. Yet they kept coming after him—indeed, he would end up with eight homers against Washington, but would walk just seven times. And here, six hours after the Nationals' clubhouse filled with laughter, Jones drove a pitch from Ayala deep to center field, the home run that sent Washington to yet another loss.

In his office afterward, Robinson considered the scene. There'd been a time back in May when the Nationals had been swept in Cincinnati and lost five of their first six games on a road trip. Back then, as they packed their bags, Robinson had approached the club-house stereo, trying to figure out how to turn it on, even after another loss. Back then, he'd needed levity. He'd needed to prop his team up, to remind them everything would be okay. By this point, though, in Atlanta, he needed to tear them down, to remind them everything was far from okay. When the team arrived home for a weekend series against Philadelphia, things were different. There would be no more music, not before games, not even at the behest of the starting pitcher, who usually controlled the stereo as part of the buildup to that first pitch. There wouldn't be music even after wins, should they manage to actually win any more games. There would be no more videos or movies, unless someone wanted to watch a tape of that night's opposing pitcher. There would be no more card games, a staple throughout the season.

"I need focus," Robinson said that day before the Nationals hosted the Phillies. "I need energy. I need attention on the things that are needed to win baseball games."

The Nationals lost that night, a listless effort against the Phillies. The announced crowd of 28,939 was the smallest at RFK Stadium since June, the smallest since the team was in first place.

Two days later, Jim Bowden stood in his box above the playing field at RFK Stadium, slightly down the third base line. Bowls of pretzels and popcorn, a fruit plate, and drinks sat on tables along the back wall. They went largely untouched. Bowden, by this point, was well aware of the fragile nature of his team's clubhouse, of the rules Robinson had instituted, and he was spending time shuttling back and forth between players and coaches in the hours before games, trying to take the team's pulse. Bowden was loath to have chemistry, or lack thereof, be the downfall of the first team to play in Washington in thirty-four summers. Through all the craziness, there was still a chance, and Bowden knew it. He was optimistic on this day, because the sun was shining, because the worst had to be over, didn't it?

And then Brian Schneider, the Nationals' catcher, drove a three-run homer out against the Phillies. Every single person in Bowden's box jumped for joy. There were his four youngest sons. There was his fiancée, Joy. There was Squire Galbreath, one of his oldest friends and closest advisors. And in the midst of another season-saving win, there was hope evident in all the fist-pounding that went around, from old to young, young to old, in Jim Bowden's box.

"You don't have to have the best team to win it, baby!" Bowden yelled above the din. "We can still win it!"

Winning it, it seemed, would be the best way to ensure a future in that box, in that stadium, with the Nationals. As the Nationals headed into the final month of their first season in Washington, they had proven they were resilient. They had proven that, even with myriad personality issues, they could win when you least expected it. They had proven that they could meet their goals for attendance, for they would draw 2.7 million fans to RFK, which didn't have a single restaurant or bar on its outskirts, which didn't draw people in for a "total fan experience," to use a marketing term of the new millennium. The fans who bought tickets bought them to watch baseball games, and in that regard, the sport's return to the nation's capital was a success.

What remained, though, as Jim Bowden, the general manager, and Frank Robinson, the manager, set the rules and made the decisions and discussed ways for the team to shake their summer-long malaise, were the questions about their futures. Both men wanted to return for 2006, for Washington's second consecutive season with baseball. Neither man was signed beyond October 31. Reviews depended on whom you asked. Some of Bowden's moves, such as trading for Jose Guillen, had largely worked out, because even with Guillen's questionable temperament, he was the Nationals' most productive hitter for much of the season. Others, such as signing Cristian Guzman, were utter busts, because Guzman hit under .200 for most of the year and was in danger of posting historically bad numbers before resurrecting himself with a solid September. Robinson, too, had received praise when he challenged the home run that hit the foul pole at RFK Stadium back on Memorial Day, more praise when he took on Angels manager Mike Scioscia the following month. But fans and front office staff grumbled when he stuck with Vinny Castilla at third base late in the season. They threw their arms in the air when he waited until the middle of an at-bat to send in a pinch runner, because sometimes he seemed a step behind rather than a step ahead.

But here they were, the two men who'd constructed this team, this story, the return of baseball to the nation's capital. And neither knew who would be doing the hiring and firing for the following year. Five months into the season, Major League Baseball still owned the Nationals. There was no telling when the team would be sold.

•   •   •

JUST THREE WEEKS after Major League Baseball announced it would move the Montreal Expos to Washington, the men who run the sport made an announcement that sounded weighty. On October 19, 2004, baseball said that anyone interested in buying the franchise that would play in Washington must submit a bid, not to mention a deposit of $100,000, by November 1. The idea, at the time, was to whittle the field from perhaps nine or ten interested parties to two or three in early December, and then to settle on an owner by January. The new ownership group would then have say over everything, from the general manager to the manager to the concessions.

"We want to move the process along as expeditiously as possible," baseball president Robert DuPuy said that day. Yet *expeditious* and *baseball*, particularly when it comes to Washington, rarely belong in the same sentence. Tony Tavares remembered those days in Montreal back in 2002 when he was told there would be a decision about contraction, then was told the team would exist for another year, then was told they'd move before 2004, and on and on. So on that very same day, Tavares considered all that had to be done in Washington over the ensuing days, weeks, months. Back then, he didn't yet have a general manager. He didn't yet have a new team name. He didn't have an office, a sales force, a staff, a secretary. An owner? Now? "For me," he said, "that looks like it's an eon away."

He was right. Go back through all the deadlines. In early December 2004, the day baseball's ownership voted to officially approve the franchise's move from Montreal, commissioner Bud Selig said he was eager to get on with "finishing the last few steps, including the sale of the ballclub." Two months later, in February, while in San Francisco for an announcement about a future All-Star Game, Selig told reporters that six bidders had submitted $100,000 as a down payment, and that "I hope to have it done by early spring. It will take time to work through all of these."

Keep going. "I know what I said before, and I'll hold to my original timetable," Selig said. "I think this can be done by midsummer. The sooner the better." This came on May 11, 2005. By that point, the original timetable had undergone some serious revisionist history. And by midsummer? "We're moving along," Selig said at the midsummer classic, baseball's All-Star Game. "Last year, I made some predictions, and the year before. But the fact is, I'm very confident now that we will be done this summer, there's no question, and have a new owner." Two weeks later, when the Nationals visited Atlanta and Selig was in town: "I'm hopeful before the summer is over, we'll have a new owner in Washington. I'm sure we will."

Eight groups bid to purchase the Nationals, and the process sputtered along in a way that befit a Washington summer, with little apparent urgency, seemingly dragged down by the heat and humidity. Each potential owner had some distinguishing characteristic, some political wrinkle, that made for good conversation over expense account lunches, and handicapping the groups—"So, who's going to get the team?"—became a popular political sport in a non-election year.

There were locals, none more active in the pursuit of landing a team in the District than the group headed by Frederic Malek, a venture capitalist whose ties to Washington's political scene included working in the Nixon administration in the '70s. There, a paranoid Nixon worried, oddly enough, about Jewish employees at the Bureau of Labor Statistics. He thought they might be plotting against him. And he enlisted Malek to assemble a list of Jewish workers there.

Malek, though, endured in Washington, running George H. W. Bush's unsuccessful reelection campaign in 1992 and serving as a partner in the Texas Rangers with George W. Bush. In 1999, Malek formed the Washington Baseball Club, a group that intended to buy the team if one was ever granted. They took up petitions of people who would be interested in season tickets long before the Expos arrived. He enlisted a young businessman, Jeffrey Zients, and other partners, from former Washington Redskin cornerback Darrell Green to former Clinton advisor Vernon Jordan and Colin Powell, former secretary of state under the younger Bush.

Joining the Malek-Zients group as Beltway insiders was the family of low-key real estate magnate Theodore Lerner, whose operation was headquartered in Bethesda. Lerner's son, Mark, would run the team, and unlike Malek-Zients, it drew very little attention to itself, as anti-Washington as it can get. There was a former baseball owner, Jeffrey Smulyan, a communications executive from Indianapolis whose three-year tenure as the owner of the Mariners was not remembered fondly in Seattle because the team nearly bolted town for St. Petersburg, Florida, under his watch, because he pulled the purse strings tight, and because, by the end of 1992, he was telling *USA Today*, "I don't want to do this anymore. I'm tired of the process." Yet Smulyan reinserted himself more than a decade later, and he waged a public relations campaign late in the summer, trying to convince anyone who would listen that out-of-town ownership would be just fine. Many people, not the least of whom was Anthony Williams, the mayor, disagreed.

"Tell me, tell me, tell me," Alan Alper said one day in September, "that that carpetbagger Smulyan's not going to get the team. He'd be Bob Short all over again. He would. I'm really afraid of that."

Nearly everyone involved had some sort of political tie, some name or face that, when it popped up in the paper, people in Washington could point to and say, "He's got some clout." There was Yusef Jackson, the son of the Reverend Jesse Jackson, who ran a beer distributorship in Chicago and joined with Ronald Burkle, a billionaire who served as vice chairman of John Kerry's presidential election campaign. There was Franklin Haney, a Tennessee developer who owned property in the District and northern Virginia, and whose ties to former vice president Al Gore ran so deep that in 1999 he was indicted on forty-two charges alleging that he funneled contributions to the Clinton-Gore campaigns in both 1992 and '96. He was acquitted on all the charges. There was a former team president, Stan Kasten, who ran the Atlanta Braves during the early portion of their dominant run in the National League, whose most important political tie might have been to Selig himself, for the two knew each other from working within the sport, an asset not to be overlooked. There was William Collins, the Alexandria, Virginia, businessman who sought to bring baseball to a slice of land out by Dulles International Airport, who was joined by Albert Lord, chairman of loan giant Sallie Mae. And there was Jonathan Ledecky, a Washington businessman who once owned a stake in the Wizards and Capitals, who played off the Senators' past by forming Big Train Holdco, the name of his partnership aimed at landing the Nationals.

It was Ledecky's bid that caused the most stir during those summer months. He enlisted George Soros, yet another billionaire, to add both clout and money to his group. There was never a stronger indication that the process, the entire existence of the Nationals in Washington, was laced with political undertones. Soros was an outspoken critic of President Bush and spent millions trying to put

Kerry in the White House in 2004, as well as donating millions of dollars to other liberal causes.

And in June, a reporter from *Roll Call,* a political trade publication and an institution in the insular world of Capitol Hill for half a century, asked Representative Tom Davis of Virginia what he thought of Soros's inclusion in Ledecky's group. Davis had worked to try to land the team for his own state. He was a Republican who was the chair of the House committee that held hearings regarding steroid abuse in baseball. "Major League Baseball," Davis said, "understands the stakes" if Soros's group winds up with the team. "I don't think they want to get involved in a political fight." Republicans went on to hint that should Soros be involved in the ownership of the team, they just might look into baseball's antitrust exemption.

So here it was, a political, partisan fight over, of all things, ownership of a baseball team. But this was *Washington's* baseball team. This was the baseball team members of Congress took to watching on those summer nights, just a little more than twenty blocks from their workplace. Why not fight about who owns it? Nancy Pelosi, a Democrat from California, roared back, "The Republicans should allow baseball to remain as it is, an American pastime loved by millions, regardless of their political beliefs." The layers of the struggle to own the Nationals continued to pile on, one after the other.

"I'll tell you what," Tony Tavares said late in the summer. "Baseball's learning a lot about this city. They're learning that no matter what you think you know, there might be a surprise. And they're learning that things here work differently than they do in any other city in the country. I mean, you've got the local politicians. You've got the national politicians. You've got everyone trying to get their hands into something. It's unbelievable."

The Nationals' summer-long swoon had little, if anything, to do with the vacancy at the top, with the fact that there was no owner. Throughout baseball in the summer of 2005, there were very few trade deadline deals, and even clubs with solid ownership groups were unable to pull the trigger on deals. Washington was able to add Preston Wilson to its lineup, whether it had an owner or not (and whether he would help or not).

But the perception, certainly, wore on some of the Nationals. "We need an owner in here, man," Jose Vidro said one day late in the season. "We need to know whoever the general manager is going to be, if the general manager is [going to be] Jim Bowden or not. We need to get some people in here so we know what's going on."

At that point, the Nationals had settled into their home and still didn't know what was going on. There were two complicating issues. The first was a lawsuit involving the Baltimore Orioles, Peter Angelos's American League team up the road, and Comcast, the dominant cable supplier in the Washington region, where it served 1.65 million customers. Think back to Angelos's objections to the Expos' relocation to Washington. He did not want to share the market, one he felt was his own. But when the move became inevitable, part of his deal with Major League Baseball dictated that he would hold the broadcast rights for the Nationals, as odd an arrangement as existed in professional sports. Angelos would pay the Washington club $21 million for the right to broadcast its games, and he formed a network, the Mid-Atlantic Sports Network. Problem: There was no way to distribute MASN, unless cable systems picked it up. And Comcast already had a contract to carry Angelos's Orioles. In late April, Comcast sued the Orioles, MASN, and MLB, arguing that the cable company should be able to compete fairly against competitors when its contract with the Orioles expired at the end of the 2006 season. The wrangling went on all summer. The suit was dismissed in late July, but Comcast's sports cable channel, Comcast SportsNet, refused to air Nationals games. In September, the cable company refiled documents in an effort to start up the suit again, and the entire squabble put a wrinkle into the ownership equation that no one originally could have expected. Who would want to buy a team where another owner holds the television rights? How would this affect the price?

The second issue stalling the search for ownership was baseball's desire to have a signed lease on a new stadium with the city, a process that, predictably, hit snags and wasn't finished by the end of the season. Baseball's position was simple: There was a signed deal, and they were not changing it. Its fear was real, for if they named a local owner, either Malek or Lerner, before the lease was signed, the District Council might try to change the terms of the lease, asking the owner to contribute money to a new stadium project because a Washingtonian wouldn't take the team out of Washington, right? The Council, though, grew wary of the rising costs of land acquisition and materials to build the stadium, not to mention leery of baseball officials themselves. The whole affair dragged on through October and then through Thanksgiving and on into December.

So in July, the Colorado Rockies visited Washington. Zach Day, the floppy-haired kid who began the year as a pitcher for the Nationals but was dealt for Preston Wilson, stood in the visitors' clubhouse, wearing a gray Rockies uniform. Things were good, he said. And out of nowhere, he added, "It's nice to be with a team that has an owner."

Really? How so?

"I think those guys will feel a big difference," Day said. "You know who runs things. You know who's in charge. You know how it's going to be from day to day and you have an idea of how things will be in the future. It's just different. Those guys'll learn that when it happens."

On August 23, DuPuy said he wanted an owner named by Labor Day. The holiday weekend came and went, and there was no deal. On September 28, Selig was in Washington, back on the Hill, to testify about steroids, and was asked, yet again, about the Nationals. "We're trying to move as fast as possible," he said.

Four days later, the Nationals played their last game of the season. The following day, Tony Tavares began preparing for 2006.

"I don't know how long I'm going to be here," he said. "None of us do. Maybe forever. I can't guarantee anybody next week. Who the hell knows?"

• • •

BY THE TIME the Nationals arrived in Flushing, at Shea Stadium, just down the metal steps from the number 7 train that ran from Manhattan out to Queens, there was no accounting for their position. It was September 14, and they appeared in shambles. One pitcher, Ryan Drese, hadn't thrown in nearly a month, the victim of a torn labrum in his right shoulder, an injury that Drese and the coaching staff believed prevented him from putting his arm in the proper position, contributing to his monumental struggles, five straight losses. Another pitcher, Tony Armas Jr., hadn't pitched in more than two weeks, and he, too, was done for the year, unable to throw because of inflammation in *his* shoulder. The Nationals had tried a lefty picked up off baseball's scrap heap, John Halama, as a fill-in starter, with disastrous results. They had tried a kid who had never appeared in a major league game, one straight from Class AA, Darrell Rasner, with disastrous results. And they had tried to piece together starts from the bullpen, getting two innings here, two more there. Again, disaster.

By all rights, they should have been out of the race for the postseason, for they didn't look like a playoff team and, for most of August and September, didn't *act* like a team ready to make a push for the playoffs. And yet they won the first two games in Gotham. With the New York air unusually muggy for a September afternoon, Frank Robinson holed up back behind a quiet and cramped visitors' clubhouse at Shea Stadium, sitting behind a desk in a barren white office. There was no music in the clubhouse. There were no card games. Robinson's disciplinary decision still held, and would for the rest of the season. So Nick Johnson and Jamey Carroll stopped to check out a video of the Mets' starting pitcher that day, Jae Seo, playing on what seemed like a continuous loop on the television that was crammed next to a post in the locker room. Johnson and Carroll predicted what pitch Seo might throw in a certain situation. They guessed right, congratulated each other, then moved on. The video kept playing.

Robinson, back in his office, liked this pregame time, a chance to kibitz and dissect and analyze with whoever might be around, be it a club official or the small group of writers who traveled with the team. Sitting in his gray baseball pants and a blue mock turtleneck, Robinson looked worn down. He was asked if it felt as if his team still acted as if they had a chance. The answer was swift and sure. "No," he said. But here they were, just three games back in the race for the National League's wild-card playoff berth. Win that day to complete a sweep of the Mets, have Florida and Philadelphia both lose, and the lead would be whittled to two and a half games with fifteen to play. There was enough time. They could get enough help. Why the hell wouldn't the clubhouse feel like it was in the midst of a pennant race?

"There's no way," Robinson said. "It just doesn't. The energy, the focus, the talk, gearing up for a ballgame, to me, it's not there." They had withstood a great deal, all the injuries and the infighting. They had so often been inspiring, coming back from deficits when they looked to be dead, getting the city of Washington behind them. But now, when it counted, there seemed to be a malaise, and Robinson was surprised. "This is an opportunity that doesn't come along very often. And they've worked awful hard a long time this year, and it's still there, it's still possible. We're looking for that little extra. And you don't see it."

That afternoon, the Nationals walked out of their silent clubhouse, took a 4-1 lead over the Mets, gave it all back on a grand slam off Livan Hernandez, trailed by a run going into the ninth, tied it in the ninth because Ryan Zimmerman, as poised as a pinch hitter as a ten-year veteran, opened the inning with an opposite-field double, then won it in the tenth because veteran third baseman Vinny

Castilla hit a two-out, opposite-field single. As they showered and dressed and packed, there were, for the first time in what seemed like months, smiles across nearly every face in that visitors' clubhouse. The nine rookies in the room discovered dresses hanging in their lockers, and the annual hazing ritual was on. Travis Hughes, a pitcher, wore a denim maternity dress. Ryan Church, who had gone through the same routine as a September call-up a year earlier, sported a nice flowered number. Zimmerman, the first-round draft pick, donned a lovely red-and-black ensemble, though his teammates couldn't zip it in the back, so broad were his shoulders. And Tony Blanco, a twenty-three-year-old from the Dominican Republic, squeezed himself into a black leather miniskirt with a skintight burgundy top. "Oh, man," Blanco said when he saw the outfit hanging there ominously.

"Damn, Blanco," Jose Vidro said, looking his kid teammate up and down, checking him out. "You *hot!*"

There was, out of nowhere, a frivolity in the clubhouse, one that hadn't seemed possible only a few hours before. "Can you imagine," Jose Guillen said, "what it would be like in here if we lost? Can you imagine how quiet it would be? We'd be done. I'm telling you, we'd be done if we didn't win that game."

They boarded their bus, drag queens and all, and headed to the airport. They flew across the country to San Diego. The next night, John Patterson, the lanky right-hander who had become the team's best starter in the second half, threw a brilliant three-hitter against the Padres, one in which he retired twenty-one of the final twenty-two men he faced, resting an overworked bullpen. And the Nationals, somehow, headed into a Saturday night game on the West Coast, one that would last well beyond bedtime in Washington, still trailing Houston for the wild-card lead by those two and a half games.

Anything was still possible.

•   •   •

BACK IN THE OLD DAYS, back when he was playing, Frank Robinson hated the idea that people drew conclusions about his feelings from his facial expressions, from the fact that he didn't socialize with many people. They called him angry, and Robinson disagreed. Over the course of the summer with the Nationals, Robinson had his run-ins with pitchers, and people drew conclusions because of it. Back in May, Zach Day had turned his back on Robinson when Robinson came to get the ball early in an outing in Los Angeles, and the action required a meeting among Robinson, Day, and Jim Bowden to clear the air. Day was eventually traded. Back in June, Robinson had fined Tomo Ohka $1,000 for turning *his* back on him when Robinson came out to replace him. Ohka was traded within two weeks. He never bristled more than when pitchers couldn't throw strike one, when pitchers walked hitters, when the Nationals' pitchers failed to find the strike zone. He stuck with struggling hitters such as Vinny Castilla even though most people in the organization desperately wanted rookie Ryan Zimmerman to play. "I guess you can call it loyalty," Robinson said, "because the kid didn't get me here."

Pitchers, though, seemed different. With them, he had a quick hook, one that didn't apply to Livan Hernandez or Esteban Loaiza or, over time, John Patterson. But he had pulled pitchers in the middle of an at-bat. He'd even pulled John Halama in the first inning. Come to think of it, didn't he hate pitchers?

"That's somebody else's perception," Robinson said. "I'm not mean toward pitchers. I just don't accept a lot of excuses. I don't baby people like some people do. I think you're a man, you've got a job to do, you do the job. I don't think you have to be babied.

"And I have a certain standard for pitchers. If you're going to pitch for me, you throw strikes. I cannot stand walks. I cannot stand ball one, ball two, ball three, ball four. *I cannot stand it.* That's like putting somebody on [and saying], 'You go to first base free.' They haven't earned it. Make them earn it."

Dissertation over, he sat back and considered it all. "If that's being harsh, I guess I'm harsh."

Yet when the Nationals entered their game on September 17

against the Padres on yet another perfect day in San Diego, Robinson knew that his pitching staff was the only reason they were still within two and a half games of the lead in the wild-card race. "We wouldn't be here without them," he said.

That night was no different. With Drese and Armas injured and unavailable, Hector Carrasco, who had started just once in 557 career appearances before starting against the Mets the previous week, again took the mound in San Diego. The result was typical of this bunch, which always responded with the least-expected outcome. Carrasco threw six innings and allowed three hits. He didn't permit a run. And as the Nationals scored one in the second, one in the third, one in the fifth, one in the sixth and yet another in the seventh, Jim Bowden stood up from his seat along the third base line, just to the side of the dugout, applauding as each run crossed the plate, even as Padres fans tried to shout him down. They couldn't. It was mid-September. His team was still in the pennant race. He would stand, and he would cheer.

When Carrasco finally came out, relievers Mike Stanton and Gary Majewski neatly took care of the seventh and eighth, and all that was left to do was mop up in the ninth, for Washington held a 5-0 lead. From the broadcast booth at Petco Park, returning from a commercial and heading into the bottom of the ninth inning, play-by-play man Mel Proctor said, "The Nationals on the verge of winning their fifth straight, all on this road trip."

Exactly who was on the receiving end of Proctor's words was difficult to determine. Comcast still wasn't carrying Nationals games on its cable systems. Just more than seventy of the team's 162 games were carried on a local broadcast station, WDCA, Channel 20. Early in the season, when no cable companies or satellite broadcasters had picked up Nationals games, Proctor gave out his cell phone number over the air, asking anybody who had their eyes on the game to call him. No one did.

In this crucial game, by the time the Nationals and Padres

entered the ninth inning, Saturday had turned into Sunday back on the East Coast. September 17 had become the eighteenth, and the Nationals were not on Channel 20. So Proctor's voice went out only to the 1.3 million Washington-area subscribers to DirecTV, as well as the 135,000 who happened to get their cable through another company, RCN. A significant portion of Nationals fans were unable to watch that last inning, when their team was about to put away the Padres.

"It's also coming together in a nice way," said Proctor's partner, former major league pitcher Ron Darling. "With this five-run lead, you're able to put Bergmann out there and give Cordero another day's rest."

Good point. Here came rookie Jason Bergmann, a right-hander still a week from his twenty-fourth birthday who had pitched exceptionally well since arriving from the minors. And Chad Cordero needed as much rest as he could get. The closer had already appeared in seventy-one games, and he was tiring. His fastball, his best pitch, no longer had that late movement, and he struggled with location, which had been so precise earlier in the summer. Six days earlier, the Nationals had been on the verge of an emotional victory over the Braves at home, one in which they stormed back from a six-run deficit to take a 7-6 lead in the bottom of the eighth, one in which Ryan Zimmerman delivered the go-ahead hit, one in which the crowd assembled at RFK Stadium on a Sunday afternoon, some 31,000 people who'd eschewed the Redskins' opener nine miles away in Landover, Maryland, cheered wildly. In that game, Cordero came on to get what would be his forty-fifth save. Instead, he allowed Chipper Jones to hit a two-run homer, an absolute blast. He allowed Andruw Jones to follow with a solo shot. On the first day when the nation's capital hosted major league baseball and NFL football simultaneously, the Redskins won 9-7 over Chicago, and the Nationals lost 9-7, in devastating fashion, to Atlanta.

"I just wanted to throw stuff," Cordero said afterward. But the

Nationals' response to that meltdown was to back up their closer, without whom they would have been finished long before, because he had more saves than anyone in the majors. They won those next three games in New York, then the opener in San Diego. And Cordero would get to watch this one from the safety of the bullpen down the right field line at Petco Park.

Except, handed a five-run lead, Bergmann opened the ninth by walking the first man he faced. He struck out the next guy, Ramon Hernandez, and appeared to have settled down. Still 5-0, one out, runner on first.

But here came Frank Robinson out of the dugout. The next Padre was Brian Giles, a left-handed hitter. So Robinson wanted veteran left-handed reliever Joey Eischen. Never mind that the lead was five runs. He made the switch, and Eischen responded by getting Giles to fly out on the first pitch. Just one more out.

Eischen, though, allowed a single to the next man. Mel Proctor, manning the microphone, told whoever was watching back in Washington, "And Frank Robinson's going to make *another* change." In his box upstairs, the Padres' general manager, Kevin Towers, mockingly pointed his finger into his mouth and pulled an imaginary trigger, indicating what everyone in the park was thinking: *Just get this game over with.* The Padres fans who still remained, who hadn't poured out into the Gaslamp Quarter to party further, booed.

Robinson turned to Travis Hughes, another rookie, and Hughes allowed a single to Joe Randa, which drove in a run. The tension, nonexistent only fifteen minutes before, now filled the park. It was 5-1. There were runners on first and second. *Next!* Robinson came out of the dugout again. "And we're going to get still another pitcher," Proctor said, and he paused. "*Chad Cordero* coming in."

"Who do you want me to leave in, Bergmann?" Robinson asked afterward. "Who do you want me to leave in, Eischen? Who do you want me to leave in, Hughes? I've made the moves like I've made all year long. The moves that I thought were the right moves to try to get us out of an inning, to get three outs in the ninth inning. That's why all the moves."

All they needed was one out, and the summer could last another day, and the Nationals might be able to return to Washington, which would host nine of the team's final twelve games, still playing meaningful baseball. Give baseball fans in the nation's capital that scenario at the beginning of the season, when nearly everyone predicted the ex-Expos would finish well out of any pennant race, and they would have taken it. But somewhere along the line, expectations changed. Ten wins in a row in June will do that. Nearly two months in first place will do that. Exceptional performances from pitchers who had no history of providing them will do that. The best baseball story of 2005 had done that.

Just one more out. In his seat next to the Nationals' dugout, Jim Bowden was no longer standing, no longer clapping. His stomach turned. "You got to put that game away," Bowden said.

Cordero threw two strikes to Mark Loretta and needed one more. Robinson stood in the dugout, his arms folded across his blue Washington jacket, rocking back and forth a bit, bench coach Eddie Rodriguez to his immediate left, rocking even more. Cordero missed with a slider, but no big deal. One and two. Loretta fouled one off. Then came a slider in the dirt, and it was 2-2. "Well," Proctor told the folks back home, "this is the pitch he wants to get him on. He doesn't want to go 3-2, then the runners will be moving." The 2-2 pitch missed inside. Loretta had worked the count full. "It's getting just a little *too* interesting," Proctor said. And when Cordero missed low with ball four, it was exactly that interesting. Cordero spun around on the mound in disgust. Pitching coach Randy St. Claire came out for a visit. The bases were loaded. Padres shortstop Khalil Greene came to the plate as the tying run. Cordero toed the rubber again.

"He shouldn't have even been in the game," catcher Gary Bennett said.

It was just after 1:05 A.M. back east. Cordero missed with his first pitch and grabbed the ball back. The call was for a fastball, and he wanted it to be down and away, so that if Greene drove it, it would be the opposite way, and it would stay in the park. He wound up again. The Nationals still had a four-run cushion. But as the ball was on its way to the plate, Cordero knew there was a problem. The pitch didn't dart away from the right-handed-hitting Greene. It stayed over the heart of the plate. And Greene turned on it. "Oh, no!" Proctor called out through his microphone, and Cordero knew. "High drive," Proctor called. "Deep to left, way back there," and then the pause that precedes nearly every home run call before that bit of finality: "Gone!"

Gone. The Nationals' chances at the postseason ended right there, because even though Greene's grand slam just tied the score, Washington was finished. Cordero, who had been the hero for so much of the summer, the humble kid with the flat-brimmed hat, raised his arms in the air when the ball went over the left field wall, then let them fall limply to his sides. When he retired the next hitter, he took the glove off his left hand, held it in his right, and walked slowly toward the dugout. Three innings later, Padres catcher Ramon Hernandez hit a three-run homer off Nationals reliever Jon Rauch, and the loss was official. The ground had been there to gain, and they had lost it. The game had been theirs, and they had let it slip away.

When the Nationals gathered back in the clubhouse, there was utter devastation. Brad Wilkerson folded himself into a locker in a far corner, submerged as if he were equipment or clothing, so much luggage to be stowed away. Players sat in full uniform for ten, twenty, thirty minutes. And as they sat there in silence, no one concerned that the stereo couldn't go on, Frank Robinson walked in. The seventy-year-old man, the defiant Hall of Famer who'd hit 586 home runs and seemed to wish for the olden days when men were men, apologized to them. This one, he said, was on him. He was sorry. He had let them down. He didn't do his job.

"I felt like there comes a time where you sit here and you say you needed so-and-so to come through, and you say that's what he gets paid for, to get a hit in this situation," Robinson said after the season. "I just felt like I could've done a better job in the last couple of innings of that ballgame to possibly help win that ballgame, and I didn't do it. I don't usually second-guess myself. But we were fighting for our lives at that time. I should've gone to Cordero at the start of the inning. It was late in the season, and I didn't want to use him. But every ballgame counted. We *had* to win that ballgame."

Apology issued, Frank Robinson shuffled back to his office. During the slump of July and August, Robinson had said he could dismiss the losses, that he was unfamiliar with sleepless nights. On Saturday, September 17, he didn't sleep.

"It was different," he said. "I felt like I didn't get my job done. In the ninth inning, I was not able to put the right person out there, the right combination, to get three outs."

Jim Bowden walked out of Petco Park that night, walked back to the team hotel, the Marriott Marina, down past the train tracks and the wine shops and the Italian restaurants. It was as tough a night as he'd had all season. There was so much to think about. Assembling the team. Meeting President Bush. Having lunch at the White House, for goodness' sake. There was the winning streak. There was that sunny Sunday in Chicago when he'd been on top of the baseball world. And now, 2,300 miles from RFK Stadium, he walked back to a hotel in silence.

"It was a hard, sad night," Bowden said, "because you know it's over."

•　　•　　•

WHEN THE NATIONALS returned to RFK Stadium for their final series of the year, three games against the Philadelphia Phillies, two new stripes, red and blue, had been painted down the white hallway that led from the dank basement concourse to their clubhouse.

When they walked down one staircase from their clubhouse, then back up another set of stairs to the dugout, they felt something different under their spikes: a new rubber surface, one on which they would be far less likely to slip. They had played seventy-eight games at home. Three remained. Not a moment too soon.

On Saturday afternoon, Alan Alper sat in the upper deck of the old stadium, a Nationals jacket on his back, a Nationals hat on his head, a radio headset over his ears. His wife, Marina, sat to his left. He basked in the cool sun, peering through his glasses, and watched John Patterson, so stellar for so much of the season, give up seven runs in just five innings. Alper couldn't make the final game the next day, so this was it, his season.

"I don't know what I'm going to do without baseball," he said. "What am I going to do without my Nats?" He read everything he could get his hands on about the team. He went to as many games as he could. He listened on the radio. He watched on TV. He wore paraphernalia every day.

The Phillies pounded the Nationals that day, but sitting in the same stadium in which he had watched his Senators taken away, Alper considered baseball's return.

"I think the city is different since we have a ballclub," he said. "Maybe I *want* to believe that just because of who I am, that I'm nuts about this. But it sure seems that way to me." He would see people on the street wearing a Nationals cap, and he would stop and tell them, "I love your hat." And sometimes they would talk, conversations that wouldn't have happened a year before. "That's because baseball is back here," he said.

Two days later, the day after the season ended, Alper headed off to work. He felt his chest tighten. His coworkers called for an ambulance. And from the back of it, in the hours before doctors determined he had suffered a mild heart attack, he placed a phone call.

"I'm sure I'll be all right," he said over the phone. "But it occurred to me: This proves that my heart can't stand the idea of no more Nationals."

The following day, the Phillies would beat the Nationals again, a 9-3 loss on a pretty Sunday afternoon that ended the season. In the season's first half, Washington went 50-31 and sat in first place. In the second half, it went 31-50, perfectly symmetrical, and finished an even 81-81, good for last place in the National League East.

It was not a flawless return, to be sure. Yet it was never expected to be flawless. Emotional, infuriating, comical, surprising, ridiculous, fun, maddening, and joyous, sure. But not flawless. On that final day, after Cristian Guzman struck out to end it, the Nationals played a video tribute to the fans, and Frank Robinson and the players offered testimonials to the faithful, so loyal after just one year. At the video's conclusion, Jim Clarke, the public address announcer, offered a hearty thank-you, booming through the microphone. "We'll see you," Clarke thundered, "in *Vero Beach!*" and he held the *V* and the *e* for emphasis, rolling it out across the stadium like a disc jockey. Never mind that the Nationals train in Viera. Viera, Florida. Not Vero Beach. *Viera.* Doesn't matter. Baseball's first season back in Washington, all along, had been much more about emotion than execution.

When the players gathered near the home dugout after the game, they pointed to the fans, thousands of whom lingered afterward. They gave away bats and balls and hats and T-shirts. Chad Cordero, who had come in for one last appearance earlier in the day but was unable to record an out, pointed to them as a group. He hurled balls into the upper deck. "I got goose bumps," he said.

They did, too, no doubt, because they hung around until the final player ducked his head under the dugout and headed back to the clubhouse, back to the showers, back to the off-season. The announcement that the Montreal Expos would relocate to Washington had come 368 days earlier. Yet the Nationals who walked off that field on October 2, 2005, Washington's first baseball team in a generation, didn't know who would be their manager in 2006, didn't know who would be the general manager, didn't know who would be the owner. There was no lease on a new stadium. There was, in all honesty, still mass confusion.

But with the shadows growing long for a few moments in early autumn, the players hardly cared.

"It was," Brad Wilkerson said, "like we had a home. Finally."

Finally, Washington, D.C., had baseball.